Sheer Presence

Sheer Presence

The Veil in Manet's Paris

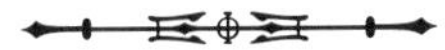

Marni Reva Kessler

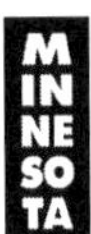

University of Minnesota Press
Minneapolis ∾ London

MM The publication of this book has been aided by a grant from the Millard Meiss Publication Fund of the College Art Association.

Earlier versions of parts of chapter 1 have appeared as "Filters and Pathologies: Caillebotte and Manet in Haussmann's Paris," *Nineteenth-Century Contexts* 27, no. 3 (September 2005): 245–68; and "Dusting the Surface: The Veil, the *Bourgeoise,* and the City Grid," in Aruna D'Souza and Tom McDonough, eds., *The Invisible Flâneuse? Gender, Public Space, and Visual Culture in Nineteenth-Century Paris* (Manchester: Manchester University Press, 2006), 49–64. An earlier version of chapter 3 was published as "Unmasking Manet's Morisot," *Art Bulletin* 81, no. 3 (September 1999): 473–89. The essay published in *Nineteenth-Century Contexts* copyright 2005 Taylor and Francis Group, www.tandf.co.uk/journals.

Published by the University of Minnesota Press
111 Third Avenue South, Suite 290
Minneapolis, MN 55401-2520
http://www.upress.umn.edu

Library of Congress Cataloging-in-Publication Data

Kessler, Marni Reva.
Sheer presence : the veil in Manet's Paris / Marni Reva Kessler.
p. cm.
Includes bibliographical references and index.
ISBN-13: 978-0-8166-4781-1 (hc : alk. paper)
ISBN-10: 0-8166-4781-X (hc : alk. paper)
ISBN-13: 978-0-8166-4782-8 (pb : alk. paper)
ISBN-10: 0-8166-4782-8 (pb : alk. paper)
1. Veils—Social aspects—France—Paris. 2. Veils—France—Paris—History—19th century. 3. Veils in art. 4. Impressionism (Art)—France—Paris. 5. Manet, Edouard, 1832–1883. 6. Paris (France)—Social life and customs—19th century. 7. Paris (France)—History—19th century. I. Title.
GT2112.K47 2006
391.4'30944361—dc22 2006023158

Printed in the United States of America on acid-free paper

12 11 10 09 08 07 06 10 9 8 7 6 5 4 3 2 1

For my mother,
Stephanie Kessler

A Charm invests a face
Imperfectly beheld—
The Lady dare not lift her Veil
For fear it be dispelled—

But peers beyond her mesh—
And wishes—and denies—
Lest Interview—annul a want
That Image—satisfies—

—Emily Dickinson

What hope of answer, or redress?
Behind the veil, behind the veil.

—Alfred Lord Tennyson,
"In Memorium A.H.H."

Contents

Acknowledgments

For a long time, I have imagined writing these acknowledgments. I have wondered what shape they would take and how I would find a way to thank the many institutions and people who have both facilitated my work and enriched my life. A refrain from Alfred Lord Tennyson's "Ulysses" kept coming back to me: "I am a part of all that I have met."

While I have not in the official sense "met" these granting entities that have supported my work both before and after my doctoral studies, they have certainly made it possible for me to do what I do. In reverse chronological order, I would like to thank the National Endowment for the Humanities, as well as the Georges Lurcy, John F. Enders, and Woodrow Wilson foundations, all of which funded my work at various points during my graduate career. I am indebted to the Department of the History of Art at Yale University, which so graciously supported me with a graduate fellowship, as well as Andrew Mellon and Robert Lehman grants for several research trips to Paris and London. Vassar College granted me a Belle Skinner Alumnae Award, which got me to Paris at a crucial moment. I am extremely lucky to have held a Mellon Postdoctoral Fellowship at the Wesleyan Center for the Humanities and a Luther Gregg Sullivan Postdoctoral Fellowship, also at Wesleyan University. While a graduate fellow at the

Whitney Humanities Center at Yale, I received useful feedback on a version of the first chapter.

More recently, a grant from the Getty Research Institute allowed me to conduct research in its Special Collections, where Ted Walybe and Kenneth Brown cheerfully helped me to find what I was looking for when no one else could. I also heartily thank Paul Arenson and Frances Terpak for their generosity in answering my many questions, with a very special acknowledgment to Tracey Schuster, reference librarian extraordinaire.

The University of Kansas has facilitated the progress of this project in many ways. I am profoundly grateful to KU for a New Faculty General Research Fund award as well as two subsequent General Research Fund Awards. Several research trips were supported by the Art History Faculty Travel Fund. Finally, but quite important, I am truly appreciative to have received a College Art Association Millard Meiss Book Subvention Grant and a University of Kansas Vice Provost for Research Book Subvention Grant, both of which have made an enormous impact on the production of this book.

Sheer Presence originated as a dissertation at Yale University, advised by Linda Nochlin, who has, for good reason, been recognized in countless acknowledgments. What I thank her for here is her unfailing support, her intellectual example, and for the sense she has personally given me of being part of a continuum, one that reaches back to our mutual beginnings in Brooklyn. It mattered a great deal when I first started out that I had such a splendid role model, and it matters a great deal now that I have such a dear friend. The members of my dissertation committee, Peter Brooks, Romy Golan, and Abigail Solomon-Godeau, offered criticism that has proved valuable as I turned the dissertation into this book. Anne Higonnet, Diana Kleiner, Maud Lavin, Esther da Costa Meyer, and Sara Suleri helped me to define the project at its earliest stage as a dissertation prospectus. Tamar Garb has, over many years, been an engaging interlocutor and friend. Her work and her feedback on mine have made me a better scholar.

At the University of Minnesota Press, I was lucky to have had the great fortune of working with Andrea Kleinhuber, who shepherded this book through the initial evaluation process with wisdom and warmth. Doug Armato has proven to be no less wonderful; I thank him for his patience with my endless questions as well as for his intelligence and skill. Katie Houlihan and Laura Westlund, both always gracious and clear, have played significant roles in getting this manuscript to completion. I thank Robin

Whitaker for her skillful copyediting. I am deeply grateful to the readers of my manuscript, Tamar Garb, Therese Dolan, and the anonymous reviewer, for seeing the potential in this project and for giving me helpful criticism.

My colleagues in the Kress Foundation Department of Art History at the University of Kansas have, both directly and indirectly, helped me to complete this project. I especially want to thank Linda Stone-Ferrier, whose friendship, humor, and daily support of me and my work go beyond any of my expectations. Charles Eldredge has consistently offered wise words and encouragement; it always cheers me to see him in my office doorway. I am grateful to John Pultz for many exchanges about work and ideas. I also thank Maud Humphrey for both practical assistance and the joy of her friendship. It is a pleasure to acknowledge my students at the University of Kansas—especially Sean Barker, Brittany Lockard, Rozanne Stringer, Debra Thimmesh, and April Watson—who have generously engaged in conversation about my ideas both in and out of the classroom. I thank Debra Thimmesh and Brittany Lockard also for their help early on in obtaining images and permissions. Heather Howard, Ann Snow, and Susan Craig of the Murphy Art and Architecture Library at the University of Kansas have helped me in ways too numerous to mention, but I hope they know I am grateful for all that they do.

The staffs of Bibliothèque historique de la ville de Paris, Bibliothèque de l'école de médecine, and Bibliothèque des arts décoratifs were always accommodating. I particularly want to acknowledge the help of Mme Françoise Portelance of Bibliothèque de l'école nationale supérieure des beaux-arts, Paris. To Mme Jacqueline Grislain I owe a special thanks for opening her homes in Paris and Brittany to me and for showing me with such delight an insider's France I will never forget.

I am grateful to the following institutions for inviting me to present earlier versions of parts of this book and for providing helpful critique and a forum for voicing my ideas: Bard College, Brigham Young University, Center for the Humanities at Wesleyan University, Dartmouth College DIA Art Foundation, Lehman College CUNY, MIT Ramapo College, Southern Connecticut State University, Vassar College, and Whitney Humanities Center at Yale University. I also delivered papers based on material in this book at annual meetings of the College Art Association, Nineteenth-Century French Studies, the International Nineteenth-Century Studies Association, and the New England Modern Languages Association.

Pam Gordon, Harold Washington, and Li Gordon Washington have fed my body and heart; I thank them for making Lawrence home to me. Caroline Jewers has given to me not only her French expertise but also the fullness of her wit and true friendship. I am profoundly grateful to Susan Kuretsky for having faith in me always; the countless conversations we have had, about the book and not, have enriched my life. The love and support of Eric Ort have sustained me over many years. Kathryn Potts, who was with me at the start, has talked with me about ideas, supported me, and many times warmly opened her home in New York to me. To Beth Handler, whom I met on our first day of graduate school and who has been by my side since, I owe enormous thanks for sharing with me her intelligence and sense of humor and for expressing her confidence in me at every turn. The calm wisdom and steady friendship of Karl Kusserow have meant more than I can say. I count the day I met Masha Belenky and Susan Hiner in Paris as one of my luckiest. Roberta Smith came into my life toward the end of the process of writing this book, but the immediacy of her friendship has made it seem as if she has been there from the very beginning.

My work has benefited greatly from conversations over the years with Linda Nochlin, Tamar Garb, Susan Sidlauskas, Ewa Lajer-Burcharth, Griselda Pollock, Hollis Clayson, Janet Wolff, and Carol Ockman, all of whom have certainly made their mark on the field of eighteenth- and nineteenth-century French visual culture. To say that their scholarship has deeply influenced my own is an understatement and an honor to acknowledge.

Masha Belenky, Martin Berger, Pam Gordon, Jürgen Heinrichs, Susan Kuretsky, and Stephanie Wiles read parts of this book, and to them I owe a special debt for provoking me to hone my arguments. At the eleventh hour, Susan Hiner graciously read a final draft of the entire book, offering not only supportive friendship but also insightful feedback. Many other colleagues and friends have contributed to this project in assorted, though extraordinarily helpful, ways: Victor Bailey, Elizabeth Breyer, Elspeth Brown, Marilyn Brown, David Cateforis, Julie Cisz, Constance Clement, Jay Coffman, Allison Covault, Susan Earle, Priscilla Parkhurst Fergusson, Michael Garval, the late Anne Hanson, Susan Harris, Tanya Hartman, Pam Lerow, Jean Lutes, Cameron McFarlane, Amy McNair, Marina Moskowitz, Mark Olson, Kathy Porsch, Ann Schofield, Beth Schultz, Jessica Smith, and Andrea Stempel.

It is a great pleasure to express my appreciation to my family. I hope that my grandmother, Eleanor Greif, knows the depth of my gratitude for her unconditional love and faith in me; having a grandmother cheering me on at this stage of my life is indeed something I treasure. I know how delighted my grandfather, Alvin Greif, would have been by this book. He never faltered in expressions of joy in all that he saw me do—big or small—and that has made all the difference. My aunt and uncle, Royanne and Gene Weiss, have been my home and family in the deepest senses. I am truly grateful to them for their love, support, and for always making me feel like I still have a home in Brooklyn. I thank Gordon and Erica Weiss for the generosity with which they have opened their home to me during many visits to Connecticut and for the limitless hours of laughter and conversation we have shared. To my nieces Emma and Sofia Weiss, I owe immeasurable gratitude for giving me their love, their wonderful ideas, and their smiles. My sister, Bethmara Kessler, has always stood by me—through life events and computer disasters. She is smart and funny, my most trusted friend, and an indelible part of my daily existence. It gives me great pleasure to know how proud my father, Arnold Kessler, would have been of this book. His infinite expressions of pride in me have worked in ways I am only now beginning to discover. It comforts me to know that his keen eye and artistic spirit helped to form my own.

This book is dedicated to my mother, Stephanie Kessler, who gave me far more than words on a page could ever capture. Her courage, intelligence, encouragement, grace, and love will always be at the heart of all that I do. Her presence and absence fill these pages.

Introduction

ALMOST IMPERCEPTIBLE but most assuredly there, a thinned wash of grayish paint with a scattering of darker dots lies across the face of the woman in the foreground of Gustave Caillebotte's *Paris Street: Rainy Day,* of 1877 (Figure 1). She and her companion establish the right side of the picture plane, the rest of which is interposed by a diffusion of people who make their ways across cobblestone boulevards lined with Haussmannized buildings. While this picture has interested scholars particularly in terms of its urban context and formal complexities,[1] none of their interpretations has noted that this woman is wearing a veil. And yet to me it is so clearly an element of the painting that shapes meaning as a whole. For in this picture of persistent diagonals, verticals, and repeating patterns, the veil reads as a whispered reiteration of the larger grids that articulate space. It mimics in microscopic form the lay of the cobblestone street and the façades and rooflines of the Haussmannized buildings that punctuate the background.

In a larger-than-life-size painting, this small veil focuses our attention; it creates a tense dichotomy between the gigantic and the miniature, which somehow helps us to parse Caillebotte's point. Indeed, the monumental scale of this work (nearly 7 × 9 feet) allows the artist to describe smaller things in intricate detail, to relate these details through finely tuned patterns, so that we understand them as parts of a larger architected whole. To be sure, the veil's presence in *Paris Street: Rainy Day* can be seen to consolidate formal and theoretical issues. It echoes shapes, reiterating their importance; it shows us just how much we need to attend to formations, both physical and cultural, in our analysis of this picture.

The veil does much more than simply fall across the face of the woman in the foreground of Caillebotte's painting. What I will show in this book is how this garment—and its visual representation—actually knots together many of the precepts determining life in late nineteenth-century Paris. It is by looking at and through the veil that was fashionable at the time, by understanding its importance at a specific moment in French history, that traditional disciplinary limits may be challenged and some familiar and some not-so-familiar images may be submitted to a fresh kind of scrutiny. And this will, in turn, reveal a more nuanced view of the society that popularized the veil.

On the basis of both visual and archival evidence, this study proposes new tactics for articulating the debates surrounding the ways in which

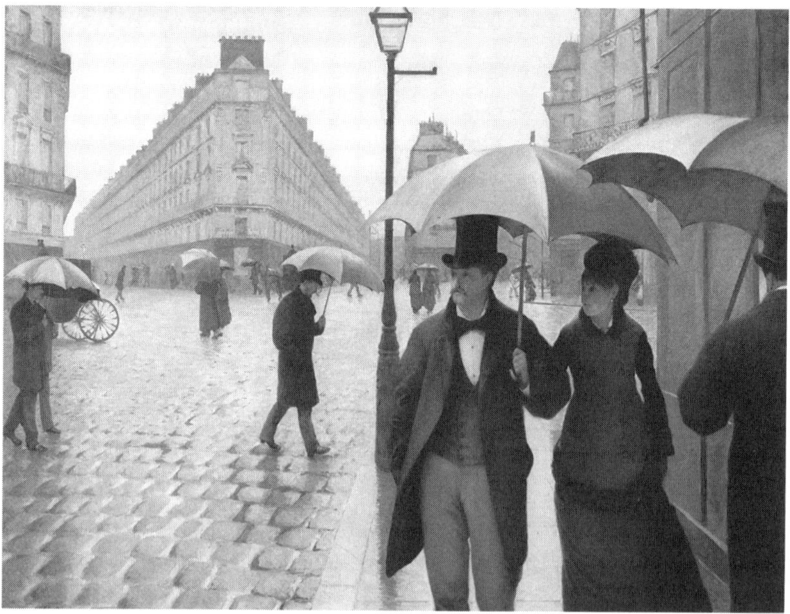

Figure 1. Gustave Caillebotte, *Paris Street: Rainy Day* (1877). Oil on canvas, 83½ × 108¾ inches (212.2 × 276.2 cm). Charles H. and Mary F. S. Worcester Collection, The Art Institute of Chicago. Photograph copyright The Art Institute of Chicago.

modern life was constructed in Paris during the late nineteenth century, a topic that has already received its fair share of attention. But what I want to do is show how the veil, as multifold object and symbol, was enmeshed in these developments and changes in French cultural history. Indeed, it was also a device that challenged some artists on a formal level. In other words, the veil was a means of exploring paint's material potential at the same time that it became a kind of topos of modernism and urbanism. Beyond being simply a fashion accessory, this Parisian veil was layered with meanings that functioned and continue to function within, to use Roland Barthes's helpful term, a "fashion system."[2] For Barthes, fashion is an organization of signifiers that, when assembled, produce knowledge about a culture. The veil was worn by stylish bourgeois women in the city and was represented in images during the Second Empire and into the Third Republic precisely because it held these multiple levels of significance. I will argue that it functioned as both an object (a garment that was worn) and a metaphor (as something that stood for and merged other, seemingly unrelated concepts). The veil even had substantial ramifications for some distinctly urban issues, such as fear of contagious disease, the readability of class, and being in fashion.

Inconsistent, translucent, opaque, and dense, the late nineteenth-century veil is a heuristic mechanism for clarifying our understanding of this particular time in Paris and some of the painting and popular imagery that helped to produce this moment. Ever-changing in its flow, the veil disperses light and shadow across the face behind it. Some were drawn tightly across the face, and some flowed loosely over it. Some veils were made of lace; others, of wool or linen. Some were compactly woven, while others had wide weaves. Some were white, and others were blue or black. Some were spotted, yet others were not. The veil's infinite varieties and nuances—its consequence of simultaneously concealing and revealing—make it an effective device with which to examine changes in urban life that began during the Second Empire and continued into the early part of the Third Republic (1852–89).[3] Like a lens that alternately blurs and sharpens, the veil is a tool that helps us to explore nineteenth-century conceptions of femininity, public health, aging, vision, imperialism, urbanism, and modernist art practices.

This veiling of the female face in Paris during the Second Empire and early Third Republic and its concomitant appearance in contemporary French painting and popular imagery frame a series of issues specific to the historical moment in which the veil became fashionable. The garment about which I write is secular and was used mainly by women of respectable standing.[4] As both object and concept, the veil thematizes the cluster of cultural conditions that structured in particular the relationship between the proper woman and the modern city that emerged under Napoleon III and Baron Haussmann. The veil was, in effect, a kind of grid through which the bourgeoise, or middle-class woman, saw the new Paris. It inhibited and intensified her vision at the same time that it disallowed easy visual access to her.

On the surface, the veil may seem simply to have affected the proper woman's vision and visibility, but its presence also consolidates the kinds of themes that challenged painters such as Edouard Manet, Edgar Degas, and Gustave Caillebotte. I concentrate mainly on these artists because of their engagement with the spectacular new spaces of Paris, its inhabitants, and its fashions. By incorporating into their production some of the very complexities and anxieties that pervaded their society, Manet, Degas, and Caillebotte handled the difficulties of depicting a moment in French history that can best be characterized as being under construction. Manet and Degas often used gestural, sometimes built-up and scumbled facture in order to convey a particularly modern and unfinished urban spectacle, while Caillebotte usually suppressed these developments beneath a slick and glossy gridded surface. Although disparate in their formal strategies, these artists were united in their refusal to adhere to strict academic conventions or subject matter. Instead, they took the challenge of representing the urban environment with all of its imperfection and spectacle.

Since detailed analysis of the works themselves is a critical component of my method, I focus closely on a limited number of paintings, photographs, and popular illustrations. Images by modernist artists provide the majority of examples, though I venture into academic art in my discussion of Orientalist painting that was popular at the Salon.[5] Drawing on the images, contemporary periodicals, fiction, and medical studies, I examine the many levels of significance that the veil and its representation both held and generated. Across a spectrum of approaches, these producers and products of visual culture charted a uniquely late nineteenth-century Parisian moment, one in which the city was undergoing extensive reconstruction. Dust was everywhere, and fashionable women of a certain status were wearing veils.

FORM

Each chapter of this book will explore layers of meaning, seemingly unrelated yet interconnected, which are alternately obscured and pulled into sharper focus by the veil. This is not an exhaustive account of the representation of the veil in late nineteenth-century French painting, nor is it a comprehensive analysis of the history of the veil. Indeed, the very subject of inquiry could not be reduced to a single narrative explaining its increased presence in Second Empire Paris and how it raises certain issues related to urban modernity. Advertised by the medical and fashion communities as a shield against the dust caused by Haussmann's renovations, the veil, I will show, also limited the proper woman's view of the modern city, aided in maintaining an ideal of femininity and youthfulness, helped to differentiate class, and was complicit in supporting stereotypes about the French colonies in North Africa.

Any attempt to identify the complexity of meanings generated by the veil and its status in late nineteenth-century French visual culture must be matched by a system of equally multidimensional pieces of evidence and method. For this reason, no single methodology on its own could be as productive as a blend of visual and textual approaches. My methodology is correspondingly hybrid as it interweaves social history, close formal analysis of images, cultural studies, feminist theory, urban studies, fashion theory, and postcolonial theory. I use the terms established by these areas of inquiry as frameworks within which to study the discursive play of some vanguard art in the larger context of other archival evidence and contemporary literature. Ultimately, I show that we can understand life and art in this particular time and place by exploring the ramifications of this previously ignored motif—the veil—that is so prevalent in the visual culture of the time. Melded formally to the city structure in which it became popular, the veil is used here as a grid, a web, a filter through which to think about the very urban problems that the veil's presence contains.

No examination of the representation of the veil, its social significance, and its uses in nineteenth-century French visual culture has previously been undertaken. In fact, there is little more than passing reference to this object that appears so often in the painting of the time. Scholars have noted, for example, its inclusion in Renoir's *Young Woman Wearing a Veil* (Figure 2), of about 1875, but none has questioned the importance of that spotted fabric both for the woman wearing it and for the society popularizing it. Instead, most have remarked on it as an object of purely artistic and visual pleasure for the viewer. Götz Adriani, for example, described this veil as a demonstration of Renoir's formal inventiveness and as something to highlight the model's ideally pale skin. He wrote: "The face is covered by the gossamer mesh of a veil dotted with black spots, highlighting the pale, delicate skin 'à la mouche' while at the same time forming the basic elements of a pointillist approach to painting well in advance of Pointillism itself."[6] Whether Renoir was in some way consciously presaging Pointillism is, to my mind, arguable. Indeed, his film of pigment with splashes of dots articulates something far more than a future stylistic shift or the hue of the surface of the face on which it is painted. The veil shapes our reading of the woman's appearance, determines how she sees, and connects her to a contemporary discourse of ideal beauty and imperialism in North Africa at the same time that it posits a formal challenge for the artist.

Surprisingly, the veil that was fashionable among proper women in late nineteenth-century France has also been virtually ignored in comprehensive costume histories, which tend to mention it only superficially, and when they do, they analyze it on a purely aesthetic level.[7] Nancy Troy rightly describes this inclination for costume historians to address mainly the formal properties of clothing when she claims in *Couture Culture: A Study in Modern Art and Fashion* that "costume history has been shaped in large measure by connoisseurs whose familiarity with individual objects enables them to attend to costume materials and the details of facture, as well as to formal and stylistic developments; but in this model, structural issues and discursive analysis are too often ignored."[8] While none addresses the veil specifically, Alexandra Warwick and Dani Cavallaro's *Fashioning the Frame: Boundaries, Dress and the Body,* Patrizia Calefato's *The Clothed Body,* Christopher Breward and Caroline Evans's edited *Fashion and Modernity,* and Ulrich Lehmann's *Tigersprung: Fashion in Modernity* have all proven to be rich sources of interlocution for me as I have completed this project. Gen Doy's *Drapery: Classicism and Barbarism in Visual Culture* investigates the history of representations of drapery, occasionally discussing the veil as a kind of drapery. Her book, while a project like-minded to mine in that it analyzes a theme/thing and its appearances in visual imagery, works across centuries without a particular interest in interpreting her object of study as both marker and maker of any given historic moment. Instead, my aim is to place the veil within a series of cultural frameworks

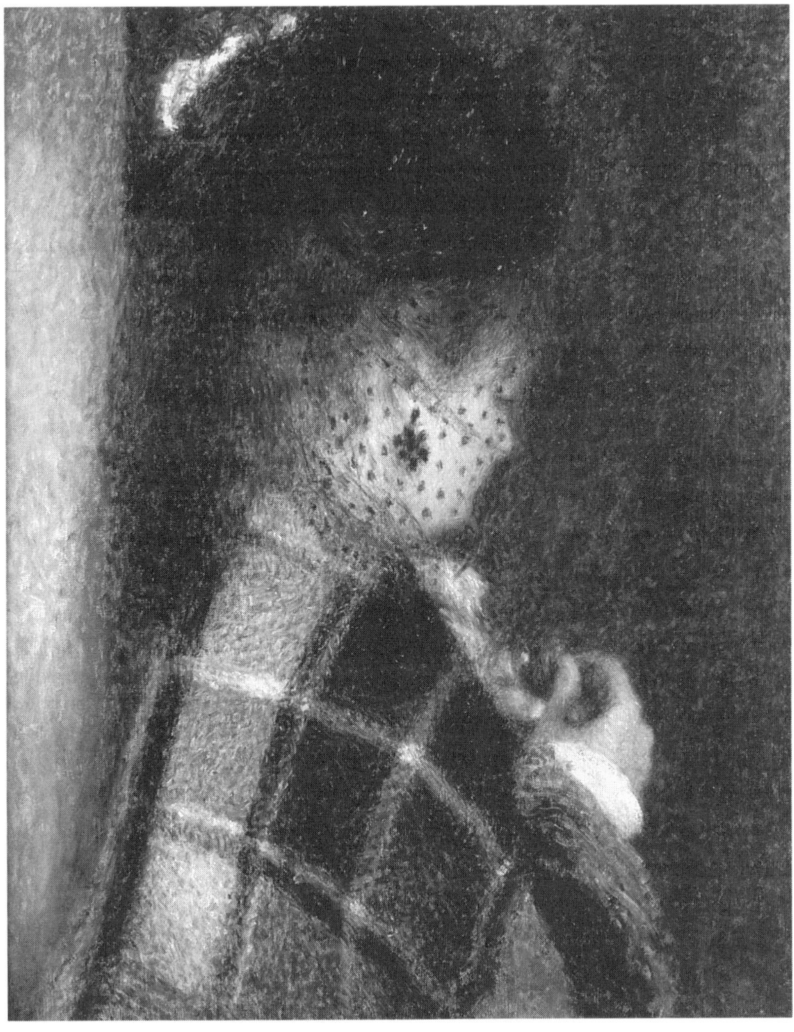

Figure 2. Auguste Renoir, *Young Woman Wearing a Veil* (c. 1875). Oil on canvas. Photograph from Preveral, Musée d'Orsay, Paris. Réunion des musées nationaux/Art Resource, NY.

so that its visual representation and its material reality may be understood not simply as a form but rather as something that is itself a layering of meanings that inscribe a formulation of the complex connection between modern life and bourgeois women.

Much has been written about the history of the Muslim veil as well as the ways in which it has been misinterpreted in certain non-Muslim societies, both historically and now.[9] While these studies have profoundly aided my research, helped to fill in gaps in my knowledge, and provided interesting theoretical models of inquiry, their goals have been different from mine.[10] Rather, I want to situate the late nineteenth-century veil as a particularly French fashion object, one that does relate to the veil of Islam but that I also see as being inflected by many other histories as well.

For my study, I have mined contemporary French fashion journals, etiquette books, periodical literature, and novels, as well as medical journals and pamphlets, all of which would have been readily accessible to a literate late nineteenth-century Parisian but are today found in archives at institutions such as Bibliothèque nationale, Bibliothèque de l'école de médecine, Centre de documentation du musée de la mode, Bibliothèque des arts décoratifs, and Bibliothèque historique de la ville de Paris. What emerges from this body of sources is a picture of a fashionable object that had wildly conflicting connections that ranged from medical discourses to ideals of beauty to painting practice to French imperialism in North Africa. My objective here is to show how these connections converge across and through the veil that was represented in the visual culture of late nineteenth-century Paris.

Histories

Of course veils existed long before the Second Empire. In their purposes and significations, earlier appearances of veils sometimes prefigure those of the late nineteenth century. And while the term *veil* is often used interchangeably in historical texts to describe both a fabric that fell across the face and one that hung around it, I will discuss here coverings that, like the late nineteenth-century veil that is my focus, fell across the face. Always a flexible signifier, the veil at times could indicate alternately a woman's status as prostitute, as faithful wife, and as widow. For example, in the Hebrew Bible, Tamar poses as a prostitute by wearing a veil so that she can seduce her father-in-law, Judah: "When Judah saw her, he thought her to be a prostitute, for she had covered her face" (Genesis 38:15).[11] Living at a time when widows were supported in their advancing years by their children, this childless widow is forced to find another way to conceive and bear a child. Tamar takes recourse to the veil, which in this case not only helps her to seduce her father-in-law but also enables her to change her status to prostitute and hide her identity.[12] In II Corinthians of the New Testament, St. Paul argues that only veiled women should be allowed to pray.

Costume historians have traced variations of veils to the ancient Near East (fifteenth to fifth century BCE, including Mesopotamian and biblical texts).[13] Middle Assyrian law (c. 1450–1250 BCE) stipulated that women of noble birth cover their faces with veils when out in public. As textile historian G. M. Vogelsang-Eastwood points out, "Concubines and 'captive' maids also had to be veiled when accompanied by their mistresses. On the other hand, the wearing of veils in public by prostitutes and female slaves was a punishable offence."[14]

We know from surviving pottery and texts that veils covering the face were popular in ancient Egypt and Greece as well. Herakleides reported that women in Thebes and Boetia around 250 BCE wore *himatia* in such a way that the "garment seems to cover the whole face like a little mask: the eyes alone peep out; all the other parts of the face are covered by the mantles. They all wear these pure white."[15] The face screen or panel, made of a piece of sheer fabric that fell from forehead to chest, appears in some Hellenistic sculptures as well. In the traditional iconography of Greek vase-painting, a wedding scene often includes a woman (the bride) holding a veil across her face. A similar gesture made by the target—or would-be targets—in mythological abduction scenes demonstrates that the bride's veil may signify modesty and a readiness for marriage as much as it indicates fear and vulnerability.

But it is Penelope's veil in Homer's *Odyssey* that is one of the most salient and well-known historical examples of the use of the veil as a garment that could indicate modesty and fidelity at the same time that it could serve as a form of protection. The quintessential Greek woman, Penelope uses her veil as a way of protecting herself from the advances of the suitors who plague her while her husband, Odysseus, is away at war. The Homeric text describes Penelope thus: "When she, shining among women, came near the suitors, / she stood by the pillar that supported the roof with its joinery, / holding her shining veil in front of her face, to shield it."[16] As commentators have noted, Homeric descriptions of Penelope's veil are often conjoined with a mention of two handmaidens who flank her. The protecting handmaidens and the veil are emblems, then, of her wisdom and virtue, unsullied and pure.

Not surprisingly, one of the richest sources of information on the history of the veil is provided by nineteenth-century social and fashion historian Augustin Challamel. Writing from within a culture that placed great importance on fashion and popularized the veil for everyday use, Challamel chronicles the history of fashion from the ancient world to the mid-nineteenth century. He points out that the use of the veil and its adornments to indicate a woman's status continued well into the Middle Ages. It was in the fourth century that the white veil began to be worn by Christian brides as a sign of purity, while the black veil came to represent mourning. And during the Carolingian period in France, which lasted from about 752 to 987, women wore veils that covered their heads and shoulders and, according to Challamel, "reached almost to the ground. . . . The veil was indispensable, being regarded as the penalty of the sin of our Mother Eve, and the hair was concealed beneath it."[17] This veil, regarded as a punishment that symbolized the original sin, was also "splendidly embroidered,"[18] and so we may infer that it equally served as adornment. In Byzantium (313–1453), respectable women were expected to wear veils both in public and in the home.

Veils also had religious significance in western Europe during the eleventh century, when they were worn by women of rank to Sunday church services. As one costume historian put it: "Religious ordinance, which had become even more powerful by becoming social ordinance, was responsible for the long retention of the veil."[19] Called dominicals, these veils were necessary for a woman to receive communion. In fact, the synodical statutes designated that women without veils had to defer receiving communion. Veils were also worn for nonreligious occasions during this period. Those of queens and princesses were encircled by crowns, and veils of widows had attached to them a bandeau that covered the throat and neck. Additionally, the length of the veil marked a woman's class status. As Challamel tells us, "The veil of a lady of gentle birth reached to her feet, but that of a plebeian might not fall below the waist."[20]

By the end of the thirteenth century, despite the fact that extreme ornamentation of the hair was out of style, women "wore a veil, as was rigorously enforced by the Church; for according to an article of the Council of Salisbury, no priest might hear the confession of an unveiled woman. This veil covered the head so entirely that it was impossible to see whether a woman had any hair or not."[21] When not at church, women wore veils with their "closely-fitted gowns, frequently ornamented with a belt of silk, or cloth of gold . . . and fur-bordered mantle. A veil, fastened on the crown of the head, flowed over the shoulders."[22] The cornette briefly took the place of the veil in the early years of the fourteenth century, when it was replaced by a headdress from which hung a veil that Challamel likens to the guimpe of a nun. During the fourteenth and fifteenth centuries, veils came back into fashion and were particularly prevalent at the court of Burgundy.

Black veils were especially popular during the reign of Louis XI, when French fashion was particularly inflected by Italian styles. Practicality intervened again during the reign of Henry II (1547–58), when, as M. Jules Quicherat reported, "For going out in cold weather . . . a square of stuff was fastened to the strings of the hood, and covered all the face from the eyes downward, like the fringe of a mask."[23] By the late sixteenth century, veils waned in popularity. As Mrs. C. D. Beebe notes in her 1880 *Lace, Ancient and Modern,* during the reign of Henry VIII, most portraits of queens do not include a veil, with the exception of bridal images. She also reports that later Queen Mary, daughter of Henry VIII and Catherine of Aragon, wore a black veil to commemorate the memory of her divorced mother and that "after her death the inventory of her effects mentions 'vales of black network,'"[24] some of which would have been incorporated as ornament on her clothing and some of which would have been used to fashion veils.

During the seventeenth century, brides of noble birth brought back into fashion white and silver veils, while women of all classes wore black ones during the summer as protection from the sun, dust, and insects.[25] Face masks, too, were seen as practical garments that could "conceal those faces to which nature had been unkind . . . or else to envelope beauty in mystery, by making its presence doubtful, and exciting the curiosity of the incredulous."[26] These masks were secured by the placement of a button-tipped silver bar between the teeth, thus altering not just the wearer's appearance but also her ability to speak.

By the time of the kingships of Louis XVIII and Charles X (1815–30), French women had adopted the British style of wearing green gauze veils attached to straw bonnets as shields against the rays of the sun. It was not until the second half of the nineteenth century in France that black or white veils began to be worn for everyday use. Initially they were donned for masked balls and at the seaside, where they served the practical purpose of protecting the face from wind and sand. But by the early 1850s, they were widely worn throughout Paris as signs of fashionability.[27] Women of style, for example, copied Eugénie's veil made of the very elaborate *point d'Angleterre,* which she wore when she married Napoleon III. Beebe claims, "The trousseau of the empress was remarkable in having laces of nearly every description employed in it, there being more foreign than French laces used."[28] Indeed, Eugénie's penchant for veils helped to popularize their widespread use throughout France at this time. She frequently wore demiveils of tulle or lace; "others were of open network, and hardly concealed the face at all,"[29] aiding the rising popularity of the many variations of this garment that would flourish especially during her husband's reign.

In Layers

While the fact that the veil had a history that predated the late nineteenth century is significant to my analysis, my concern in this book is most specifically with the version of the veil that emerged in direct connection to the changes—structural, social, cultural—happening in Paris under the rule of Napoleon III. Each chapter looks at diverse, though related, reasons for why the veil became fashionable and at the multiplicity of consequences that its popularity had, particularly for the women who wore it.

Chapter 1, "Pathologizing the Second Empire City," analyzes the importance of the veil within the discourses of medicine, public hygiene, vision, and urbanism. I position the veil in relation to the radical renovations orchestrated by Napoleon III and Baron Haussmann and the dust the construction generated. I also examine the medical evidence that established the veil as a shield against this dust—the traces of the old Paris—at the same time that I consider the visual ramifications of such veiling for the woman behind it. The second part of this chapter integrates the urban and medical material with careful expositions of Gustave Caillebotte's *Le pont de l'Europe* and Edouard Manet's *Music in the Tuileries Gardens.*

In the second chapter, "Making Up the Surface," I consider ideals of beauty and fears of aging in late nineteenth-century France and show how the veil and subtle layers of maquillage covertly participated in the fabrication of the exemplary youthful bourgeois woman. Here, I incorporate information culled from contemporary etiquette books, family manuals, and fashion journals, as well as illustrations from those texts, in order to establish the set of expectations for beauty that were pervasive for a particular class of women in Paris at the time. These expectations, I show, unexpectedly placed the respectable woman within the discourses of seduction and sexuality, the very entities that her toilette was meant to eschew. I also explore in this chapter the formal issues that painting veils and maquillage posed for the artists representing them, as I discuss the constitutive links between actual makeup and veils and their pictorial counterparts.

The third chapter, "Unmasking Manet's Morisot, or Veiling Subjectivity," provides a case study of veiling in artistic practice and analyzes the effects of that veiling on the identity of a particular sitter. Here, I focus on a group of portraits that Manet painted of the artist Berthe Morisot between 1868 and 1874. Through analyses of the cultural context, the relationship between Manet and Morisot, and the paintings themselves, I argue that these images tell us far less about the sitter than they do about the painter. Manet ultimately depicts the ideal bourgeoise, Morisot, as excessively *maquillée* and not as the respectable woman and artist she was, thus betraying not simply the complexity of his feelings toward her but also her unclassifiable status within the social order. Truly elaborate and complicated uses of paint and canvas allow Manet to veil, both metaphorically and literally, the semblance of one of his most challenging colleagues. These paintings, while not entirely inconsistent technically with others in Manet's oeuvre, are nevertheless quite unusual. They are repetitive and highly confounding, and they depict the woman who would become Manet's sister-in-law.

Chapter 4, "The Other Side of the Veil," examines the intersections between the French veil and its discursive other, the Muslim veil, in order to consider their particular and linked responsibilities in the composition of late nineteenth-century French imperialism. The increased popularity of the veil in Paris fashion coincided with the 1850s, 1860s, and 1870s, decades marked by the expansion and maintenance of the French empire in North Africa. This chapter will thus speculate on the mutual borrowing between France and its Orient and demonstrate how the veiled French woman was, like her Muslim counterpart, invested in affirming certain colonial stereotypes. Through close analyses of veils in contemporary photographs and illustrations, as well as in paintings by Manet and Renoir, I show how the visual culture also participated in the persistence of French colonial interest in North Africa. This chapter then examines what I term avant-garde Orientalist painting, by looking at Edouard Manet's *Young Woman in Oriental Costume,* of 1871, and its relationship to French imperialist ideologies.

Ultimately, this book will demonstrate that the veil and its representations are always politically, socially, and culturally determined. I have chosen to begin this study in 1852 and to end in 1889, for these are especially significant points on both the modernist trajectory and in the history of France. The chapters themselves do not necessarily follow chronologically, for strict yearly progression does not allow for the active integration of shifts, subtleties, and discrepancies into the reconstruction of a piece of history.

The year 1852 marks the opening of the Second Empire, when Napoleon III assumed the role of emperor and appointed the Baron Haussmann the prefect of the Seine. This time also represents a watershed in the development of ways of communicating through illustrated periodicals and innovative marketing strategies, as well as stricter rules concerning appropriate fashion. The desire for change and technological advancements helped to provide the breeding ground for the formal invention of a ready-made clothing industry, the means by which to distribute those garments rapidly, and the disposable income necessary for buying those goods. Improvements in weaving and sewing methods also supported this expansion of the clothing industry. Perhaps the most influential factor in the growing importance of fashionability, however, was Napoleon III and Empress Eugénie's celebration of lavish clothing. Given this context, the Second Empire's witnessing of the increased popularity of the veil is not at all surprising.

If the early 1850s in France saw the explosion of a periodical literature that helped to popularize fashion, then 1889 was surely not the endpoint. Yet I close the main text of this book with the year 1889, when indigenous colonial people were imported from various French colonies and displayed at the Paris Universal Exhibition. It was on the Champ de Mars that colonial villages were constituted for the viewing pleasure of a mostly European audience, and it was here that the French veil literally came face-to-face with the Muslim veil.

This book does not purport to offer a history of veils and veiling practices, cross-culturally or otherwise. What I do want to provide here is an examination of one of the historical contexts, late nineteenth-century Paris, in which certain kinds of veils became à la mode and the ways in which these garments were represented in and filled with meanings for the visual culture of the time.

Dense or light, white or black, dotted or not, long or short, veils produce nuanced views of the women behind them and, in turn, shade our interpretation of French painting and history during the second half of the nineteenth century. The veil worn by the foregrounded woman in Caillebotte's *Paris Street: Rainy Day* may be small, but it is a fundamental element of the picture as a whole. Like a barely visible road map, it helps us know where to look. And once we do start to look carefully, the image suddenly blooms into an ever-widening sequence of grids, the very warp and weft of the new Paris. This painting is so engaged with the urban environment that we cannot but notice that even the woman's dress is architectural. Both formal convention and trope, the veil offers us a fresh lens through which to see the flaring of boulevards and the locus of change that was late nineteenth-century Paris.

1

Pathologizing the Second Empire City

Dusts

The foreground of a photograph taken by the Studio of Delmaet and Durandelle sometime in 1867 or 1868, during the construction of l'avenue de l'Opéra, is filled with rubble and dust (Figure 3). This picture documents a particular moment in Paris's pathology, a moment characterized by cultural chaos, disorder, and change. Garnier's unfinished Opera House sits just shy of the center, flanked by buildings in varying states of completion. The foreground of this image contains the fragments of what had been there before, the ruins, the shattered bones of buildings and paving stones. Forming a kind of mosaic of the past, the rubble lingers at the physical surface of the photograph in abstracted patterns. Simultaneously indexical and dead and always a measure of change, this debris represents the metamorphosis of the physical city, and it also charts changes in late nineteenth-century social ideologies. At this time in France, dust and dirt became tropes for social anxieties over a perceived breakdown in class structure and moral behavior. While dust had always proliferated in Paris, the transformation of large sections of the city between 1852 and 1870 by Napoleon III and Baron Haussmann raised even more. On a literal level, a perceptible veil of dust settled over Paris, but what I want to show is that this dust was actually directly related to limiting bourgeois women's engagement with aspects of urban life and culture. For Haussmann's dust generated the need for women to be veiled, which, in turn, changed how women saw and were seen in the spectacular new city.

The dust of Haussmann's Paris, then, must be seen not simply as bothersome sediment but also as a cultural artifact of the city's historical moment.[1] Dust and the actual veil its presence inspired in French fashion are the historical remnants that allow us to trace shifts in ideologies that inflected the position of bourgeois women in Paris during the second half of the nineteenth century. Indeed, the veil, which was ostensibly a means of protecting the woman from the filth of the construction, also controlled how she experienced the city. And although at least three types of urban maskings occurred in Haussmann's Paris—the unifying fabric of the new buildings and boulevards, the dust of the deconstruction and construction that fell over the city, and the subsequent veiling of the female face—my focus here will be on the last two and how they fit together to produce a framework for reading the conditions determining life for some women in modern Paris. While everyone was controlled in some way by the circulating grids of grand boulevards that veiled the new city and by the dust of the renovations that also mediated experience, the respectable

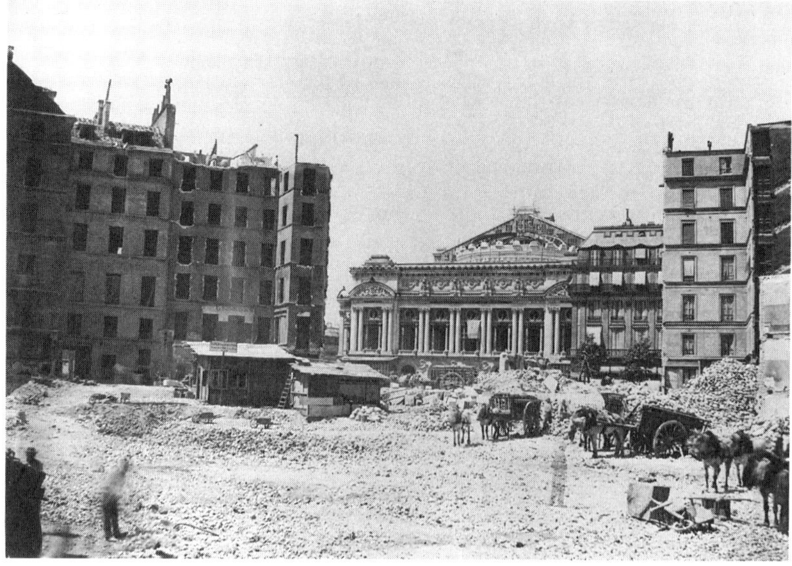

Figure 3. Delmaet and Durandelle, *Percée de l'avenue de l'Opéra* (1867 or 1868). Photograph. Bibliothèque de l'école normale supérieure des beaux-arts, Paris.

woman was doubly limited by the system. The physical changes in the city defined her passage through Paris at the same time that her vision was further narrowed by the veil across her face. To push this point further, I would even argue that the veil's popularity at the time should be read as a visual manifestation of the bourgeoise's particularly vexing status in the new city.

To be sure, the veil was only one of the devices that shaped women's lives during and after the Second Empire.[2] As the old city was erased by Haussmann's buildings and boulevards, cultural imperatives increasingly erased proper women from parts of public life, for women who wanted to maintain their respectability were actively discouraged from visiting certain areas of the city and from walking unaccompanied at all. Although not a transparent representation of social reality, an excerpt from Jules Michelet's *La femme* of 1859 epitomizes a strain of the dominant ideology that endeavored to restrict proper women's activity:

> She [the bourgeoise alone] can hardly ever go out in the evening; she would be taken for a prostitute. There are a thousand places where only men are to be seen, and if she needs to go there for some reason, they are amazed and laugh like fools. For example, should she find herself delayed and hungry at the other end of Paris, she will not dare to enter a restaurant. She would be an event, she would be a spectacle. All eyes would constantly be fixed on her.[3]

Thus, Michelet describes how a woman walking about the city without an escort was subject to inaccurate evaluations of her status. Mingling with the masses became, for a woman of respectable standing, increasingly unfamiliar and somewhat dangerous. Many interior public spaces were also circumscribed by strict rules of propriety. The artist Berthe Morisot recounted her experience at the opening of the Salon of 1869 in a letter to her sister, Edma. In it she describes her panic at realizing that her escort, Edouard Manet, has disappeared:

> For about an hour Manet, in high spirits, was leading his wife, his mother, and me all over the place, when I bumped headlong into Puvis de Chavannes. . . . he asked if he might accompany me for a few minutes. I wanted to see the pictures, but he implored me so eagerly. . . . Such conversation might have appealed to me had I not found myself confronted at every step by familiar faces. What is more, I had completely lost sight of Manet and his wife, which further increased my embarrassment. I did

> not think it proper to walk around all alone. When I finally found Manet again, I reproached him for his behavior.[4]

Cognizant of the social consequences of walking through the Salon unaccompanied, Morisot admonishes Manet for losing her. She has clearly been so socialized by the stipulations of bourgeois society that she does not think it proper to walk around alone even at the Salon, which was a big part of her professional life.

A now well-known journal entry by the young, unmarried, expatriate artist Marie Bashkirtseff, a contemporary of Morisot and Mary Cassatt, not only demonstrates the effects of these limitations on women's behavior but also confirms the existence of these circumstances well into the 1880s, when she wrote in her diary:

> What I long for is the freedom of going about alone, of coming and going, of sitting in the seats of the Tuileries, and especially in the Luxembourg, of stopping and looking at the artistic shops, of entering churches and museums, of walking about old streets at night; that's what I long for; and that's the freedom without which one cannot become a real artist. Do you imagine that I get much good from what I see, chaperoned as I am, and when, in order to go to the Louvre, I must wait for my carriage, my lady companion, my family?[5]

Bashkirtseff is particularly aware of her desire to have the freedom to wander about the city alone. As an artist, she especially recognizes how her vision is affected by certain cultural restrictions, acknowledging how her chaperons, her carriage, her lady companion, and her family limit how and what she sees.

The newly articulated geography of Paris and the risks associated with unaccompanied travel clearly constricted respectable women's circulation in the modern city. In effect, just when sidewalks made strolling in the city less messy and more enjoyable, the proper woman was restricted from having free use of them. As the renovations redefined and further codified zones of public and private, masculine and feminine, working class and bourgeois, the city progressively came to signify the world of labor, politics, and education, commonly, though not exclusively, perceived as the realm of men.[6] Public parks and uniform building façades were constructed in an effort to rejuvenate the health of the city and its inhabitants, to create the illusion of social equality, and to mask Paris's conflicts. The face of the city was literally and figuratively effaced by dust, veils, and façades, its signs of difference and politics smoothed over in order for it to appear, at least on the surface, coherent and unmarked by friction.

The veil, like Haussmann's façades, could regularize difference, since it also obfuscated signs of personal uniqueness.[7] In an 1863 issue of *Le journal des demoiselles,* one writer noticed the ways in which veils created the appearance of uniformity: "In the midst of these white dresses and all these veiled faces, even a woman's mother would have difficulty recognizing her."[8] While it did not obliterate the presence of the woman beneath it, the veil complicated the individualized features of the face.

As women began to look more and more homogeneous, so did the buildings and boulevards that were being constructed around them. Indeed, one of the objectives of Haussmann's work was to produce a city of consistently congruous surfaces and pleasing spaces.[9] Like the veil across the woman's face, the beautiful and clean boulevard could conceal or divert attention from what was behind it, around the corner, or two or three streets away, where there remained the same dirty and narrow paths that instigated the need for changes in the city in the first place.[10] Paris obviously benefited greatly from Haussmann's buildings, parks, and boulevards, which enabled traffic, air, and water to circulate more easily. However, the program involved disguise, the production of filth, and the displacement of parts of the population in order for the city to look untouched by class distinctions.[11] The grand boulevards further standardized Paris's appearance, opening out sections that had been narrow, expanding and systematizing the field of vision.

At the very same time that broad fields of vision were facilitated by Haussmann's vistas, fashionable veils functioned dialectically to restrict the respectable woman's view. The veil was even further integrated with the very structure of the new city, since one of its primary functions was to protect the proper woman from the dust of the renovations. Yet, while it screened out some dust, the veil also filtered what the bourgeoise saw. This need for the manipulation of vision is linked to the unfounded fear that direct visual contact with the now more conspicuous prostitute in the city would contaminate the respectable woman's character. By midcentury, especially after the construction of wide boulevards and the destruction of areas that were previously locales for brothels, prostitutes were even more noticeable in Paris. Additionally, the prohibitive rents in the Haussmannized districts of the city forced many prostitutes onto the street, making them appear to be more numerous than before. Even though the prostitute was regarded as a necessary evil of bourgeois society, she nonetheless had to remain undetectable in public. In fact, one of the main goals of the regulationist movement, spearheaded by Alexandre Parent-Duchâtelet in the 1830s, was to ensure the invisibility of the venal woman. He claimed that civil authorities were obligated to design methods for keeping prostitutes as unnoticeable as possible. Parent-Duchâtelet's subjective and highly flawed system of regulating prostitutes, based on his own personal analysis of the women themselves, their clientele, their living conditions, and their behavior, attempted to categorize and register prostitutes. His work was both symptomatic of and an instigation for spreading fears of social contagion.

Contemporary accounts promoted a moral panic as they warned of the abundance and visibility of prostitutes in the city at this time. For example, in his well-known guide to Paris of 1869, James D. McCabe Jr. noted the prominence of the demimonde:

> You cannot go into any public place in Paris without meeting one or more women that you will recognize at a glance as belonging to the class known in French society and fiction as the Demi-Monde. You find them at the theatres, in the concert halls, in the Cafés, on the Boulevards, in the Champs Elysées, and at Longchamp they have almost driven respectable women from the ground. Before you have been in the city a week, you will be convinced that these women are very numerous.[12]

What seemed to be an escalation of the number of prostitutes in Paris only increased preexisting concerns over class mixing and class confusion. This, coupled with the growing popularity of mass-produced clothing, which made it economically feasible to disguise conspicuous signs of class difference, catalyzed the need for a means of both distinguishing the respectable woman from the prostitute and keeping the bourgeoise from directly seeing the prostitute. Émile Zola articulates this problem of not being easily able to determine the status of a woman in a passage from *The Ladies' Paradise,* based loosely on Paris's first department store, the Bon Marché, written in 1882, and set between 1864 and 1869. In a conversation between Hutin and Favier, rival salesmen at the new department store, Hutin asks Favier about the extent of his most recent customer's purchases: "'Well! And your courtesan?' asked Hutin of Favier, when the latter returned from the pay-desk, where he had accompanied the lady. 'Oh! A courtesan,' replied the other. 'I fancy she looks too lady-like for that. She must be the wife of a stockbroker or a doctor, or something of that sort.' 'Don't tell me! It's a courtesan. With their grand lady airs it's impossible to tell now-a-days!'"[13] Not only does this passage address the challenge of differentiating courtesan from respectable woman, but it also illustrates the ways in which classes readily mixed in the new spaces of Paris.

Octave Uzanne, a cultural critic deeply invested in maintaining the ideology of separate classes, helped to generate worries about class mixing in the new city. He wrote in his nostalgic essay "Les cocodettes du Second Empire": "Life's new opportunities produced almost immediately a general abandonment of the reserve which had been the line of demarcation of sedentary aristocracy's existence. All social classes found themselves mixing little by little."[14] The broadening of Parisian streets, a by-product of which was the increased visibility of the people on them, in an ironic twist also further solidified the perceived need for more firmly established class divisions. The veil, I would argue, became a device of discrimination within this visual crisis, since its presence or absence could indicate a woman's status.[15] Émile Zola illustrates this point well in his novel *Nana* when Satin, who is vying for a place in Nana's show, is spotted "wearing a hat and a little veil, and trying to look like a lady paying a call. 'A real little trollop she is!' murmured Prullière."[16] For all of her efforts to look like a lady by wearing a hat and a veil, Satin remained a woman of dubious virtue in the unsuccessful guise of someone of a higher class.

Even though any woman could conceivably wear a veil, contemporaries believed that the manner in which she wore it, in concert with its design and her posture, would signal her class. In *Le journal des demoiselles* in 1857, for example, one author recognized the importance of a woman's deportment in establishing her social position when he wrote: "In Paris, the manner of wearing and of placing a hat or a dress is still difficult to comprehend. One can recognize a hat by Mesdames Bricard and Callmann only on the head of an elegant woman; on the head of a common woman, it could be by anyone."[17] Government officials took measures to facilitate the readability of a venal woman's class. In addition to restrictions on their behavior and the times of day during which they could solicit clients, prostitutes were subjected to strict clothing guidelines.[18] They were required to wear understated clothes and regulation-sized hats or none and were prohibited from adorning themselves with accessories that called attention to their appearance.[19] Even contemporary writer and cultural critic Charles Blanc weighed in with his assessment of the veil: "This transparent veil, whose filmy material is so prettily called *tulle illusion,* is perhaps only a means of attracting attention, and of making more conspicuous what there is an appearance of wishing to conceal."[20] Therefore, the veil, an accessory that contemporaries believed called attention to the woman wearing it, was codified as bourgeois or aristocratic, partly to enable this taxonomy of the social order.

A Key to the Bridge

This question of class distinctions—is she a proper woman or is she a prostitute?—has been at the center of scholarship on Gustave Caillebotte's *Le pont de l'Europe,* of 1876 (Figure 4). The status of the woman in the foreground of the painting has already been debated, but I want to contribute to this debate, since it is clear to me that a key to understanding the woman's class, her veil (a key provided by Caillebotte himself), has been overlooked by other scholars.[21] Situating this image within the discourse of the veil, dust, and urbanism, which I have begun to establish in this chapter, will open up our reading of it. This painting of grids and veils visually articulates some of the thematics of life in the new Paris. In fact,

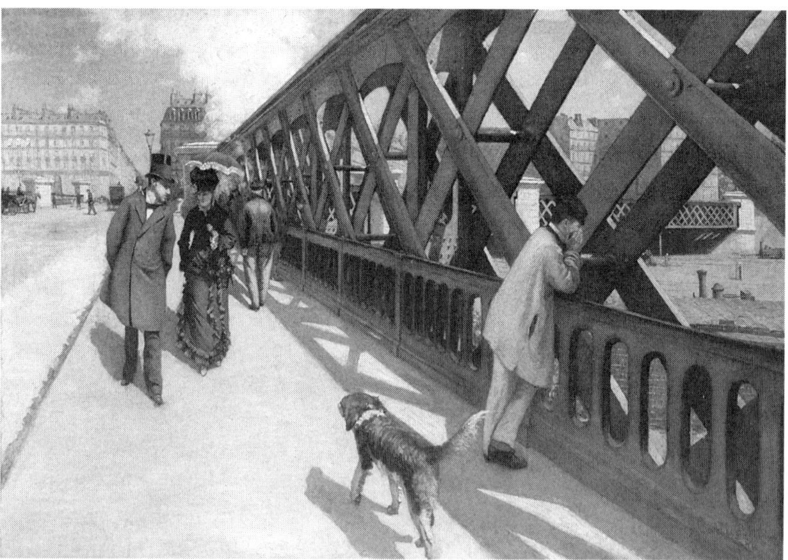

Figure 4. Gustave Caillebotte, *Le pont de l'Europe* (1876). Oil on canvas. Musée du Petit Palais, Geneva. Photograph by Studio Monique Bernaz, Geneva.

this image actually responds to and creates a dialogue among issues of class confusion, modernity, pollution, visuality, the development of industry, and, ultimately, the uneasy relationship between the bourgeoise and Paris—all characteristic aspects of life in the new metropolis.

Simply put, *Le pont de l'Europe* depicts people walking in a distinctly Haussmannized section of the city. Caillebotte has chosen this view, this spot, deliberately, for it allows him to describe not only le pont de l'Europe and all of its griddy intricacies but also the congruent façades of Haussmann's buildings. Called the "iron star" by Émile Zola in *La bête humaine*,[22] this bridge merges the new with the newer, makes connections both literal and metaphorical for the inhabitants of the new city. Indeed, the very use of a bridge (an object that is "ambiguous everywhere," to quote the French cultural historian Michel de Certeau)[23] as the stage for this painting helps to undermine the potential for a simple reading of it. Caillebotte makes his point clear: we are meant to consider the relationships of the figures in the picture within the context of Haussmann's Paris and all of the ambivalence and confusion that existed in it.

The perspectival rush across le pont de l'Europe, completed in 1868 and a symbol of technological advancement, culminates beyond the edges of the canvas at the convergence of six newly built and evenly orchestrated streets. Since regularity and coherence were two of the goals of Haussmann and Napoleon III's scheme, the streets in this painting should be read as interchangeable, as standing for the other streets in the radiating grid of the new city.[24] Thus, the street in the background and the two we fractionally see through the girder of the side of the bridge on the right become synecdoches for the other renovated parts of Paris. One could even say that contained here, in miniature terms, is the grand plan of the entire city.

The veiled Parisienne, near the center of the canvas, strolls through this network of protracted vistas and plunging diagonals. Her path runs parallel to the iron girders that function themselves as a magnified veil, through which puffing clouds of smoke, buildings, train tracks, and a trellis are partly visible. Like the bridge's ironwork, the balustrade in Caillebotte's *Balcony Grill*, of 1880 (Figure 5), effectively performs the work of an architectural veil, further illustrating the artist's interest in perspectives that capture the ways in which urban viewing practices were circumscribed. In this painting, irregular swirls of black paint assert the flatness of the canvas at the same time that they foreground the complex relationship between two of the most basic structures of Haussmann's Paris: the balcony and the street. The interstices of the grillwork are filled with the bright flickers of a passing carriage, a street cleaner, kiosks, lampposts, and a macadam-covered street, collapsing *matière,* that which it represents, and the surface of the canvas. The balustrade, like the Xs of the bridge's girders, cuts through whole objects, limiting what we see, filtering our view, making clear the condition of being veiled in the modern city.[25] What seems then, at first, to be an insubstantial veil across the top of the face of the woman in *Le pont de l'Europe* assumes a more dramatic importance when we consider it in relation to Caillebotte's career-long interest in examining the

Figure 5. Gustave Caillebotte, *Balcony Grill* (1880). Oil on canvas. Van Gogh Museum Enterprises B.V.

restriction of urban spectatorship. He presses us to think about the circumscription of her vision, since he depicts her with three objects—a hat, a parasol, and a veil—all of which would alter her field of vision.

The veiled woman's enigmatic positioning in relation to the man at her right has inspired conflicting readings of her class that have ranged from prostitute and courtesan to *bonne bourgeoise.* I would say, though, that a decisive explanation of her status is impossible. While the veil may be understood as distinguishing her as a woman not for sale, its presence, as well as all of the meanings inherent in it, is undercut by the possibility that the woman may be alone in the city. Some of the signs of her respectability are there. Her glance in the general direction of the man who may be accompanying her and not at the city before her contributes to a reading of this woman as proper, since strict etiquette rules recommend that any woman not wanting to be mistaken for a prostitute avoid eye contact with strange men in public.[26] Further evidence of the possibility of her status as proper is suggested by a well-developed study for the painting in which the man and the woman are depicted walking side by side. In it, she looks straight ahead; he seems to cast his gaze in her direction. Most of the subsidiary figures have not yet been put in, but the basic composition is there. Caillebotte has already worked out the swish of the woman's skirt and the tilt of the man's coat in this final sketch. The buildings in the background firmly take their positions. Even some of the shadows have already been determined, patches of thickly laid-on white epitomizing the filter of light through the girders.

Obviously, this final study is a close relation to the finished picture, now populated by more figures but compositionally quite the same, except for the way the main man and woman are depicted. Caillebotte's gesture of pulling them apart in the painting must be understood, then, as a conscious one, one that he knew would change the meaning of the picture as a whole. His deliberate insertion of a gap between the two figures is what actually *creates* the confusion about the woman's status, since it produces a reason for wondering whether she is or is not accompanied by the man to her right. As an embodiment of simultaneous disconnection and potential fusion, this thin slice of scumbled shadow and up-tilted pavement becomes a point of tension, a point of contention. Indeed, by introducing this gap, Caillebotte proposes multiple readings of this woman's class, despite the veil across her face, at the same time that he destabilizes a definitive assignation of her class. The gap is seemingly subtle spatially. It does not take up much canvas at all—only a small sliver, really. And yet its presence is so consequential, for it dissolves all easy interpretations of the woman's status.

Whereas the main characters in the foreground of *Paris Street: Rainy Day,* of the same year, are physically united and assuredly a couple, the figures in *Le pont de l'Europe* hold unstable positions. Since both images are contemporaneous and both concern themselves with Haussmann's Paris, its even façades and long vistas, a comparison of the main figures in each is entirely appropriate, even necessary. The man and woman in *Paris Street: Rainy Day* are united by the synchronic turn of their heads; they are also physically fused with her arm linked through his, his elbow fitting perfectly the curve at her waist. He holds the umbrella that covers them both, drawing them even more closely into the same space. Although the gentleman who rushes into the picture at the extreme right is going to knock umbrellas with them, possibly disconnecting them, causing one or both to stumble, at this moment they are firmly fixed.

It is the comparison of this part of *Paris Street* with its pictorial analogy in *Le pont de l'Europe* that makes the distance between the man and the woman in the latter that much more significant, that much more conspicuously there. By forcing a space between these figures, by adorning the woman with a veil, by marking out her glance, Caillebotte articulates in visual terms the nexus of perplexing connections between the woman and Haussmann's Paris at the same time that he makes unstable the class of this veiled woman. In keeping with a late nineteenth-century modernist tendency to render deliberately ambiguous images, the artist has constructed a painting that is laced with one of the most exasperating issues for contemporary bourgeois society: the difficulty of determining the class of a woman in the city. This figure's veil, more than any other aspect of her ensemble, may reveal her status. Indeed, Caillebotte includes it in order to make this woman at once a *bonne bourgeoise,* a courtesan, even a *flâneuse.*

This Parisienne's condition as the only obvious woman on a bridge populated by a scattered configuration of male figures further complicates the painting. In fact, the only other women in this composition of sixteen people and a dog are nearly indiscernible at the extreme left.[27] We have to work to decipher the two women, each made up of merely a few quick strokes of milky blue with some white. Their formal marginalization in the picture's structure further underscores the importance of the veiled woman along the focal point. Behind her, a puff of smoke, the trace of a recently passed train, rises. This smoke leaks through iron railings and effaces part of a Haussmannian façade, only to resolve itself in a mingled coalescence with the clouded sky. The smoke forms a visual frame for the head of the veiled woman, suggesting a connection between her and the marks of modernity.[28] Even her veil, really only a thin, grayish whirl of pigment, casts a smoky haze over her eyes and nose, offering an optical parallel to the smoke snaking across the building in the background.

To push this analogy between veils and the formations of modernity further, we may read the lattice work of the bridge, its intricate reticulation of crossing diagonals, as an exaggerated veil. The girders, like the threads of a veil, visually disperse and pull into sharper focus that which lies behind them. This bracketing of vision is put into active play by the figure in workers' blues who peers through the Xs of the bridge. The grid controls the parameters of what he sees, yet, unlike the veil, it does not superimpose itself *across* what he sees. This passage in the painting, this stilled moment in which a worker has stopped to check out a passing train, reminds us that the experience of all inhabitants of the new city was regulated, albeit to differing degrees, by grids. In fact, the formal construction of le pont de l'Europe itself reiterates, in reduced terms, the most spectacular grid determining life in Paris: the actual format of the new city, a series of widening concentric circles, or a radiating grid.

Caillebotte's painting charts a circuit among grids, smoke, veils, the new city, men, and women. Even the seemingly inconsequential details of modern life, such as veils and spaces between people, are consequential in this carefully crafted picture. Using this reasoning, we must read the shiver of smoke behind the veiled woman's head as having larger ramifications than its presence in the painting may at first indicate. Again, Caillebotte employs the diminutive to visualize major troubles in French society even as he lightly touches an almost pellucid grayish white pigment to the background of his image, whirling the paint behind the veiled woman's head and then increasing its viscosity as he pushes it back through the bridge's girders, one of its posts, and across the building façade beyond it. I believe that Caillebotte means for us to relate the smoke in the painting to other kinds of air-clouding substances such as dust, because the parallels between this image and the actual urban circumstances surrounding its production are so noticeable and compelling. For, considered within this set of connections, the concomitant escalation of the popularity of the veil with the filth from the destruction and construction of buildings becomes anything but coincidental.

The Medicalization of Dust

I want to continue to suggest here that the popularity of veils in Haussmann's Paris was only tenuously linked to fashion. Rather, their increased usage was more specifically connected to fears of class confusion, to the dust emitted by the razing of parts of Paris, and to the coincident, if not resultant, rise of scientific and medical discourses at the time. In other words, the renovations of the city generated dust, which in turn led public officials to study its effects and to warn of the dangers of inhaling it. As an actual presence and as a concept, dust conflated fears of physical contamination and moral degeneracy. In Alexandre Parent-Duchâtelet's studies of the 1830s, for example, the discourse of dirt provided a vehicle with which to link sewers, filth, and putrefaction to prostitution and, by extension, prostitution to the potential contamination and destruction of bourgeois society.

Given the ur-history of dirt and debris and the belief at the time that these substances were hazardous to public health, the dust emitted by Haussmann's renovations induced considerable alarm, worsening already significant anxieties over the health of the city's inhabitants. Zola's description of construction on le rue Neuve-Augustin in *The Ladies' Paradise* is a good, although fictional, indication of a contemporary's reaction to this dust: "At the slightest gust of wind, clouds of plaster flew about and covered the neighbouring roofs like a fall of snow. The Baudus in despair looked on at this implacable dust penetrating everywhere—getting through the closest woodwork, soiling the goods in their shop, even gliding into their beds; and the idea that they must continue to breathe it—that it would finish by killing them—empoisoned their existence."[29] For the Baudus, who own a shop on a street where a department store has been built, the dust symbolizes both the end of the old Parisian system of small business and the beginning of the new, more competitive market created by the *grands magasins*, as well as a health hazard. Both metaphorically and literally, the Baudus perceive that the dust has the ability to poison and kill not just their financial livelihood but their physical bodies as well. Slightly earlier in the novel, Denise Baudu, the heroine, observes from the street the gradual destruction of her uncle's store as a result of the "great thoroughfare to be opened from the Bourse to the new Opera House, under the name of the Rue du Dix-Décembre. . . . the opening would make a great hole in these streets, letting in the sun and air." However, using Denise's perspective a paragraph later, Zola undermines the positive aspects of Haussmannization and building of department stores: "As the Ladies' Paradise became larger, The Old Elbeuf seemed to get smaller. The young girl thought the windows looked blacker than ever, and more and more crushed beneath the low first storey. . . . the damp had still further discoloured the old green sign-board, a sort of distress oozed from the whole frontage, livid in hue, and, as it were, grown thinner. . . . the dust was invading the counters and drawers, whilst an odour of saltpeter rose from the bales of cloth that were no longer moved about."[30]

In addition to the damaging consequences of the dust of the construction, Paris after 1850 faced even more problems caused by other kinds of pollution. More directly than before, the city was affected by industry, which had, prior to that year, taken place mostly in suburban areas.[31] The razing of entire parts of Paris, in combination with the acceleration of industrialization there, resulted in a substantial increase in air pollution, which, in turn, necessitated the study of its effects on the health of the population.

While an organized French national health movement had begun under the Bourbon Restoration, it was not until the Second Empire that more serious inroads were made in Paris itself. As industrialization and urbanization flourished between 1852 and 1870, air and water pollution, identified as problems earlier in the century by Lavoisier, Boussingault, and Cloquet, increased as well. The overcrowding of work spaces, in conjunction with an awareness of the impurities emitted by steam engines and bitumen and rubber factories, caused concern, and by the middle of the century the bourgeoisie was obsessed with filth, degeneration, and infection.[32]

Important inroads in the analysis of airborne materials toward the middle of the nineteenth century were, in fact, indirectly facilitated by these urban health problems that were generated by industrialization and perceived to be linked to moral and social decline.[33] Beginning in the 1860s, public hygiene and urban hygiene became part of the discourse of medicine, thus requiring that doctors consider health in broader, more urban terms. For example, Louis Pasteur, a leading proponent of the concept of contagionism, connected the minuscule to larger questions when, in 1862, he analyzed the composition of dust and organisms in the air and related his findings to public health. Perhaps the most telling example of this intense interest in air and its effect on Parisians was the practice, common by the 1850s, of taking air samples from active parts of the city, such as around l'Opéra, la place de la Concorde, and le jardin du Luxembourg at varying times of day and studying their dust content.[34]

The work of public hygiene and its influence on medical discussion and practice grew increasingly important to the people who were living in a dusty and continually changing Paris.[35] In *La revue scientifique* in 1889, one writer confirmed this interpenetration retrospectively: "It is incontestable that hygiene has made tremendous progress in the past twenty years, as much in the realm of pure science as applied sciences; in particular, urban hygiene, which is developing parallel to the science of microbes, has taken on considerable importance."[36]

The rhetoric of urban hygiene grew out of long-standing fears, which the architectural changes of Paris simply exacerbated.[37] Indeed, the very formation and success of an urban hygiene movement, a field so engaged with the problems of the new metropolis, illustrate the depth of anxieties over disease, which the transformation of Paris brought closer to the surface. The stagnant pools of water and constricted streets of the old Paris posed certain health risks; however, their elimination raised others. In 1848 the Comité consultatif d'hygiène publique was established to advise the government on issues pertaining to public health. And the Organisation de médecine publique was developed to address the quality of the air, dustier and dirtier than before, and its effects on the health of Parisians.

"Many epidemic diseases are contagious, and these contagions travel in air currents, wind, and clothes," claimed Benoist de la Grandière, articulating the previously unsubstantiated, yet commonly held, fear that disease spreads through the air.[38] In 1882, Robert Koch identified the tubercle bacillus, the living microorganism responsible for the spread of tuberculosis, discrediting Pidoux and the others who opposed theories of contagionism by arguing that the disease was inherited.[39] Koch's work represented a shift in what David S. Barnes has called the "historiography of medicine," for it validated the hitherto controversial germ theory, proving that certain diseases were contracted through contact rather than through heredity.[40] Adding further to the important inroads of Koch, Dr. Jules Rochard, an influential hygienist whose *Traité d'hygiène sociale* and *Encyclopédie d'hygiène et de médecine publique* were owned and consulted by many French families, reiterated that dust carried the lethal tubercle bacillus: "The microbe, agent of contagion, exists above all in dust."[41] Gaston Bonnier also catalyzed concern over the dust in the air, claiming, "Dust is certainly dangerous because it contains living germs, in particular bacteria, which transmit certain illnesses such as tuberculosis, diphtheria, and the flu."[42]

Although Haussmann's architectural changes can arguably be blamed in part for increasing dust and fear of disease, ironically the structure of his buildings discloses an even longer-standing concern about infection through people's physical proximity to the dirt on the street. In an effort to lessen the possibility of bourgeois contact with lower-class germs and street dust and the diseases that they harbored, many of Haussmann's buildings were equipped with balconies. These balconies were intended, in part, as protected extensions of the bourgeois interior into the city.[43] High enough above the circulating masses of people and germs, the balcony enabled the bourgeoisie to witness life below without necessarily being contaminated by it.[44]

Gustave Caillebotte's *Balcony Grill* becomes, within this context, an illustration of the ways in which the balcony separates the public from the private, the filthy from the sanitary. A view through the balcony of Caillebotte's home on le boulevard Haussmann, this painting takes as its subject the iron grill that physically and visually isolates the man who sweeps the dusty macadam-covered street below from the family inside. It differentiates the space of contagion from the less threatening interior of the *haut bourgeois* home. At the right edge of the picture, the artist even includes a flash of a shiny green leaf from a potted plant on the inside of the home in order to provide the perfect "natural" domestic counterpart to the presumably unhealthy public street below. Caillebotte's painting of the partition between the dusty street and the pristine space of his family home may thus be seen as a visual exegesis of the fears and ideologies that science and medicine fueled through their elaborate public warnings. Indeed, he would have known that scientists had been studying the effects of dry ground sweeping since the late 1850s, for much was made of its ill effects in widely circulated contemporary periodicals, and he certainly would have understood the importance of a clean home, since this was extensively publicized as well.[45] A scientifically based causal connection between dust and health linked dirt with morality. In other words, a clean and healthy home became a measure of moral goodness, while a dusty and dirty home or street was equated with degradation and disease.

By the middle of the century, the growing field of medicine was promoting its beliefs through a propagandistic blend of scientific knowledge, politics, and ethics.[46] Bourgeois women in particular were targeted by the medical community and encouraged to shield themselves from any kind of contamination, mainly because they were thought to be more susceptible to disease and because they were considered responsible for maintaining the physical and moral health of present and future generations. In a popular journal of family health, this fusion of science, women, morality, and the good of the country is apparent in Maurice Barenne's dogmatic and prescriptive words: "Woman is the fervent soul of the family. . . . She is munificent by nature. . . . the health and happiness of women, this is the health and happiness of all people."[47] Women's health and, by extension, the health of the family were clearly of great concern to late nineteenth-century doctors, some of whom worked with government officials to institute what they considered to be appropriate rules of hygiene and behavior for respectable women in the new city.[48]

When Robin and Pouchet examined dust particles during the cholera epidemic of the late 1840s and discovered that dust contained choleric material,[49] contemporaries were given the scientific substantiation they needed for advocating that proper women protect themselves by veiling their faces. Dr. Emile Beaugrand's *L'hygiène ou l'art de conserver la santé* of 1855, a popular household health guide, boasted of the veil's ability to guard the face from the elements: "[T]he white or colored veil . . . protects the face from cold during the winter, and, during the summer . . . keeps the eyes safe from dust and the too-strong rays of the sun."[50] A writer named Cléophée supported this idea in her (or is it a man using a feminine pseudonym?) column, "Modes, fashions et causeries," for *Les modes parisiennes:* "One finds also at the House of Violard [*sic*] the most beautiful laces of Chantilly and the most wonderful black quipures that one can possibly imagine, then the light voilettes which are necessary for protection from the mists of autumn."[51] Obviously, the idea that veils could help shield the face was catching on. Cléophée describes the ubiquity of the veil after rainy weather a year later in 1855: "After the rainy days of fairly moderate temperature, the frost has come to harden the mud and spread a glaze over the streets of Paris; on this wintery mirror a white layer of snow has fallen; Paris resembles a Russian city: the women's faces are hiding under thick veils."[52] In a later edition of the widely read journal, another critic has this to say: "The lightest and most diaphanous voilettes, which were lowered at the end of the session over more than one pretty face to protect them from the mist outside, also came from the House of Violart."[53] Though writing about the hat of the woman who rides horses, Charles Blanc gives us yet another example of what contemporaries believed a veil could do: "A man's hat has long been looked upon as classic in the costume of a woman on horseback, whose only way of asserting her sex is by wearing a veil, under pretence of protecting her eyes from the dust and sun."[54]

Still, not all veils were understood as being effectual means with which to guard the face. In an 1863 issue of *La mode illustrée, journal de la famille,* the *voile de loup,* or wolf veil, is described as being quite successful for this purpose: "The round voilettes are always in fashion, even though they are absolutely inadequate for protecting the face. We recommend to our readers the wolf veil of which we publish the drawing and the pattern, it will give them [the wearers] incontestable service, in every season."[55] Since no studies seem to have been conducted on the veil's ability to inhibit the passage of airborne contaminated particles, I would suggest that the veil—and its medical materialist justification—served simply to curb an escalating social anxiety over germs and disease.

Obviously dust fell on men, women, and children of all classes. Yet the medical community's directives were pitched at bourgeois women.[56] Although working-class women, especially laundresses, were most affected by the tuberculosis and cholera epidemics, it was still bourgeois women who were invited by etiquette books, fashion journals, and the medical community to use veils. Since concerns over germs and disease were the motivating factors behind the bourgeoisie's desire to mark out clearer class distinctions, it makes sense that the veil would have been an active agent in helping to maintain those divisions. For the visibility of the unveiled lower-class face to the bourgeoisie was crucial at a time when viewership signified a type of mastery. Thus, the presence or absence of a veil may be seen as both a display of class power dynamics and an indication of real fears associated with disease and infection.

Émile Zola's *Nana,* begun in 1878, provides a contemporary's recognition of the importance of an unveiled face in determining both the status and the health of an individual, who happens to be, in this case, a prostitute. He wrote: "And around this grotesque and horrible mask of death, the hair, the beautiful hair, still blazed like sunlight and flowed in a stream of gold. Venus was decomposing. It was as if the poison she had picked up in the gutters, from the carcasses left there by the roadside, that ferment with which she had poisoned a whole people, had now risen to her face and rotted it."[57] Nana's physical deterioration from smallpox, which insinuates as well her moral deterioration from prostitution, visibly manifests itself across her face. Zola's detailed description of Nana's transmogrifying face serves to underline the importance of its visual accessibility and thus, by implication, the unobstructed accessibility of all prostitutes' faces. Consequently, the practice of veiling only respectable women seems to have been both a function and an inhibitor of bourgeois fears of contamination by the working and lower classes.

Ironically, this classing of the veil denied its use to those who most needed the protection it offered from the inhalation of dust. Sartory and Langlais blamed the high rate of tuberculosis and cholera among ironers and laundresses on their poor working conditions and their handling of dust-embedded clothing: "In laundry facilities, there is a profusion of dust, and hanging dirty laundry can be considered dangerous, since it spreads a cloud of dust containing a large quantity of microorganisms."[58] The brushing and banging of clothes resulted in the release of dusts, both adulterated and not, linking the bourgeoisie and the working classes in a way far more dangerous than casual contact on the streets. In addition to the apparent disregard for the health of laundry workers whether through their own ignorance or volition, clothing from contaminated homes was not disinfected, further increasing the possibility of infection both for the laundresses themselves and for the families to whom the clothes in their facility belonged.[59] In the *Revue des cours scientifiques de la France et de l'étranger* in 1870, John Tyndall quoted J. B. Dancer, who suggested that people whose work involves the production of excessive amounts of dust wear "*respirateurs*."[60] Surprisingly, despite both the hazards associated with the profession and the admonitions of doctors and scientists, the visual and textual evidence suggests that laundresses did not actually use *respirateurs*, or any mouth or nose covering for that matter. While it was an imperfect means for filtering impure particles, the veil would have been effective in keeping some contaminants out. The site of cleansing and purification was, unexpectedly, a space that actually generated disease.[61]

While the medical community was alarmed by the staggering death rate among laundry workers, little effort was made to improve their working conditions or to educate them in the proper handling of infected garments. Edgar Degas's *Laundresses*, of 1884–86 (Figure 6), painted after an earlier version of 1876, depicts the kind of cramped and bleak spaces in which these women worked. Even the yellowed and scumbled background of the painting, the masterful result of oil paint on thickly woven canvas, becomes the visual equivalent of the dusty and murky atmosphere in which the laundresses performed their jobs. The picture represents two women; one is hard at work, shoulders stooped intensely over a shirt sleeve, while the other yawns so widely that her mouth opens into a perfect oval. This kind of behavior, the absentminded breathing in of large quantities of dusty air, would have increased one's chances of contracting an airborne disease. And although Degas's images are anything but fixed or reportorial, they certainly function across scientific, medical, and artistic discussions.[62] This picture, whether Degas knew it or not, exposes what was evidently a challenge for public officials: the even distribution of information about epidemic disease.[63] This woman signifies the ignorance of the working-class female vis-à-vis scientific research. As long as the inhabitants of the most poorly ventilated spaces of the city remained uninformed of the

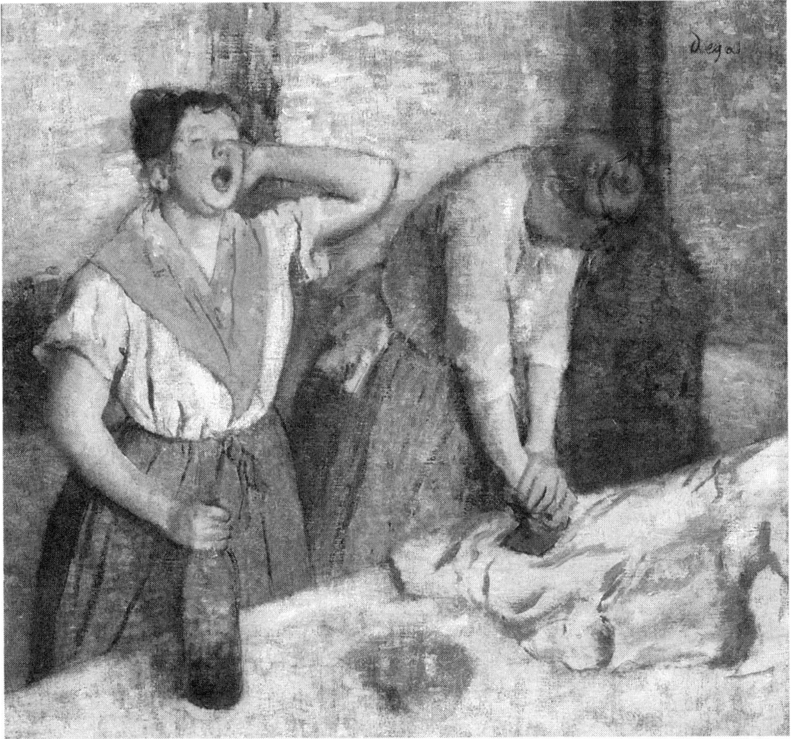

Figure 6. Edgar Degas, *Laundresses* (1884–86). Oil on canvas. Photograph by Hervé Lewandowski, Musée d'Orsay, Paris. Réunion des musées nationaux/Art Resource, NY.

consequences of their unhealthy work and living environments, modern medicine would prove ineffective in combating the spread of epidemic disease in the spectacular new city.

Even the backgrounds of Degas's earlier pictures of ironers reverberate with a hazy sense of dust-infused air. For example, in *Woman Ironing*, begun around 1876 and completed by 1887 (Figure 7), which is just one in a series of similar images, an ironer emerges through a mesh of alternating thicknesses of paint. The gauzy transparency of some strokes combined

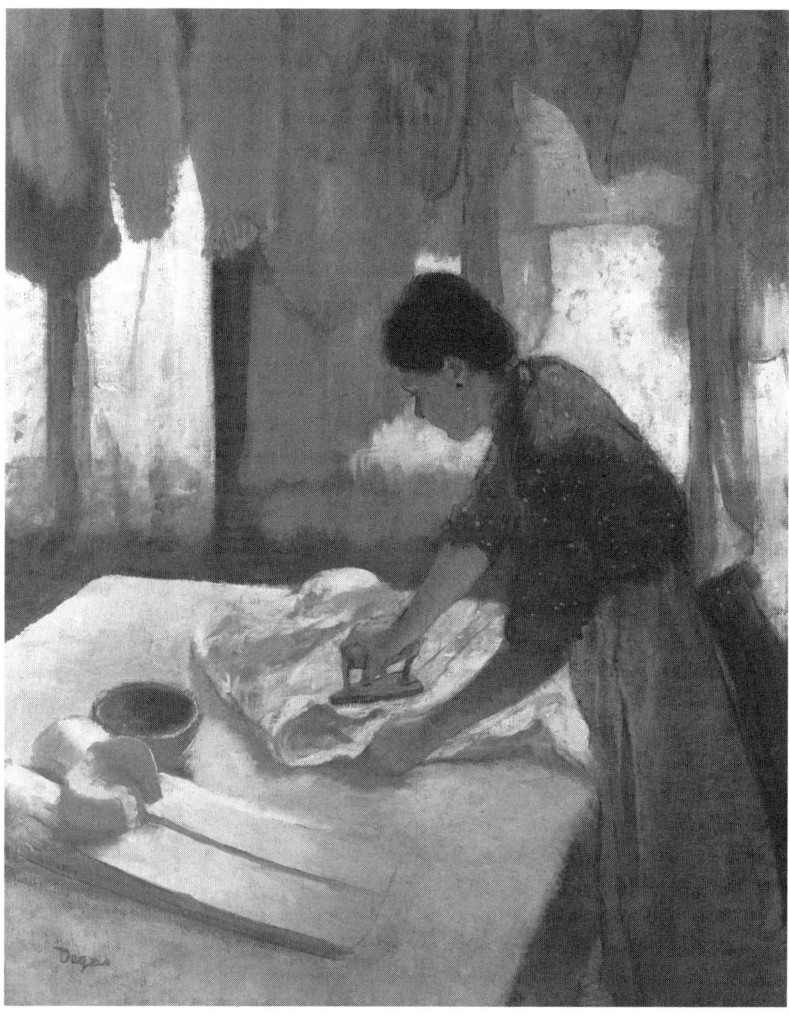

Figure 7. Edgar Degas, *Woman Ironing* (begun c. 1876, completed c. 1887). Oil on canvas. National Gallery of Art, Washington, D.C. Collection of Mr. and Mrs. Paul Mellon.

with the lushness of others allows Degas to evoke the dense and steamy air that would have filled the laundry worker's lungs. Light passes through the fragile curtains, really just scumbled white paint, only to be blocked in parts by the colorful array of shirts that hang before them. Even the ironer's plodding and deliberate gesture emphasizes the oppressiveness of the air that surrounds her. Both composition and technique facilitate the visual evocation of what Degas must have recognized about the circumstances within which this part of the population worked.

Reformists earlier in the century had been more interested than those in the later half were in improving the living and working environments of workers and the poor.[64] Louis-René Villermé, who, along with Parent-Duchâtelet, was a member of the hygienist movement, exposed the need for legislation and institutional change to improve conditions for the laboring classes. Some effort was made during the second half of the nineteenth century to lower the death rate in working-class sections of the city by advocating the importance of ventilation and sunlight in the interior of the home. Yet, these areas remained as restricted and dark as they had been before studies found that the rays of the sun and proper aeration could hinder the survival of such lethal microorganisms as the tubercle bacillus.

David S. Barnes has, in fact, argued that "[w]orking class wives and domestic servants were implicated in the spread of tuberculosis through slovenly housekeeping and direct contamination. Nevertheless, they were rarely, if ever, the ultimate targets or endpoints either of social etiologies or of charitable intervention."[65] Young women who attended school were educated in the gravity of keeping a sanitary home, of cleaning clothing, and of breathing fresh air.[66] The Société de médecine publique et d'hygiène professionnelle de Paris, for example, distributed books and pamphlets to students, one of which included a detailed and "scientific" chapter titled "Of the air . . . impurities of the air: Dust, gaseous substances, miasmas, contagious viruses, microbes, bacteria."[67] Other texts strongly suggested that all clothes be brushed and shaken every day.[68] Yet this information remained available to only a select segment of the population, since the successful disbursement of this knowledge depended on a degree of literacy.

Seeing through the Veil

The veil shielded those women literate enough to understand the directives that warned of dust's unhealthy composition and wealthy enough to afford the family health books, etiquette manuals, and fashion journals that described the uses of the veil. A fashion journal of 1860, *La mode illustrée, journal de la famille,* boasted, "This new type of veil offers advantages with regard to its charm and the useful service it renders in protecting the face entirely from wind and dust."[69] This is surely an overstatement of the veil's actual ability to protect the face entirely, yet it is part of the symbolic discourse of the veil that circulated widely and magnified its actual usefulness. And while women were encouraged to adopt veils to shield themselves from sun, dust, and wind, those same veils did more than simply protect; they also affected the way respectable women were seen in the city.

The veil's facility in altering appearance is well documented by contemporary observers, who often remarked on its ability to hide the face. In 1852, one writes, "[T]heir bonnets are more elaborate than ever; their little faces are lost in layers of laces and little ribbons."[70] An image from an 1860 issue of *La mode illustrée, journal de la famille* (Figure 8) is just one of many examples of the kind of veil the author describes. Made of tulle, lace, and a *soutache* of silk, the complex weave of this garment, the *voile à barbes* (a veil with Newgate frills), all but disguises the woman who wears it. This is the veil that protects "the face entirely from wind and dust," according to the description that accompanies it. But this particular veil also alters the topography of the face beneath it. Its intricate web almost obliterates the mouth and nose, each caught behind the decorative lower half. The eyes remain vaguely there, punctuated by broad arches meant to emblematize eyebrows. The absence of all facial features but the eyes calls attention to the ways in which the veil jeopardizes vision on both sides. The densely woven veil, then, could mark out an aesthetics of power for the woman behind it. She could be both seer and not seen. Her identity could be concealed at the same time that her veil revealed her status as bourgeoise.

While the veil inhibited easy visual access to the woman behind it, it also encouraged the concentration of the gaze of the viewer who looked at her. The very constitution of the veil itself, really an elaborate system of densely or loosely woven threads, sometimes flecked with dots, as in an image from an 1864 issue of *La mode illustrée, journal de la famille* (Figure 9), surely declares that its function is not necessarily only that of protecting the woman from the gaze and the elements. A screen of irregularly organized loops of thread, the veil in this image brands the face so that skin and fabric read as one plane. It does not mask the face behind it, but rather it causes us, and of course the woman, to look through it. Forced to look even more closely to synthesize all of the parts of the woman's scotomized face, the viewer becomes virtually enmeshed in the viewing system. So, while the veil could, to varying degrees, perform the work of concealing, an outside viewer could decrease that degree of concealment by looking more closely to sharpen the blurred face on the other side.

Even though some veils undercut the pleasure of the viewer, allowing the wearer to resist absolute surveillance, a critical issue remained: the veiled woman's vision was somewhat impeded. The veil of the Second

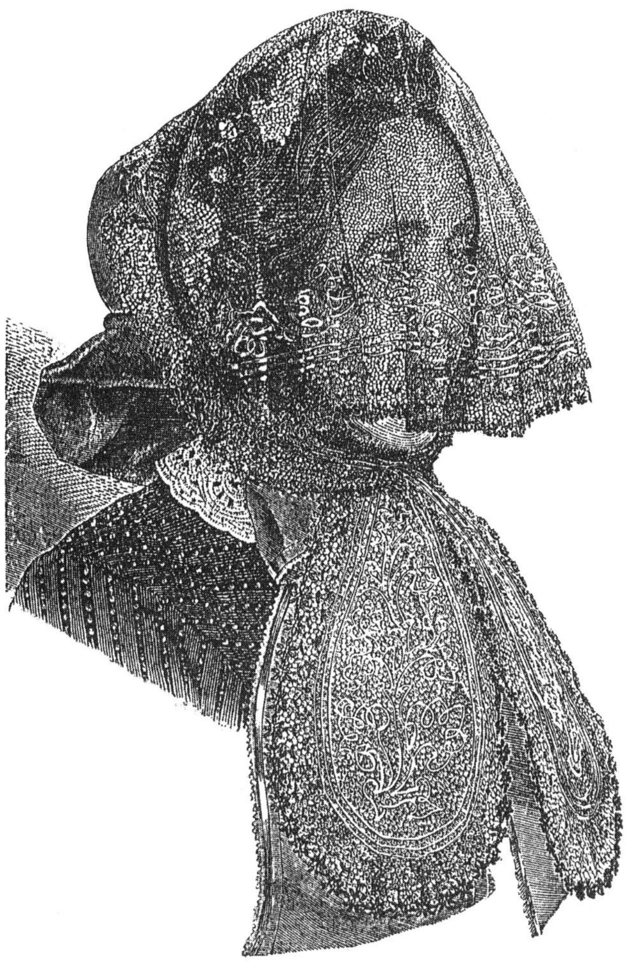

Figure 8. *La mode illustrée, journal de la famille* 14 (April 1, 1860): 106. Engraving. Bibliothèque des arts décoratifs, Paris.

Empire was the filter through which the bourgeoise's view was "purified." While fashion journals, etiquette books, and the medical community encouraged the use of veils by bourgeois women from the 1850s through the 1880s, by 1890, doctors began to vocalize their concern that they obstructed vision. In an article titled "Contre les voilettes," one writer acknowledged the work of a doctor who "has just declared war against the voilette. He affirms that it is deadly to the eyesight. . . . dotted veils appear to be the most dangerous."[71]

Doctors were not alone in recognizing that the veil could be harmful to vision. In her etiquette book of 1893, Baronne Staffe exclaimed, "Veils,

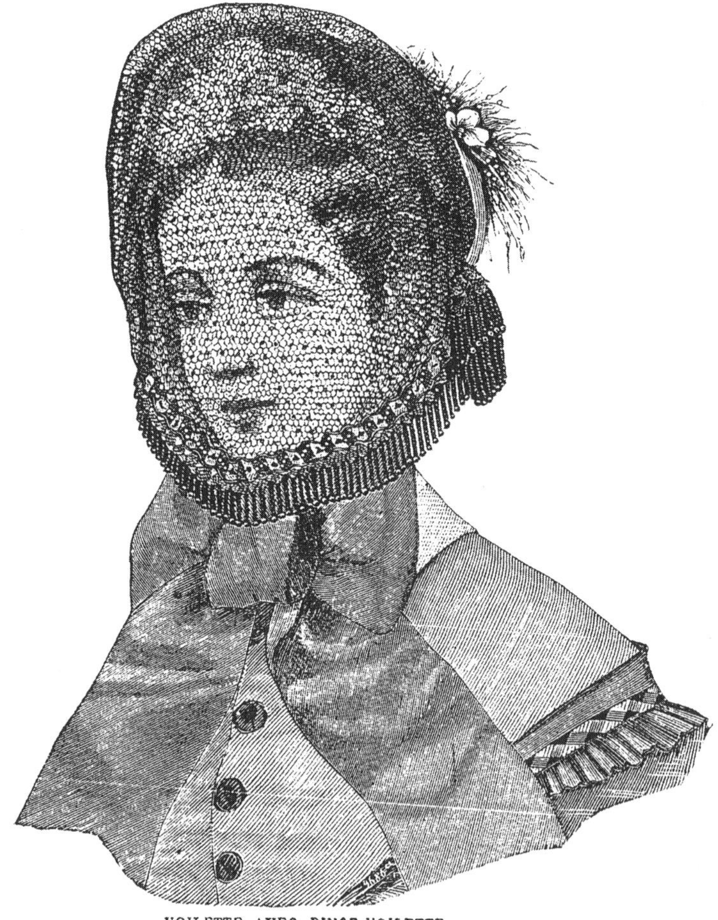

Figure 9. *La mode illustrée, journal de la famille* 21 (May 22, 1864): 164. Engraving. Bibliothèque des arts décoratifs, Paris.

and certainly dotted veils, are quite injurious to eyesight."[72] The fashionable dotted veil had interfered with respectable women's vision long before social and medical authorities deplored its use.[73] During the Second Empire, however, and for the first twenty or so years of the Third Republic, little public evidence suggests that veils did anything other than protect miraculously against dust, sun, and wind and obscure signs of aging and the absence of ideal beauty, two issues that I will address in the next chapter. And while other varieties of veils were worn prior to 1852, when Haussmann began the work of realizing Napoleon III's scheme, those veils tended to be more loosely constructed and had less-urban functions. During the 1820s and 1830s, demiveils and voilettes, most of which were thin and did not cover the entire face, were popular mainly at bathing resorts but also in the city, where, according to a writer for the *Journal des dames et des modes* in 1834, "the vogue is for demiveils. Demiveils of tulle are worn well with hats of *demi-toilelle*."[74]

French fashion journals of the 1850s through the 1870s, the comprehensive analysis of which is a useful indication of some social trends, continually demonstrate the popularity of the veil at the beach and in the countryside, where air was presumably healthy. But more important for my argument, these same periodicals chronicle an explosion of the wearing of veils in the city, where air was less healthy. Unlike earlier veils, the type worn during the Second Empire was enmeshed with the city structure itself. Not only did its form roughly mimic the radiating grid that translated a mostly circuitous, medieval city into a more modern one, but it also screened the face from the remnants of the old Paris. It became popular in a culture and time that was driven by improvements in technology and by a fascination with fashion—in clothes, in architecture. The veil of the Second Empire was bound to the discourse of the new city, functioning as a visual and physical filter between the woman who wore it and modern Paris.

While vision had always been connected to knowledge, technological advancements and the subsequent specularization of life in general instigated an even greater awareness of the visual in the second half of the nineteenth century.[75] Since visual knowledge of the spectacle of the modern city could threaten the proper woman's position in society and lead to her downfall, it makes sense that the bourgeoise was actively encouraged to veil herself when in the city. As Anthea Callen has pointed out in relation to the late nineteenth century: "[K]nowledge, temptation and containment were all equated with the visual: the eye was the organ both of revelation and of control. . . . Looking was, therefore, an activity to be discouraged in women—whose submission to an assertive male gaze/sexuality was its guarantee of meaning, and thus power."[76] The veiling of the respectable woman, indeed the deliberate discouragement of her looking, was a means of controlling her exposure to both the city and the male gaze and even her sexuality.

The *flâneur,* or Baudelaire's paradigmatic man about town, had the privilege of observing the city through the anonymous and less obstructed gaze, while the bourgeoise had a veiled view.[77] This hierarchy of vision was enforced not through strict dichotomies but rather through the proper woman's weakened vision. Not blinded by the veil, she was nevertheless held back, protected, and shielded from modern life. Since a proscribed vision of modern Paris was symbolically equated with a controlled exposure to modernity, the respectable woman's vision had to be somewhat obfuscated. Her limited access to Paris already restricted by institutional structures, the proper woman was further detached from public life by the physical barrier of the veil.

Considered within the discourse of late nineteenth-century visuality and veiling, Edouard Manet's *Music in the Tuileries Gardens,* of 1862 (Figure 10), a picture of fashionable Parisians enjoying a concert on a Sunday

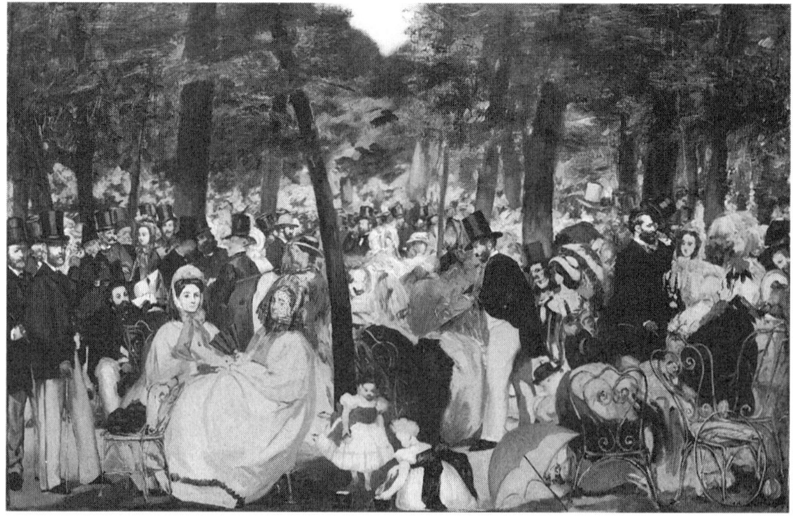

Figure 10. Edouard Manet, *Music in the Tuileries Gardens* (1862). Oil on canvas. National Gallery of Art, London.

afternoon in le jardin du Tuileries, may be read as tracing the mediation of vision for bourgeois women. What did the five veiled women see when they left the gardens through the west exit and faced the broad expanse of la place de la Concorde? They must have seen it through a shifting and changing grid, sometimes punctuated by black dots, as in the case of Madame Loubens in the foreground of the painting. The five most obvious veils in this painting chart five intensities of seeing in Haussmann's city. The two thinnest veils, worn by the women behind the blue and yellow bonnet-clad figures in the foreground, would disrupt vision less than the black veil of the woman (Manet's mother) who faces the gentleman in a top hat (Manet's brother), to the right of center. She is so encased in her veils—we see only a swatch of dark hair and the vague indication of an eye—that her presence is read only through that which visually liquidates it. In other words, her identity has been obscured by the very veil that actually defines her space in the painting.

Still, no one is more elaborately veiled than Madame Loubens, in the foreground of the picture, and no one's vision is more highly filtered than hers. The heaviness of her particular veil is further exaggerated by the lighter, sheerer one worn by the woman who walks directly behind her. A fabrication of black netting and dots, Madame Loubens's veil brands a relatively small part of the canvas's surface. However, Manet heightens the effect of her veil by performing the clever ocular trick of practically twinning Loubens with her pictorial counterpart, Madame Lejosne. Besides the difference of the presence and absence of a veil, both are dressed in almost identical yellow capes and bonnets with large blue bows. They are slightly off mirror images of one another, a convention often found in contemporary fashion plates.[78] The visual comparison between the two most conspicuous figures in an excessively populated painting only magnifies the impact of Madame Loubens's veil both on her and on the viewer. It infiltrates her visual field, reminding her of her position within the social hierarchy by continually calling attention to the ways in which her view of the Tuileries is caught within the netting of her veil. Because it happens to be one of the most fashionable veils of the day, which is readily apparent with a quick perusal of the pictures in the many fashion journals published at the time, its significance is further elevated, especially for the women looking at the painting who own similar veils.

For the viewer, Loubens's veil formally screens her face, simultaneously distinguishing her from Madame Lejosne and providing a paradigm for reading the painting as a whole. For it is here, in this small passage, that layers of paint become metaphors for levels of engagement with the city. In other words, if we understand the veil as a trope for some of the complexities of modern life, then Loubens's veil in the foreground works as a blueprint for the entire picture, enabling us to see displaced veils and veiling practices throughout. The complicated play of patterns at the surface of *Music in the Tuileries Gardens* causes wrought-iron chair backs, parasols, hats, playing children, and trees to function as filters through which we parse the threads of the painting, really a microcosm of the intricate design of modern Parisian bourgeois society. Even the structure of the composition itself performs the work of a veil, simultaneously dispersing and forcing the proliferation of random particles into some semblance of clarification. And like a cloud of dust, the picture perpetually renews itself, shifting some things into focus, others into obscurity, and then back again. As a modern reader, I find myself trapped in an elaborate nexus of black suits and dresses, top hats, and trees. I have to labor through this tangle in order to decipher the veiled women in the painting. Not considering the potential of the women whose backs are turned to the viewer, there are five, as I count them, but they at once evade the gaze and are captured by it.

Even the faces of some of the unveiled women are, in effect, veiled by the thick layers of paint that constitute them. For example, Madame Lejosne's face is alternately impastoed and thinned, readable on multiple planes simultaneously. At once *matière* and skin, the paint and the weave of the canvas become the veil through which we read her likeness. Unlike the faces of the men at the edges of the left side of the canvas (those of Manet and his brother), with their more crisply delineated details, Madame Lejosne's face is blurred by dabs of fleshy pigment. She is closer to us than the figures to the left of her, yet we see her through more actively applied brushstrokes. Like her counterpart, Madame Loubens, Madame Lejosne is veiled, at least in formal terms.

Just as in Caillebotte's *Le pont de l'Europe,* both women and men in Manet's elaborate tableau are implicated in the web of the new city. For Caillebotte, iron girders and vast rushing streets circumscribe the passage of people through modern Paris, whereas Manet threads choice members of Parisian society through a labyrinthine entanglement of people, trees, and chairs. And while these crowds and uniform streets somewhat veiled life for all inhabitants of Paris at the time, it was specifically women's vision that was further held in by veils. The respectable woman's engagement with modern Paris was inscribed on a grid that both empowered her, for she could be somewhat hidden, and occluded her vision. These women were prevented from fully experiencing the spectacle of the new city, and what opportunity they did have was further limited by the veil. If only on a subtle level, the veil was a means of redirecting the female gaze, of lessening the amount of visual contact a woman had with the city so that her public respectability could be preserved.

Gustave Flaubert recognized the gendered division in accessibility to urban life—and life in general—when, in 1857, he wrote in *Madame Bovary*, from the pregnant Emma's perspective:

> She hoped for a son; he would be strong and dark; she would call him George; and this idea of having a male child was like an expected

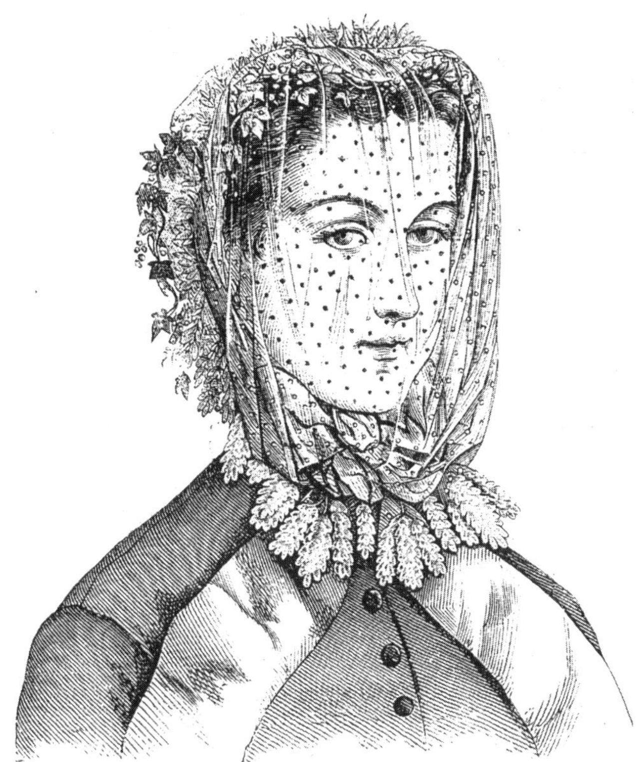

VOILE LAMBALLE, DE CHEZ Mme AUBERT,
RUE NEUVE-DES-MATHURINS, 6.

Figure 11. *La mode illustrée, journal de la famille* 32 (August 5, 1866). Engraving. Bibliothèque nationale, Paris.

> revenge for all her impotence of the past. A man, at least, is free; he can explore all passions and all countries, overcome obstacles, taste of the most distant pleasures. But a woman is always hampered. Being inert as well as pliable, she has against her the weakness of the flesh and the inequity of the law. Like the veil held to her hat by a ribbon, her will flutters in every breeze; she is always drawn by some desire, restrained by some rule of conduct.[79]

Emma muses here about what she sees as the advantages of life for a man and the disadvantages of life for a woman. Flaubert/Emma uses the veil as a metaphor for women's position in 1850s France. The woman's will, and as I read it, her freedom, which Flaubert likens to a veil, is always both

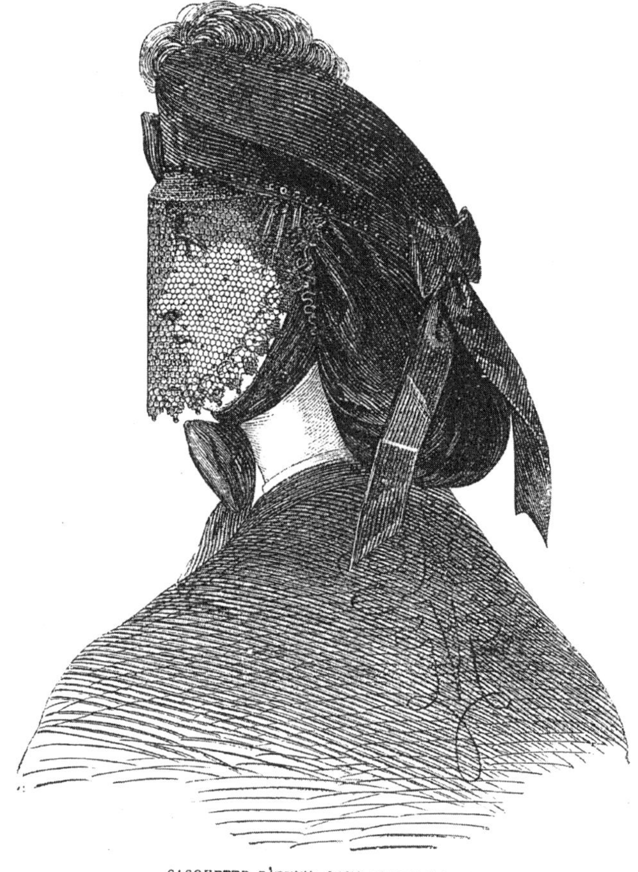

CASQUETTE D'HIVER POUR JEUNE FILLE.

Figure 12. *La mode illustrée, journal de la famille* 8 (February 19, 1865). Engraving. Bibliothèque des arts décoratifs, Paris.

in process and inhibited. This passage enacts a dichotomy between male and female, between free and not free, between unveiled and veiled. And even though Flaubert's oppositional assertions are heavy handed, his text, like the veil to which it refers, still serves as a filter through which to view a contemporary's take on the position of the respectable woman at this time. She was certainly distanced from Paris through restrictions against her entry into specific parts of the city. However, an underconsidered, yet significant, means of inhibiting the bourgeoise's view and experience of modern Paris was through the veils she was encouraged to wear by contemporary fashion journals and by the medical community. Some of these veils were light and filmy, even barely noticeable. If it were not for its dots and subtle folds, the veil illustrated in an 1866 issue of *La mode illustrée, journal de la famille* (Figure 11) would be almost undetectable. Still others, such as one dating from February 1865 (Figure 12), were so dense and starched that they resembled armor. This type of veil functioned not simply, and probably only minimally, to protect a woman from dust, wind, and germs. Giving her the power to be hidden from full view, the veil simultaneously decreased a woman's power to see the city without mediation. The veil, then, affected how the bourgeoise was seen, and, more important, it inflected what she saw.

2

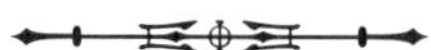

Making Up the Surface

The Ideal *Bourgeois Visage*

Not only was the late nineteenth-century French face connected to a discourse of urban pathology and visual inhibition, but also it was a locus of attention for both textual and visual explorations of aging and ideals of beauty. The face could register a woman's age more readily than could her body, which would have been corseted, clothed, hidden, smoothed over, and perfected.[1] Photographs commissioned by the Countess de Castiglione shortly before her death in the 1890s expose how the face could be exploited as a space for an attempted revision of the visual manifestations of age even when the youthful body was beyond recall. As Abigail Solomon-Godeau has pointed out in her important essay on these and earlier photographs of Napoleon III's mistress produced by the firm Mayer and Pierson, by the time these pictures were taken, "the countess has become stout and possibly toothless. She seems, as well, to have lost much of her hair. Nonetheless, her face appears unlined (it was probably retouched on the negative), her eyebrows are penciled, her eyelids shadowed."[2] Solomon-Godeau focuses especially on a photograph taken around 1895–98 in which the countess's face is elaborately made-up, so overdone in fact that her eyebrows look like they have been pasted on. Every effort has been made across the countess's face to restore her to her youthful position as one of the most beautiful and desirable women in Second Empire Paris. Lines have been magically erased, makeup has been applied, and what is left of her hair has been curled and fitted under a black lace mantle. And yet the image of her clearly uncorseted and aged body only emphasizes the futility of such efforts to eradicate the evidence of her advanced maturity.

Another photograph of the countess from this series, "The Ermine Cloak," further indexes the importance of the treatment of the face in attempting to construct a visual ideal of youthfulness. She is no less ostentatiously adorned than in the previous image, yet here the countess has chosen to place a spotted black veil across her face in order to subvert the potential for an unmediated reading of her.[3] Ironically, this particular veil works counterproductively to pull her excessively made-up face into even sharper focus. The important thing here is not the visual proof of the impossibility of truly changing the markers of her age but rather the misguided attempts she used to try, however futilely, to make herself look younger. And once again these efforts took place not across her aging body but on her face, the most available and public surface for the relentless display of age.

Significantly, contemporary scientific and beauty sources identify dust, which circulated especially readily during these years, as a main contributor to the premature maturation of the female face. Providing some of the most useful examples of Second Empire attitudes toward women's aging and beauty, especially since she wrote one of the most widely read columns on the subject, Emmeline Raymond claimed, "[T]heir principal enemy is dust, which hardens the skin, encrusts itself and settles there so that it can never more be removed if one waits too long to fight it. One must therefore constantly wear a veil when one goes out, frequently and carefully wash the face, and not fail to wash it before going to bed."[4] Not only were women led to believe that the veil could protect them from inhaling potentially contaminated dust, but also the veil was advertised as having the ability to keep that same dust, considered to be detrimental to the surface of the skin, from falling on the face and catalyzing an imagined cataclysmic aging process.

Jules Michelet, one of many contemporary writers who lavished attention on the details of women's behavior and appearance, also regarded the face as the most accessible site for the inscription of age: "We have a cruel severity toward women in judging them precisely by what fades the most, the face."[5] In his oblique attempt to position himself as sympathizer, Michelet further reinforces the importance of a youthful face, one that is not "faded." He goes on to say, "It is not rare for the body itself to be twenty-five years old and for the face [to appear to be] forty."[6] Obviously, the visible took primacy over the factual, and the critical thing was not to look older than one actually was or to look as young as possible.

One of the key components in maintaining the appearance of a youthful and unlined face was the appropriately chosen veil. As one writer in *L'express des modes* instructed: "Veils of lace coming down too far over the front of the face make women look older. For lace to be used to its full charming effect, and the diaphanous quality that is its principal element, it must be worn in a manner that allows the light to play between the face and its delicate networks of threads."[7] The veil was a layer between the face and the outside, a screen dispersing light. Its full charming effect, as well as its diaphanous quality, could lessen the visibility of wrinkles. Depending on its weave and its position across the face, a veil could create the desired illusion of uniformity and agelessness.

The paradox of the veil, its ability to impose lines in order to blur others, lies at the heart of its popularity at a time when descriptions in etiquette books and fashion periodicals meticulously postulated that ideal beauty was youthful and unaffected by the passage of time. For example, in her *Le cabinet de toilette,* Baronne Staffe made these claims for the veil: "The old and tired woman will do marvelously well to cover her hair (even if it is still beautiful) with a mantilla of lace, which will disguise the attacks of age . . . and graciously frame her face. An old woman with an uncovered head is frightful. The light shadow of lace conceals many of the ravages of time."[8] Laces that frame and shadows that cover orchestrate an elaborate scene of prevarication, if we are to believe the words of Baronne Staffe. In order for the fiction to be successful, aging facial skin would lie at the bottom of a series of palimpsestic accretions, of piled up and increasingly dissembling planes. The face could thus be reconstituted beneath layers of pulverized powder, fabrics, light, and shadow, produced as a kind of canvas, as a site for manufacturing the illusion of youthful beauty.

Foundations

The base of this tiered pastiche of lace and light and shadow is the skin, over which would have been smoothed whitening substances, sprinklings of almost invisible rice powder, and carefully applied subtle smudges of rouge. A writer for *Les modes parisiennes* described the effect of these layers of maquillage: "On a fresh complexion, this rouge is like the down that covers a beautiful fruit. On white skin, Guerlain white stretches and blends like milk on alabaster."[9] The skin is played on by material substances. It is speckled by rouge and prickled by downy, almost imperceptible crystals of powder, yet its surface remains impenetrable. The face itself, its color imperfections and fine lines, is subverted by maquillage.

These conventions of contemporary beauty, which advocate a plane of flesh played on by dustings of whiteners, powders, and cremes, both translucent and reddened, brand the face as a particularly important terrain at the same time that they detract attention from it. If the veil is the textile, the text on, under, and through which are inscribed some codes of bourgeois propriety, then the layers beneath the veil—the face and the maquillage used to perfect it—need to be examined as participants in the construction of that ideal. A finger smoothes on whitening agents and dips into a jar of rouge, a brush drags across a palette and into a pot of velvety rice powder, suffusing a canvas with color, writing across a face. The skin is the canvas, the makeup is the facture, and the female face is set up as an object on which can be inscribed the text of supreme beauty.

Contemporaries' regard for the surface of the female face as a canvas on which beauty could be described is articulated by Rétif de la Bretonne in *La femme jugée par les grands écrivains des deux sexes.* He writes, "Real beauty consists of medium height and good proportions, noble and delicate features, and beautiful skin. 'It [the skin] is a canvas that nature formed,' said Vandermonde, 'to merge there the most beautiful colors in all their variety: now it gives bloom to lilies and roses; now one sees only the somber violet, or the dark fruit of the myrtle.'"[10] The woman's skin is likened here to nature, regarded as a space on which floral tones blend. The discriminating use of color, just enough to conjure up the lilies, roses, violets, and myrtle described by Vandermonde, was key to composing perfect beauty. Others corroborated this rhetoric using words from the natural world, in this case the elderberry flower milk and snail creme, to promote the use of cosmetics: "For the face, it is the elderberry flower milk, snail creme, extract of benzoin; in a special cupboard there are marvelous rouges and cosmetics: crimson from China, the queen's rouge, Damascus rouge, extracts of roses for the lips; there is white of pearl, and lily powder. The skin undergoes a transformation under these marvelous compounds, the fine and satiny skin exhales a sweet scent."[11] Still, some fashion journal writers argued that the use of any makeup at all was problematic.

Quoting from the *Dictionnaire des gens*, one author claimed, "*Fard* [heavy makeup] is a composition that has the property of making old women a little more ugly, and young women a little less pretty."[12] This writer was probably referring to cosmetics that could be seen, that looked extremely artificial, and not to the light powders that most proper women used, which, as we shall see, many sources considered innocuous.

The perfect crafting of one's maquillage, which meant the suppression of its visibility, was integral, then, to the successful production of a proper face. Indeed, contemporary fashion journals and etiquette manuals were filled with instructions and advice for achieving the exemplary *bourgeois visage*. Most helpful in the establishment and reinforcement of the cultural paradigm was the distinction that was aggressively made between the artificial face and the properly composed one, for the former was associated with a lack of respectability. This distinction grew, in part, out of the belief at this time that cosmetics could damage and prematurely age skin, an effect particularly undesirable for a bourgeoise, whose beauty was defined in relation to how youthful and clear-skinned she could appear to be. Referring to occupations in which makeup was a professional necessity, such as acting, Paul Gastou expressed some long-standing beliefs: "Heavy makeup rapidly damages and ages the skin, whence the obligation to keep it on for the shortest time possible and, immediately on removal, to combat the negative effects with soothing and softening moisturizers (lotions and cremes)."[13] On another level, the actual components of makeup were even more feared, since so many contained lead and other substances that were beginning to be understood as being equally poisonous, even lethal.[14]

By the beginning of the 1860s, Emmeline Raymond, in her weekly column for *La mode illustrée, journal de la famille*, continually warned of the physical dangers associated with the use of maquillage: "[M]akeup is a poison! . . . Makeup, which contains arsenic, whether its base is antimony or bismuth, acts on the stomach in a short interval of time, where it disrupts its functions: inducing vomiting, making breath fetid, and deteriorating teeth."[15] As early as 1854, one writer for *Les modes parisiennes* pointed out: "Makeup is a fine dust composed of carbonate of lead and of limestone, soft and creamy to the touch and it adheres easily to the skin; however, this lead, absorbed by the latter [skin], may have a deleterious consequence."[16] Despite the known hazards connected with makeup usage, it was still being manufactured with substances known to have ill effects on the human body even into the early twentieth century.[17] In 1900, a Dr. Vaucaire warned of the detrimental physical consequences associated with zinc, lead, and other chemicals and active elements that companies continued to include in the fabrication of makeup: "The first and most important [rule of facial hygiene] is the abstention from the use of all makeup. The skin's surface must function normally, and the presence of these foreign substances can only prevent absorption, secretion, or excretion from occurring."[18] Dr. Vaucaire recommended that women use rice powder, because "[i]t is better to cover the face with an inert powder than to allow it to be covered by dust."[19]

And yet, the layer of rice powder had to be subtle, since the extensive employment of cosmetics was regarded as vulgar, as being the domain of the actress and the prostitute. Indeed, these two categories were linked in the minds of contemporaries, not only because of their perceived association with sexual promiscuity, but also because of their similarly dramatic usage of makeup: "The actress should exaggerate its [the cosmetics'] effects because of the distance and the lights, but the coquette imitates her foolishly, considering that, instead of attracting men, she forces them to step back . . . in order to judge the effect."[20] The overly made-up face, permissible for the actress, who had to be seen from afar, is imitated by the prostitute in order to attract or to be more attractive to men. Yet when seen from too close, at least according to this writer, the coquette dissolves into an overdone and foolish imitation of the actress.

Cora Pearl, the English-born courtesan who made her fortune in Second Empire Paris (she was at one point the mistress of Napoleon III's brother) and was well-known for her extravagant use of cosmetics, found a way to tone down yet still indulge in the elaborate toilette affiliated with the actress. She covered her eyelashes in glittering powders, spread a gamut of unexpected hues on her eyelids, and used colors ranging from milky tones to orange on her skin.[21] She prided herself on possessing enough money to be able to have her clothes made by Charles Frederick Worth, Empress Eugénie's couturier. In her memoirs, Pearl—never understated in her self-aggrandizement—even claims that she was singlehandedly responsible for popularizing makeup usage in Second Empire Paris:

> It was about this time . . . that I brought to Paris the habit of making up. Some of the ladies of the theatre had the habit of retaining their stage makeup during the late evening, but with ludicrous results, for

> their faces appeared pink and orange. . . . I had the idea that it should be possible to apply a lighter paint which would enhance the visage without making it ridiculous, and experimented at first alone, painting my face with tints of various colours, even including silver and pearl; I also used a dye from London to make my red hair yellow. When I first ventured forth after such an experiment, I was much admired; and soon after I had requests from other ladies to show them the art.[22]

Pearl set her face up as a canvas on which she could "paint" using various colors. She differentiated her technique from that of the actress, whom she regarded as looking ridiculous if still made-up when offstage. Yet Pearl's narcissistic description of painting her face with silver and pearl, not to mention dying her red hair yellow, sounds as extravagant for the streets of Paris as she thought the made-up actress appeared to be. And while Pearl does not directly discuss the class distinction that was widely associated with maquillage, she does allude to it even as she conflates, perhaps inadvertently, courtesan and actress.

A fascination with this aspect of some women's toilette is portrayed in contemporary fiction as well. For example, in a famous passage from *Nana,* Émile Zola indulgently describes his heroine's makeup ritual. Watched by Count Muffat, the Marquis de Chouard, and the prince, Nana prepares herself for her show.

> [Nana] covered herself with rice-powder, taking great care to avoid putting any on her cheekbones. . . . [She] turned round for a moment with her left cheek very white, in the midst of a cloud of powder. Then she suddenly turned serious, for it was time for her to put on her rouge. With her face once again close to the mirror, she dipped her fingers in a jar and began applying the rouge below her eyes, gently spreading it back towards her temples.
>
> . . . She dipped her paint-brush in a pot of kohl; then, putting her nose close to the glass, and closing her left eye, she passed it delicately between her eye-lashes. Muffat stood behind her, watching. . . . And try as he might he could not turn away his eyes from that dimpled face, which seemed fraught with desire, and which the closed eye made so seductive.
>
> . . . Her face and arms were finished now, and with her finger she put two broad strokes of carmine on her lips. The Comte Muffat felt more disturbed than ever. He was fascinated by the perverse attraction of Nana's powders and paints, and filled with frantic longing for the young woman's painted charms, the unnaturally red mouth in the

> unnaturally white face, and the exaggerated eyes, ringed with black and burning fiercely, as if ravaged by love.[23]

Zola does not focus on the moment when Nana changes her costume for the show, but rather he recounts the details of her makeup application and the feelings that this act and the maquillage inspire in the count. The count understands Nana as "unnatural," because she is painted, exaggerated, ringed with black, stroked by carmine, and therefore different from his respectable wife, whom (as Zola tells us) Muffat has never even seen putting on garters. Everything about Nana's toilette inspires desire for her in the count, who feels a "pious repugnance" toward his own wife. Nana's artifice attracts him. Her dusts and perfumes and rouges and creams render her simultaneously irresistible and the epitome of vice for Muffat, who, at one point, describes Nana as the devil. Her makeup becomes the outward sign of her carnality, her mark of vulgarity, the very thing that makes her so enticing to the count.

This link between maquillage and disreputable women is one way to account for the widely held understanding that the proper woman, in order to be recognizable as such, had to remain only delicately made-up. The lascivious connotations ascribed to heavy makeup use and the known health dangers associated with toxic elements in cosmetics make it unsurprising that the bourgeoise was advised to control her use of them. Conversely, the encouragement of women of other classes to indulge in maquillage is also unsurprising. Not unlike the classed double standard recommending that only upper-class women veil their faces to limit their inhalation of dust while other unveiled women remained more susceptible to contamination, the known hazards of makeup were ignored and certain working-class women were still sanctioned, even exhorted, to wear it in large quantities. Like the veil, but in reverse, makeup was an index of social standing.

Degas's *Women on a Café Terrace, Evening,* of 1877 (Figure 13), illustrates some of the ways in which visible maquillage and vulgarity were interconnected at this time. Three of the four main figures in this pastel over monotype are elaborately made-up, their reddened lips and kohl-outlined eyes carefully articulated. They are each seen in profile, which could, in the hands of another artist, mean the limitation of information. Yet Degas marks them clearly as artificial and coarse creatures through their vivid red lipstick, their facial types that do not conform to standards of ideal beauty, and their colorful hats. The thumb-to-mouth gesture of the central figure, who alone does not sport crimson lipstick, has been interpreted by Hollis Clayson as a detail that encourages us to read "the scurrilousness of the street prostitute and to collapse further the distinction between work and play for the prostitute's mouth."[24] This gesticulation compounds what is not so subtly conveyed by the profiled faces of her comrades. She wears a vibrant and powdery periwinkle dress with a shockingly flamboyant red and blue bow. This figure, as well as the two women at the margins of the composition, with their red lips, hats, dresses, hair, and earrings, further highlights the link between prostitution and vivid ornamentation. Prostitutes were indeed abundant on the streets and in the cafés of Paris in the second half of the nineteenth century, and they were often perceived, at least by Degas and by many of his contemporaries, as being highly artificed and vulgar types.[25]

Referring to the numerous and excessively cosmeticized women of disreputable standing who populated the streets, Emmeline Raymond wrote with the confidence that her readers would deduce what sort of women she meant:

> Seeing them with their faces painted white and red, their eyebrows colored, their eyes encircled in black, like those of King Charles's little

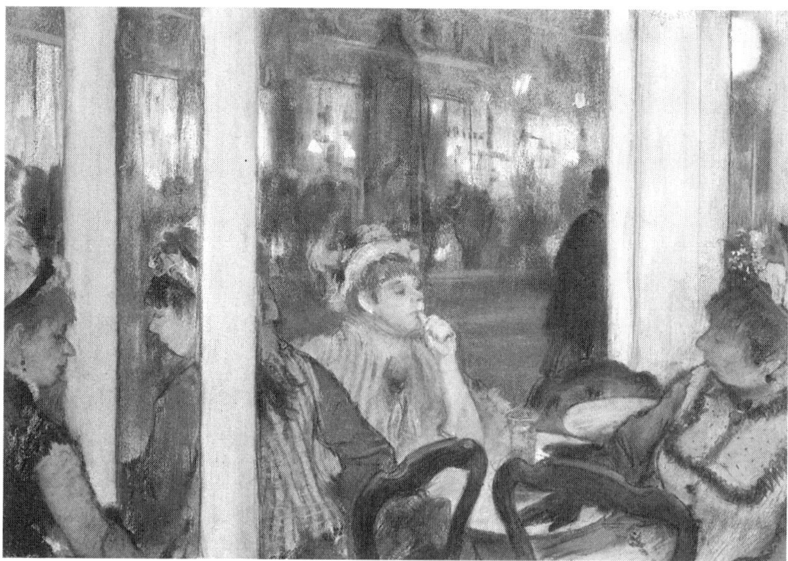

Figure 13. Edgar Degas, *Women on a Café Terrace, Evening* (1877). Pastel over monotype. Musée d'Orsay, Paris. Réunion des musées nationaux/Art Resource, NY.

> dogs, one is gripped by pity for the ridicule they bring on themselves and for the ills which are in store for them: these artificial faces, these walking phantoms, cause indignation at the same time as they produce laughter; it is impossible to respect a made-up woman; the permanent falsehood of her face seems to imply other, more serious falsehoods.[26]

The message was clear: an intensely overdone face marked a woman as being unrespectable, untrustworthy, easily comparable to ridiculous little dogs.

The heavily suggested makeup on the face of the model in Manet's *Woman Reading,* of 1878-79 (Figure 14), is, in fact, one of the primary factors that has led some interpreters of the painting to question the woman's social class.[27] Along with her stein of beer and the appearance that she is alone in a public café and despite her relatively refined-looking clothing (purchasable for a low price at any department store), this woman's excessively maquillaged face disallows any easy categorization of her position. On a canvas covered mostly by permutations of greens, grays, and blacks, the lusty red of the model's artfully applied lipstick, the color of which is repeated at the bridge of her nose, her chin, the top of her right cheek, and in the foliage above her head, takes on a specific importance. These displaced lipstick-red marks make little sense in their context among the green leaves, yet they help to propound the significance of a tiny passage in the painting: the woman's lips. Indeed, the seemingly stray marks mimic not only the color but also the approximate shape of the model's pursed lips, the upper one a more deeply saturated ruby, the lower one almost persimmon. This heightening through both color and form of what could have been an insignificant part of the painting allows Manet to foreground the artifice of the woman's appearance, making every other contrivance of maquillage in the picture more readily apparent.

In technical terms, the woman's face itself is not really built up. Yet, Manet conveys the sense of a thickened mask of makeup by using the grain of the canvas to sculpt pigment. The eyes are thinly painted, even scratchy, as black paint is teased out by the threads of the canvas. The left eye has three discernable lines running down it, the result of the canvas's weave making its way through the pigment, or perhaps it is the paint making its way through the canvas's weave. The two work together, *matière* and the surface on which it is applied, particularly at the eyes and at the collar, where the canvas, covered by thin, dry paints, approximates the texture of black and white tulle.

Flesh-colored tones simultaneously assemble and erase the woman's face.[28] Whereas these pigments establish the plane of her cheeks, they also cancel out the bridge of the nose in favor of a more flattened, exaggerated, and smoothed-out effect. A universal yet specific *parisienne* type emerges from this simultaneous reduction and clarification of facial features. The sitter's nose is so distilled that it is both an inverted visual echo of her top lip and simply a brownish bird-shaped mark on the canvas. And her cheeks are so highly artificed that they take on a hue achievable on a human face

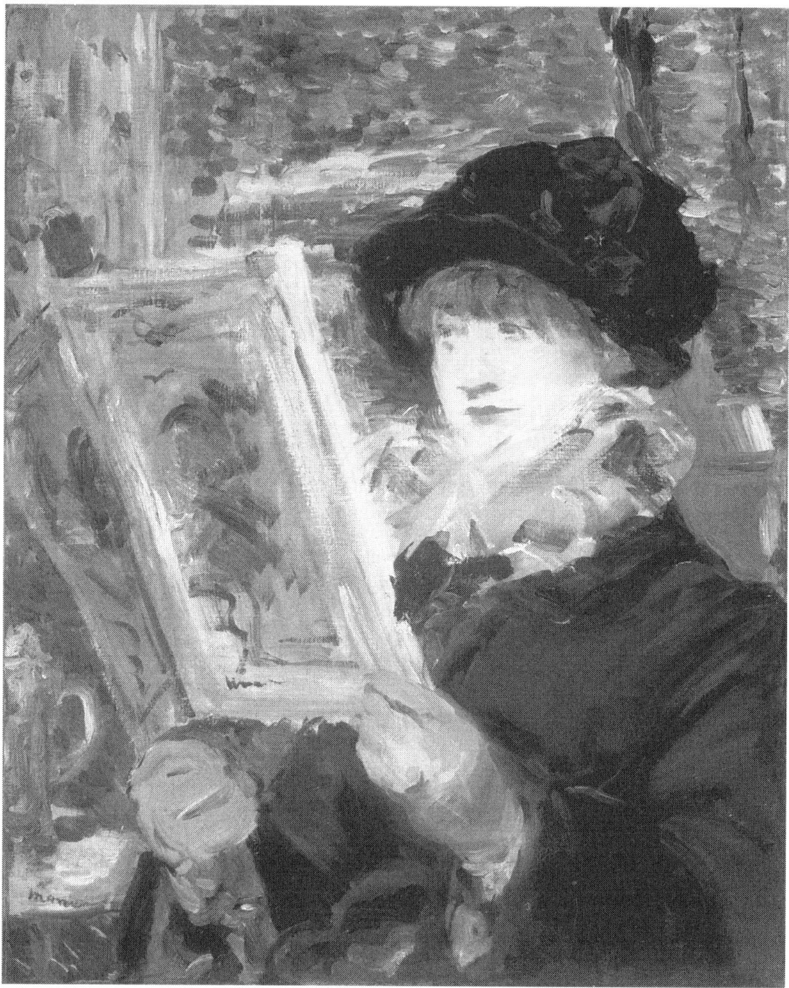

Figure 14. Edouard Manet, *Woman Reading* (1878–79). Oil on canvas, 61.2 × 50.7 cm. Mr. and Mrs. Lewis Larned Coburn Memorial Collection, The Art Institute of Chicago. Photograph copyright The Art Institute of Chicago.

only through the use of the kinds of foundations, rouges, and rice powders that were being marketed at the time.[29]

Manet carefully frames the woman's conscientiously crafted and irregularly edged face by topping it with a floppy black hat, which he underscores with an erratic fringe of bangs and the loosely articulated tulle collar. This collar all but sets the face apart from the body, declares its independence from the body, further calling attention to the face's particular significance within the painting's fabric. Even the broad brushwork throughout the entire composition, itself constituted by a veritable lexicon of strokes and splotches, reiterates the comparison Manet is making between the painting's construction and the constructedness of the woman's appearance. That the figure in the picture is reading an illustrated journal, the cover of which is indicated by the sketchiest marks of gray, blue, and black, additionally accentuates this reciprocity at the same time that it tells us she is not necessarily literate.[30] Even though we cannot determine the subject of this periodical's illustration—although we can probably assume that this is meant to represent a fashion journal, since they circulated so widely at the time and since the model is attired so fashionably—its presence provides an important visual clue that further helps our understanding of the image. Like a painting within a painting, this object reaffirms the unreadability of the picture as a whole at the same time that it becomes a space for Manet to articulate the connection between the artfulness of representation both in visual imagery and in the fabrication of feminine beauty. In the end, the female face succeeds as the most highly artificial level of representation, for our eye is continually drawn to the part of the canvas, the part of the face, where the lips covered in pigment imitate the effects of maquillage.[31]

Manet's *Victorine Meurent*, of 1862 (Figure 15), explores this physicality of paint as it merges with the sense of cosmetics in perhaps an even more marked way than *Woman Reading*. Done early in Manet's career, this picture is also the artist's first that features Victorine Meurent, who would go on to model for seven more paintings including *Olympia* and *Le déjeuner sur l'herbe*. In this image, a veritable close-up of Meurent's face, *matière* establishes simultaneous surface and depth. Where Manet cuts through flesh at Meurent's slightly twisted neck with a thin black ribbon, where threads of skin-colored paint splatter a bit over the left side of the ribbon, the artist detaches head from body. Meurent becomes here all face. If considered according to the helpful concept of *visagéité*, promoted by Gilles

Deleuze and Félix Guattari in the 1970s, Meurent's face is a politics, a semiotic system of significance and subjectification. Her face—any face—is produced by and specific to a moment in history. It is a landscape, a territory to be mapped. They write: "*The face* . . . is naturally a lunar landscape, with its pores, planes, matts, bright colors, whiteness, and holes: there is no need for a close-up to make it inhuman: it is naturally a close-up, and naturally inhuman."[32] In some sense Meurent's face in this painting is just this type of wide expanse, a kind of close-up that gets so close that even the pores seem to be readable.[33] Manet uses scale, format, and *matière* to overrepresent in such a way that this face appears to be a close-up when it really is not one. As it relates to Susan Stewart's suggestive idea

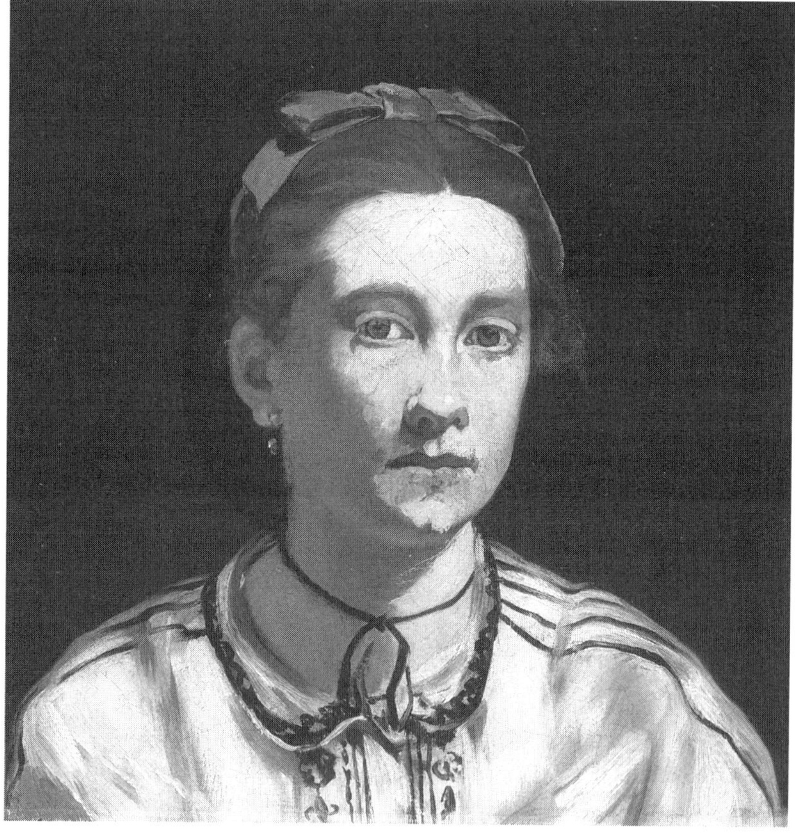

Figure 15. Edouard Manet, *Victorine Meurent* (c. 1862). Oil on canvas, 42.9 × 43.8 cm. Gift of Richard C. Paine in memory of his father, Robert Treat Paine 2nd, Museum of Fine Arts, Boston.

of the face as a "deep text," Meurent's face needs to be read as such, as glazes in layers, but also as accretions of meaning.[34]

A coagulated blend that calls to mind concrete mixed with sand, the surface of Meurent's face is nowhere consistent, everywhere flawed, and not at all the ideal of beauty that the popular press claimed was achievable through discrete deposits of rouges and rice powders. At Meurent's chin, Jean Clay sees a wreckage: "this wreckage, this collapse of matter, these deposits in *excess*—as on Victorine Meurent's chin . . . where nothing but a lack of strength, an indifference to the mimetic, forces the artist to break the curve of the face with thick daubs of light ocher."[35] I would like to expand on Clay's notion of crumble and buildup to argue that I see here also a simultaneous distillation and amplification of Manet's point. Using choppy, synoptic strokes of muddled pigment, Manet undoes static illusionism at the same time that he marks the female face as the site on which to explore with abandoned freedom the parallel between paint and maquillage.

The figure of Meurent is just emerging from a flat, placeless background. Her icy blue hair bow further pulls her head and shoulders out of airlessness and into a creamy articulation of smudges and blurs. The broad area of bleached forehead (made all the more pronounced by its juxtaposition with the model's red hair) melts into a jagged edge of shadow at her right temple and cuts down through her mottled cheek. A cosmetic pinkness is there, at the shadowed bit of cheek, that migrates into a less saturated version of itself where we imagine the light hits. We can detect a faint (almost invisible) touch of this blushy hue on the edge of the left cheek as well. The pink is especially there on her lips; a worn-away pale smear at the bottom and a deeper crimson on top. Under her eyes, shadow reads simultaneously as dark eyeliner. And her eyebrows are thickly pigmented, especially her right one, which arches unnaturally down into the corner of the bridge of the nose. It also appears as though Manet is representing some thickening substance—the kind of powders women used then—on Meurent's eyelashes. Or is he simply highlighting the lashes, a part so often suppressed by other artists who do not want to interrupt representational polish and perfection? Taking paint to its extreme possibilities of saturation and density, an extreme that suggests maquillage, Manet asserts a kind of impenetrability of the face, even when unveiled. Hue and texture affirm its artifice, the face's inherent status as a sequence of accretive layers, the end result of which is deception.

The Parisienne's Veil

Charles Baudelaire, the well-known poet and social critic and a close friend of Manet, expounded on the importance of obvious and extreme artifice in the construction of a feminine beauty of a particularly classed sort. "Woman has to astonish and charm us; as an idol, she is obliged to adorn herself in order to be adored," he claimed in his influential and widely read essay "In Praise of Cosmetics."[36] Baudelaire's use of the term *woman* is perhaps not universal but rather a reference to women of specifically non-bourgeois standing, the kinds of women who are unaccompanied in the streets and at cafés, as in Manet's *Woman Reading.* For Baudelaire's woman, adorned and thus adored, charms through an elaborately fabricated surface. Set up as an idol, his woman's face is fragmented and torn from the body, turned into a site for embellishment. He goes on to detail the steps in the production of the artfully artificial face:

> [Woman] . . . must . . . borrow from all the arts the means of raising herself above Nature, the better to conquer hearts and rivet attention. . . . anyone can see that the use of rice-powder . . . is successfully designed to rid the complexion of those blemishes that Nature has outrageously strewn there, and thus to create an abstract unity in the colour and texture of the skin, a unity which, like that produced by the tights of the dancer, immediately approximates the human being to the statue, that is to something superior and divine. As for the artificial black with which the eye is outlined . . . its black frame renders the glance more penetrating and individual, and gives the eye a more decisive appearance of a window open upon the infinite; and the rouge which sets fire to the cheek-bone only goes to increase the brightness of the pupil and adds to the face of a beautiful woman the mysterious passion of the priestess. . . . Maquillage has no need to hide itself or to shrink from being suspected; on the contrary, let it display itself.[37]

According to Baudelaire, woman is eye and cheek, fragmented surface, synthetically unified by rice powder. This concept of woman being an abstract unity is paradoxical, especially given the ways in which abstraction works in painting to limit the legibility of a painted image. By comparing the "abstract unity in the colour and texture" of the rice-powdered face to the tight-covered legs of a dancer, Baudelaire is also displacing the body onto the face. As Abigail Solomon-Godeau has pointed out, "Tights were virtually the prerequisite for the transition of carnal flesh into the sublimated, sculptural form of aesthetic, albeit eroticized, delectation."[38] If we use this logic, it would seem that by equating the woman's face with the legs of the dancer, Baudelaire is drawing on a set of allusions that are freighted with a long history of sexual innuendo, however sublimated this association may appear to be.

Thus, even without a veil, the woman's face is veiled, its status as artifice and erotic object constantly recorded across its surface. Baudelaire's prescription likens the female face to a statue; the outlined eye, framed, to a painting, a window of illusionistic potential. Erased by makeup, the face is re-made-up through the orchestration of its veneer. It becomes indistinguishable from that which covers it. Maquillage is, in effect, the nonbourgeois woman's veil. It colors and sculpts the face, alters its appearance. It also calls attention to the woman who wears it while simultaneously mediating the gaze that looks at her. Makeup, then, is a layer over the face, a mask that maintains the fiction that feminine beauty is carefully organized artifice.[39]

"It matters but little that the artifice and trickery are known to all, so long as their success is assured and their effect always irresistible," Baudelaire wrote in his treatise.[40] But it does matter that the "artifice and trickery are known to all," for it is this knowledge that may, in some small way, reenfranchise the woman. Like the effect of the veil on the face, makeup can undo the order of intelligibility, making unmediated views of a woman impossible. Feminine beauty, according to this reasoning, is an ocular conceit, a kind of mask, for which the woman is partly responsible. In other words, the woman may determine how successfully she tricks the viewer by the ways in which she applies her maquillage.[41] Baudelaire's version of ideal beauty, then, does not hide the fact that its basis depends on dupery and artifice. Like the veiled face, the made-up face exposes its seams by foregrounding its own construction. If you come too close to the elaborately made-up woman, she will disintegrate, she will be reduced to her structure, and her face will become threateningly illegible.[42]

Baudelaire goes on to describe the ways in which his ideal female face vaporizes into an accumulation of its layers of production:

> [Woman] . . . is a divinity, a star . . . a glittering conglomeration of all the graces of Nature, condensed into a single being. . . . She is a kind of idol, stupid perhaps, but dazzling and bewitching, who holds wills and destinies suspended on her glance. . . . Everything that adorns woman, everything that serves to show off her beauty, is part of herself. . . . No doubt Woman

> is sometimes a light, a glance, an invitation to happiness, sometimes just a word; but above all she is a general harmony, not only in her bearing and the way in which she moves and walks, but also in the muslins, the gauzes, the vast, iridescent clouds of stuff in which she envelops herself.[43]

Baudelaire's archetypal woman is contained within vast festoons of muslins and gauzes and iridescent fabrics. That which she uses to adorn, that which she layers on herself, becomes inseparable from her. Surface becomes depth as these gauzes and muslins define her as dazzling and bewitching. The woman is the function of the objects that decorate her, and she becomes the epitome of mystery and seduction. She holds wills and destinies suspended on her glance, and she takes on the mysterious passion of the priestess. She is, for Baudelaire at least, a tease, a seductress determining the progression of attraction. Her maquillage and the clouds of stuff in which she embellishes herself promote a scene of seduction in which the viewer is captivated and the woman is rendered irresistible.[44]

If we understand maquillage as a kind of veil, since it covers the face, redefines it, and marks its class, then the overlap between the bourgeoise and the prostitute or between the bourgeoise and the actress is clear. Reading these veils in relation to each other and to Baudelaire's exhortations of the bewitching aspects of feminine embellishment reveals that the bourgeoise's veil, in fact, actually further complicated her position in late nineteenth-century Paris. For some of the characteristics associated with the veil, particularly its ability to render the woman behind it seductive, mysterious, and coquettish, had to have been translated onto even the proper woman who wore it. Indeed, the veil always carried with it specifically erotic connotations, no matter who the wearer. While the veil helped to differentiate classes of women, inhibited the proper woman's inhalation of germs, and circumscribed the wearer's view of the new city, it also ironically reinscribed the bourgeoise within the framework of sexuality. The veiled bourgeoise could be simultaneously sexy and asexual, seductive and distanced, mysterious and known.

The connection between a woman's appearance and her ability to dupe was widely articulated by the contemporary visual and textual culture. In 1866, in *L'express des modes,* a journal intended for consumption by a presumably female bourgeois audience, one writer claimed, "The appearance of women is as deceptive as the reflection of objects in the water."[45] If this refers to the image of the bourgeoise, and I am assuming that it does, given the context of the statement, then we can infer that the lines of demarcation between the elaborately maquillaged nonbourgeoise and the proper woman are perhaps not as firmly drawn as one would think (or as contemporaries would have liked). Although she was not to overdo her makeup, for the heavily made-up face was identified with vulgarity, the respectable woman was still, according to this statement, able to manipulate her appearance, to fool those who looked at her. If her makeup had to remain subtle, in part because of the poisonous materials used in its preparation and in part to distinguish her from her prostitutional counterpart, the veil was an object of artifice that could enable the proper woman to vacillate between a straightforward adherence to propriety and a staging of falsity, mystery, and sexuality.

An image from an 1887 issue of *La mode illustrée, journal de la famille* (Figure 16) illustrates this visual convergence of eroticism, temptation, and mystery on the presumed bourgeoise, who, thus construed, takes on the appearance more typically associated with the less than reputable woman. Her body in profile, her head tilted to her right so as to give up more of it to view, this woman wears an elaborate hat and a spotted demiveil, carries a fan, and holds a flower in her gloved hand. The rhythmic arpeggio of fan, hat, and veil evokes the air of a seduction. The woman cagily looks out from behind her veil, she holds her fan up to the left side of her head, and a secret is enacted, for she is now visible only to the viewer of the image. Of course, the fact that this illustration was meant to be seen mainly by a bourgeois female audience complicates its meaning, for the implied narrative, inspired by the tilt of the head, the gesture of the fan, and the momentary glance through the veil, generates the question of who is seducing whom.[46] Still, if the logic of the fashion journal works on the premise that the reader is meant to copy what she sees, to wear the outfit for the pleasure of those who look at her, then the seduction has taken place. By drawing inspiration from an image so clearly marked by a language of erotic potential, the bourgeoise could have invested herself with the qualities we have been led to believe were wholly dissociated from her. She could quite intentionally ally herself with deception and seduction.

In their inspiring book on fashion and its relation to the erotic body, Alexandra Warwick and Dani Cavallaro claim, using the metaphor of the wrapped gift, that "[t]he parcel itself is sealed, anonymous, possibly amorphous. It could contain anything and everything. The parcel itself is uncanny in its silence and mysteriousness: something about its deliberate

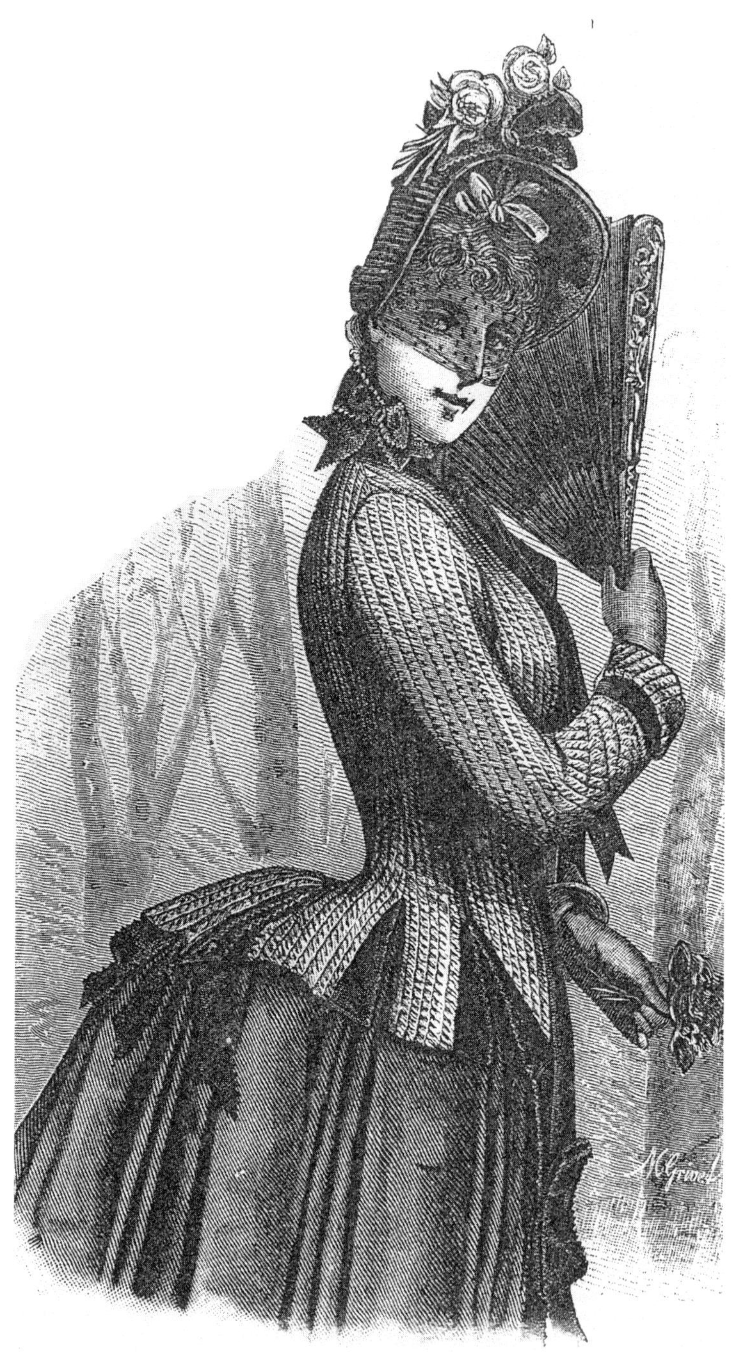

Figure 16. *La mode illustrée, journal de la famille* 17 (April 24, 1887): 133. Engraving. Bibliothèque des arts décoratifs, Paris.

secretiveness may even make it slightly off-putting. But the ribbon reaches out to us. It seductively provokes us to undo it, to fiddle with the knot."[47] The veiled face leaves us forever fiddling with the knot, the thing that stands in our way, the thing whose absence will allow us to know truly the threat that lies on the other side.

Perplexing the Veil

Some contemporaries considered veils to be charming and sweet: "A half-veil of black lace, attached around the hat, and producing a light shadow over the eyes, lends an indescribable sweetness and yet another charming quality," claimed a writer for *Le miroir parisien* in 1861.[48] But others found veils disconcertingly multivalent: "I know of nothing more troubling, more cajoling to the eye, more soft, adorable, and tickling to the touch than these light, sparkling, transparent veils," asserted Octave Uzanne, writing of the 1850s.[49] Uzanne is simultaneously fascinated and disturbed by the mystery of the veil and what has been hidden behind it. Yet it clearly exists for his pleasure, for it provides a screen on and through which he may project his feminine ideal. It is soft, adorable, sparkling, and transparent. It is also tantalizing, since it catalyzes both visual and tactile associations. It allows him to imagine how it would feel (soft, tickling to the touch) and what is behind it, for it is both tangibly there and not (light and sparkling but also transparent). The veiled face provokes Uzanne to want to see behind what troubles and compromises his vision. This face becomes a space for the coalescence of a narrative of mystery and seduction.[50] It both defers and enables satisfaction, for impossibility and potentiality constantly undercut one another across the veiled woman's face.[51]

Contemporary examples of the seductive aspects of veils abound. For Gustave Flaubert's Frédéric, in *La première éducation sentimentale,* seeing a group of elegant, veiled women pass in a carriage while he is out walking through le bois de Boulogne sends him into a kind of ecstatic reverie. Flaubert writes: "He was walking in the bois de Boulogne, he was noticing the pretty horses and the fine gentlemen, the varnished carriages and the plumed coachmen, and the society women with pale faces, whose veils, ruffled by the wind, were wafting outside the door of the carriage, passing under his nose with the sound of silver bracelets."[52] The veils, which float under his nose, are evocative for Frédéric. Their essence and glide mingle with the whole of the scene—the site of a polished carriage, the jingle of silver bracelets, the beautifully dressed women and men—creating an optical but also a sensory experience, a seduction of sorts.

If Jean Baudrillard is right when he concludes that seduction occurs outside vision, then the veil, since it simultaneously hides and reveals, is the appropriate motif for producing the effects of mystery and temptation.[53] He writes, "The fury to unveil the truth, to get at the naked truth, the one which haunts all discourses of interpretation, the obscene rage to uncover the secret, is proportionate to the impossibility of ever achieving this. . . . But this rage, this fury, only bears witness to the eternity of seduction and to the impossibility of mastering it."[54] The desire to know what is behind the veil, according to Baudrillard, stages an elaborate but impossible seduction. The veil then, is a device of masochistic pleasure for the viewer: the need to see behind it is perpetually thwarted.

To push this point further, the veiled face may be understood as a synecdoche for the partly revealed body, which, like the face, is both present and not, both satisfying and perplexing. The veiled face is also always erotic, a partly viewable site that incites desire. Roland Barthes asks the question: "Is not the most erotic portion of a body *where the garment gapes*?" He goes on to say, "[I]t is intermittence, as psychoanalysis has so rightly stated, which is erotic; the intermittence of skin flashing between two articles of clothing (trousers and sweater), between two edges (the open-necked shirt, the glove and the sleeve); it is this flash itself which seduces."[55] Even though Barthes's examples are bigger, cause bigger ruptures for the introduction of an erotic narrative, I would argue that he could just as easily have included the veiled face in his list of places on the body where gaps generate desire. For what is the veil *but* gaps? Each space in the veil is edged by a thread, a frame, and it is this dichotomy between empty and charged, between there and not, that inspires the seduction of the viewer.

When he discusses in *The Fashion System* the ways in which fabrics of different weight, weave, and heft affect the potential for an erotic response, Barthes finds garments that are most transparent—gauzes and mousselines—are more likely to succeed. He even provides us with a table that runs from opaque to invisible, with openwork and transparent falling in between. He situates "veiling" and "veiled" under transparent and later goes on to note, "[T]o the extent that the garment is erotic, it must be allowed to persist here and disintegrate there, to bc partially absent, to play with the body's nudity."[56] The veil most certainly persists here and disintegrates there, revealing flashes of secret flesh that intoxicate the person who looks at it.

Given the codes of propriety for bourgeois women, it is unexpectedly the proper woman's face across which all of these flashes of secret flesh and eroticism occur. In chapter 1, I analyzed the ways in which the veil was deployed, through elaborate medical justifications, in order to inhibit the proper woman's view of the new and what was considered to be the vice-infested city. I also discussed the ways in which the veil was a means of differentiating the respectable woman from the prostitute at a time when visual appearances were growing alarmingly similar. Here, I want to suggest that while the veil did these things, ironically it also re-placed sexuality and even a type of agency onto the bourgeoise. Like its function as an actual physical layer over the face, the veil's consequences are multiple and coterminous. It could simultaneously defer the projection of sexuality onto the bourgeoise by marking her as respectable and also reinvest an erotics in her because it is a device that is always already loaded with sexual implication.

So, in a paradoxical twist, the veil, that object meant to ensure respectability, actually reinscribes that which it seeks to suspend: sexuality. Contemporaries recognized this incongruity—the veil's concurrent capacities to arrest erotic allusions as well as to reinforce them—in both advocating its use by the proper woman and remarking on the alluring aspects of wearing it. For example, Henri Bouchot pointed out the ways in which a veil could render the woman beneath it mysterious: "After the exhibition of 1855 a respectable woman . . . is the most mysterious and the most indecipherable person who could be; at the very most a bit of sweet little face can be perceived in the mass of flounces, amongst the hives, the ribbons, the demiveils."[57] The veil works to hide the face, to make the woman behind it mysterious and indecipherable. Yet, the face remains there, beneath the veil, its surface simultaneously under erasure and indelibly played upon. Within this set of conditions, the veil becomes a device for both the woman's pleasure and the pleasure of the person who looks at her.

When a writer for *Le moniteur de la mode* made the claim in 1853 that "[n]othing is as beautiful as a hood of lace that gracefully frames the face and at the same time protects it from the cold,"[58] the effects of the veil on both the viewer and the wearer are again articulated. It frames the face for the voyeuristic pleasure of the person who looks, turning it into a separate object, divided and set off from the rest of the body but always referring to the unseen body. And for the wearer, the veil has more pragmatic applications, since it presumably helps to shield the face from the cold, although I cannot imagine how effectively it could have done this. Describing a group of female shoppers' reactions to piles of lace for decoration and the making of veils at the Ladies' Paradise, Zola articulates a kind of female frenzy: "The lace was passed from hand to hand. The ladies were astonished . . . fascinated, intoxicated. The pieces were unrolled, passed from one to the other, drawing the admirers closer still, holding them in the delicate meshes. On their laps there was a continual caress of this tissue, so miraculously fine, and amidst which their culpable fingers fondly lingered."[59] The shoppers fondle the fragile lace passionately. The department store, with its elegant and desirable contents, becomes not simply a place for shopping but also a site for the expression of female pleasure. Arguable practical justifications aside, the really interesting, if not confounding, thing about the veil and its popularity among the bourgeoisie in late nineteenth-century Paris is the way in which it inevitably aligned the proper woman with sexuality, both covert and not.

Still, underlying this seemingly innocuous quote about the veil both framing and protecting is not just the pleasure but also the anxiety that the veiled face catalyzes, for it allies the woman with artifice (because she is framed) and with vision, which is interrupted (again because she is framed). Veiled, she can be youthful and the epitome of ideal beauty. Yet she can also be associated with deceit—for her veil hides something from view—and with seduction. Edgar Degas's *At the Races*, of 1876–77 (Figure 17), a close-up view of two women who are likely engaged in conversation, exemplifies this dialectic of pleasure and fear that the veil generated. Covered by veils, hats, and parasols, these women have no faces. In this image, the representation of the female face becomes its very antithesis. For here, paint becomes the suggestion of fabric straining across faces, actually obliterating facial features as it skims the terrain. Instead of being a representation of two particular women, the painting depicts them as universalized, tropic figures who stand for the visual frustration associated both with wearing a veil and with trying to see through to the woman on the other side of it. This painting enacts what Lacan would later notice: that despite the perpetual desire to know what lies behind it, there is nothing behind the veil. He writes: "[I]f one wishes to deceive a man, what one presents to him is the painting of a veil, that is to say, something that incites him to ask what is behind it."[60]

So much in this picture reads as surface, not face, for the dots on the veil worn by the woman on the right are essentially superimposed across the blank canvas of face underneath. Degas uses the back edge of the gold chair, shot through with the sunny pink of the woman's dress, to hold in the right border of the picture. He crudely hollows out the green underside of the cream-colored parasol—the perfect *repoussoir* to direct our attention—and impastoes the colorful flowers of the hat on the woman at the right. The veiled faces in the foreground formally frame the small passage of the sandy-colored ground that is meant to be in the distance, but by more thickly building up that sandy color, Degas pulls foreground and background onto a single plain, thus consolidating them. In these ways, Degas consistently calls attention to surfaces and the play of *matière* across them, asserting the materiality of the paint that veils the canvas and plays against the veils that are painted. Simply put, facture hides canvas, while veils hide faces. Degas works, one could say, to make it plain that pigment blots out blank surface, the nothingness behind Lacan's veil. There is nothing behind either, for the veiled face and the canvas are each vacant vehicles. Playful yet dangerous, the veil of the woman on the left may be read

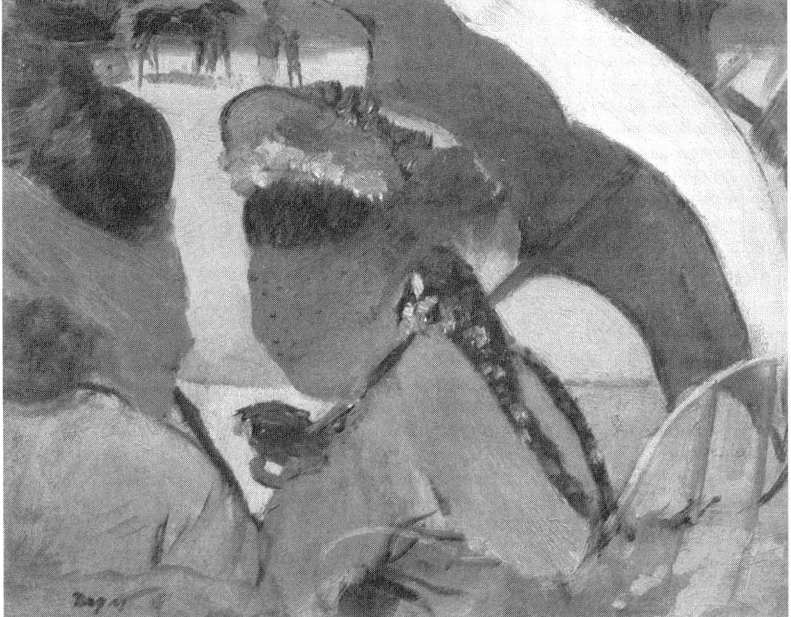

Figure 17. Edgar Degas, *At the Races* (1876–77). Oil on canvas. Private collection. Photograph copyright Robert Lorenzson.

as purely surface decoration, as the result of the careful pull of a brush, only minimally loaded with periwinkle blue paint, diagonally across her cheek and out past the margin of the picture. Yet this mythical face across which the artist drags his paint never existed in the first place, and in the end, it becomes an empty screen, a play of *matière* over blank surface.

Degas's obliteration of the two women's faces in this image is understandable, especially since some of the actual laces used in making veils could, in fact, create this effect of obfuscating the face beneath. Some were light and airy, yet others were extremely densely woven and intricately patterned. The latter could surely have made seeing the face on the other side difficult, at times nearly impossible. I see a strong link between the actual fabric Degas is painting and his conception and use of the paint itself as a kind of veil, a material presence covering over something else. In the case of *At the Races* there is a direct connection between *facture* and that which it represents, between the veil of oil paint and the veil it epitomizes in the picture.

While much of Degas's work is concerned with exploring the tangibility of his media, some of his late bather pictures of the 1890s are especially related to this interest. Pastels and paints virtually screen over the fleshy bodies that their combinations and linkages are meant to establish. The artist scratches pastels over paper, paint over canvas, over the women's bent and twisted bodies. In effect, he veils these bathers with coats of pigment, forces us to see through grates, and scores, and hatch marks down to the bodies. They are there beneath coverings of pinks, yellows, purples, flesh tones, black, and white pastels, all of which behave much like the layers created by a veil.

Degas can be subtle, as in *The Morning Bath,* from approximately 1895 (Figure 18), in which he achieves the overall effect of having the viewer feel as if she is seeing through a veil to this scene of a woman entering a tub. Hazy and frenzied pastels convey, along with the cast-aside curtain, the sense of activity in the picture, lending it a narrative—if we can call it that—quality. For here we are led to speculate that this woman, a prostitute, has just emerged from the unmade bed in the foreground. The vibration of pastel seems to propel the woman, and our eye, forward into the tub at the same time that it also renders the picture out of focus, a semblance of confused and shaky, yet carefully crafted, strokes.

Degas's interest in the formal and ocular tricks achievable through the manipulation of *matière* is also evident in *In the Omnibus,* a black ink

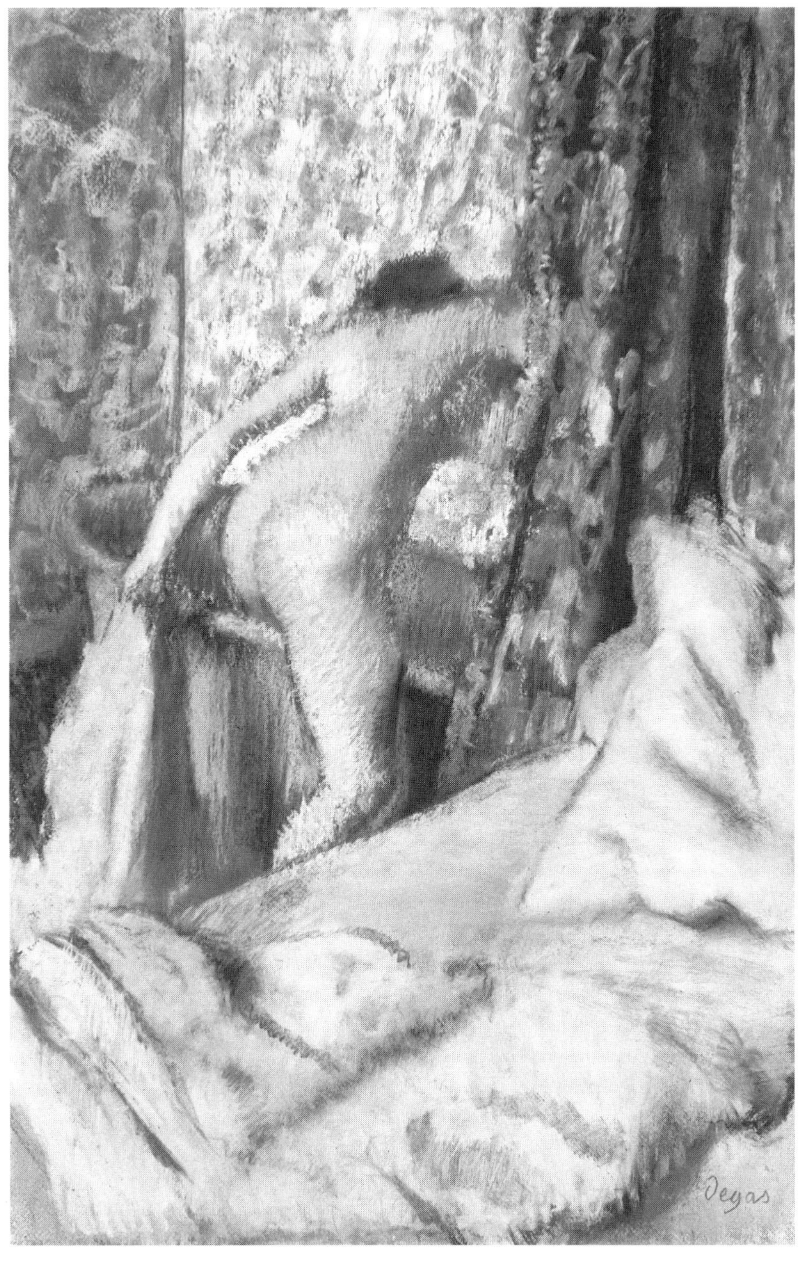

Figure 18. Edgar Degas, *The Morning Bath* (1895). Pastel on tan wove paper, 70.6 × 43.3 cm. Mr. and Mrs. Potter Palmer Collection, The Art Institute of Chicago. Photograph copyright The Art Institute of Chicago.

monotype of 1877–78 (Figure 19). Here the veil becomes an excuse for exploring the materiality of the veil on, in this case, paper. With the brush of a finger over thick black ink, Degas indicates the problematics and consequences of the veil. He expertly turns a smudge into a spotted short veil, or voilette, and thus makes what could be a straightforward face more difficult to read. Indeed, the face of the woman, already seen in profile and thus partly hidden, is rendered a blur. Her eyes seem to be the only truly readable part of her, and yet they really are not. Merging with the dots of the veil, her left eye is especially wrong, and her right eye takes the form of a strip of ink. Her nose is simply an outline, a suggested protrusion interrupting the line of the face. And she has no mouth. The formal juxtaposition of her and the overeyed gentleman who sits behind her only emphasizes the fragility of the woman's ability to see. Through the window of the omnibus is an indecipherable view, perhaps a visual suggestion of the overall sense of the veil's capacity to trouble seeing. In this

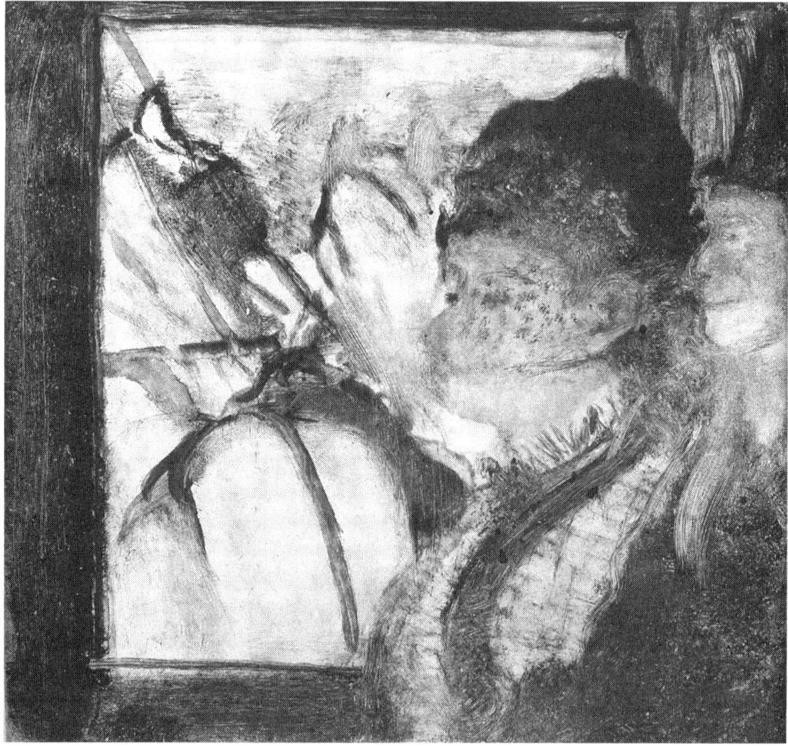

Figure 19. Edgar Degas, *In the Omnibus* (1877–78). Monotype in black ink. Musée Picasso, Paris. Réunion des musées nationaux/Art Resource, NY.

relatively small space on a piece of paper, Degas has exposed the underpinnings of feminine adornment and the fact of its constructedness.

At the same time that it covers over the specificity of the face, the veil becomes a blank screen on which may be projected an ideal beauty. Like the prostitute's maquillage, the bourgeois woman's veil changes and distorts, effaces the appearance of that which is underneath it. The veiled face is a vehicle on which the viewer may envisage what is codified as desirable beauty. Still, it always conceals something from view and simultaneously succeeds in marking the veiled woman as secretive and deceptive. As Mary Ann Doane has put it in relation to the filmic image, the veil "is most materially a question of what can and cannot be seen."[61] Of course, the veil in painting works similarly, for it too establishes parameters of vision. Its very presence calls attention to the unseen, the hidden, the secret, the part we cannot see that we want to see. It is the object that incites visual frustration at the same time that it eases it.

In late nineteenth-century Paris the veil proliferated in meaning. It was saturated by medical and class justifications. And it was also supposed to conceal overt signs of age. Furthermore, it could create unified and perfected faces. However, the mark of deception was also recorded across the veiled face, for the veil was intimately bound up with a discourse of seduction thought to be—or is it that it was hoped to be?—unconnected to women of reputable standing. Like the licentious woman's maquillage, the veil's unexpected double, it sexualized the *bonne bourgeoise.* The veil could, thus, be interpreted on multiple planes, each of which could simultaneously privilege and undercut the subjectivity of the woman beneath it. In the final analysis, the veil is as complicated as the intricate weave of its surface and has as many layers of significance as the layers it and its shadows infinitely create. Is this Degas's point in choosing to skim surfaces, in teasing fabrics across faces, undoing them as he went along? I imagine that he wanted us to see in his mysterious close-up of effaced women a visual articulation of the complexity of late nineteenth-century French femininity and how it could intersect with an inventive art practice.

3

Unmasking Manet's Morisot, or Veiling Subjectivity

As I argued in chapter 2, the postulates of fashion and cosmetics in late nineteenth-century Parisian culture conspired to fabricate an ideal bourgeois face, a face that foregrounded its surface as simultaneously smooth and highly artificial. Covered by the thinnest layer of rice powder and topped off with a veil, this face could appear to be ageless, even, and regular, not lined and variable. The creation of the impression of youth was, therefore, critical to the proper woman's toilette. Why then does Edouard Manet, in his series of paintings of Berthe Morisot, go against this social expectation by representing her with an increasingly convoluted facial terrain that would have been inconsistent with contemporary notions of perfect beauty for a woman of her class? By using elaborately impastoed facture in these paintings, by cosmeticizing her face with thickened pigments, by effacing her features, Manet is quite directly positioning Morisot within a category of femininity that would have stood outside bourgeois propriety. By building up the surface of Morisot's face and resisting the seamlessness associated with youth, Manet does not conform his portrayals of her to the standards of beauty and perfection established by contemporary etiquette books and fashion journals. Indeed, I would say that he actually visualizes the very problematics of representing respectable femininity in these pictures of Morisot. And perhaps he is also visually constituting the precariousness of the position of the woman artist—her unclassifiable status—during the second half of the nineteenth century. His depictions of her were, of course, determined by both external codes and his own impulses, the full character of which we will never know. One could say that in these pictures the ideal bourgeoise, or rather Manet's ideal bourgeoise, is collapsed into modernist painting conventions. In this group of images, which is a cultural microcosm of a sort, a late nineteenth-century ideal of femininity was both formulated and resisted. The challenge is to begin to understand why Manet did this and how his formal decisions determined for a long while how we thought about Morisot.

Even though Morisot was a respected artist who showed and received a great deal of praise at the annual Salon and all but one of the impressionist exhibitions, the historical understanding of her has been inflected by Manet's representations of her. In too many instances, Manet's portraits of her have come to stand for Morisot, her life, her artistic production. In fact, the frontispiece of the catalog for the posthumous exhibition of her work held in 1896 is a portrait of Morisot by her long-time friend and colleague Edouard Manet. Similarly, the cover of the 1987 edition of the *Correspondence of Berthe Morisot* shows not one of Morisot's self-portraits (or any of her other works, for that matter) but rather a painting of her by Manet.

Neither Manet's portraits themselves nor the alliance between the two artists is simple or clear. They met through Fantin-Latour, they socialized, and they relied on one another for professional advice. Manet even introduced Morisot to the man she would later marry, his brother Eugène. During the years in which Morisot sat for Manet, their friendship was that of a married man and a proper unmarried bourgeoise. Obviously, the friendship between Manet and Morisot was far more complicated than we can ever know. So are Manet's paintings of Morisot, which neither fit easily into a framework of bourgeois respectability nor conform to pictorial expectations. Instead, they gradually and systematically trouble the borders of both propriety and representation. For these images are marked by a language of excess that effaces as much as it depicts Morisot, masking her beneath layers of paint, veils, and fans. This chapter will seek to excavate some of the levels underlying the process of picturing so that a less obscured version of the painter Berthe Morisot, and her relationship with Edouard Manet, may be unmasked. For it is his paintings of her, in their enigmatic complexity, that provide the most compelling clues to the nature of their alliance. As visual manifestations of what had to be hidden in a relationship circumscribed by bourgeois propriety, these paintings must be understood as they are mediated by the terms of desire and artistic rivalry. Broadly handled brushwork, variegated textures, startling asymmetries, and certain freighted objects—all part of a discourse of unrespectability—become the means by which Manet hid his feelings toward Morisot. In other words, in order to keep his emotions contained below the surface, he gradually built up the surfaces of the paintings, thus marking his pictures of Morisot with what I will interpret as the tensions and contentions of their association.

Manet represented Morisot eleven times between 1868 and 1874 in oil, watercolor, and print.[1] This suggests not only that she was a convenient model but also, more important perhaps, that he was absolutely fascinated by her. In fact, as Anne Higonnet points out in her biography of Morisot, seven of these portraits of Morisot were listed in Manet's estate inventory at his death in 1883.[2] Whether he kept the images because he was dissatisfied with them, because they were unfinished, or because they held a special significance for him is purely speculative. Manet's need to repeat Morisot's likeness—his need to shape it, to help it take shape—is, I think, clear. He painted his wife, Suzanne Leenhoff, perhaps his most accessible model, only five times and usually in highly unidealized, even frumpy ways. Manet portrayed his other favorite model, Victorine Meurent, eight times, usually in disguise, most notably as the courtesan Olympia and as a naked lunch picnicker in *Le déjeuner sur l'herbe.*[3] Meurent's status was different from Morisot's. As an official artist's model she automatically occupied a dubious position, for models at the time were often considered social outcasts, even labeled prostitutes, since so many, out of financial necessity, had to supplement their incomes by providing sexual services.[4] Even though she was also an artist (she exhibited three times in the Salon), it appears that Meurent was forced to model to support herself.[5]

Whatever the reality of any given studio situation, modeling was closely related to a discourse of sexuality. It is partly this association between a lack of respectability and modeling that made Morisot at first reluctant when Manet asked her to pose for *The Balcony* in 1868. While women of her class often commissioned and sat for their portraits, this painting was neither commissioned nor a portrait of Morisot. She was not a paid model in costume or a *bonne bourgeoise* simply sitting for her portrait. For this first picture in what I would call a series of images of Morisot by

Manet, Morisot apparently recognized her complicated position, because she had her mother accompany her at each sitting (or perhaps it was her mother's idea).

From the very start, the relationship between Manet and Morisot was circumscribed by the rules of gender and class propriety. While the impressionists and their circle frequently modeled for one another, Manet never posed for Morisot. This is not at all surprising, as it would have been socially unacceptable for a married man of Manet's class to have sat for hours while a young woman painted him.[6] However, Manet expected Morisot to put everything aside to pose for him. She most likely did this willingly, perhaps to escape from her own painting, which, at a time when proper women of her age married and did not become professional painters, was a source of consternation for her, or perhaps it was simply because she enjoyed Manet's company. In fact, after Manet's death in 1883, Morisot wrote to her sister, Edma, illustrating the degree to which her close association with Manet had affected her:

> If you add to these almost physical emotions my old bonds of friendship with Edouard, an entire past of youth and work suddenly ending, you will understand that I am crushed. . . . he also had an intellectual charm, a warmth, something indefinable.
>
> . . . I shall never forget the days of my friendship and intimacy with him, when I sat for him, and the charm of his mind kept me alert during those long hours.[7]

Morisot felt Manet's death in a physical sense, noting the intimacy she had shared with him and his charm and intelligence, yet she made it clear to her sister that her feelings were based on old bonds of friendship. Her language is charged with the kinds of complexities that I will show are also characteristic of Manet's portraits of her. Both a text and a subtext, a surface and its constituent layers, are built into the relationship between these two artists. Superficially, their alliance is strictly collegial, yet, as in Manet's portraits of Morisot, an underlying narrative of attraction and infatuation runs just below an imperfect veneer of middle-class respectability.

The Balcony

Based on Manet's sighting of a group of people on a balcony in Boulogne-sur-Mer in 1868 and obviously related to Goya's *Majas on a Balcony*,[8]

Manet's *The Balcony,* of 1868 (Figure 20), serves as a template for his subsequent images of Morisot. It begins a trajectory of pictures that become increasingly difficult, their surfaces so built-up and worked over that the facture actually becomes a veil limiting legibility. In this painting, four people, all friends or relatives of Manet, are either on or are entering a balcony. Violinist Fanny Claus, who played duos with Manet's wife at the piano and who would later marry Manet's friend the sculptor Pierre Prins, is in the process of either putting on or removing her yellow kid gloves. Her dress buttoned almost to the neck, she looks slightly comical and prudish, with a large flower dangling above her summarily indicated eyes, really just black paint, smudged probably by Manet's own fingers or his palette knife. Her feet improbably hitting the floor, she can only be seen as less substantial, as somehow less fully realized, in comparison to Morisot's seductively torsioned body and better-developed and forceful facial features.

Claus becomes the foil against which Morisot is measured, not only because she is the other woman in the painting, but also because Manet links the two through color. Whereas the other figures wear black, Morisot and Claus are dressed in white. The green of Morisot's choker plays against the dab of green leaf above Claus's eyes and the green parasol that she holds. Even when color is not necessarily pulling together the parts of the picture occupied by the women, form is; Morisot's red fan and Claus's parasol inversely echo each other, opening out the painting, harnessing in the formal relationships between them.

A study for *The Balcony* further links the women in white.[9] In this earlier image, Claus is the seated figure, the position that Morisot holds in the final picture. This transposition of one woman with another establishes an enigmatic connection between the two, one that remains even after Manet shifted to another canvas, put the final touches to his decisive painting. The curious relationship between Claus and Morisot in *The Balcony* did not go unnoticed by critics such as Jules Castagnary, who, in *Le siècle* in 1869, projected a family narrative onto the picture: "On this balcony I see two women, one quite young. Are they sisters? Are they mother and daughter? I cannot tell. . . . one is seated and seems to have taken her place merely to enjoy the view of the street; the other is putting on her gloves as if to leave. These conflicting postures baffle me."[10]

Perhaps equally baffling, besides Castagnary's speculation that Morisot and Claus could be mother and daughter, is that Morisot is so much more

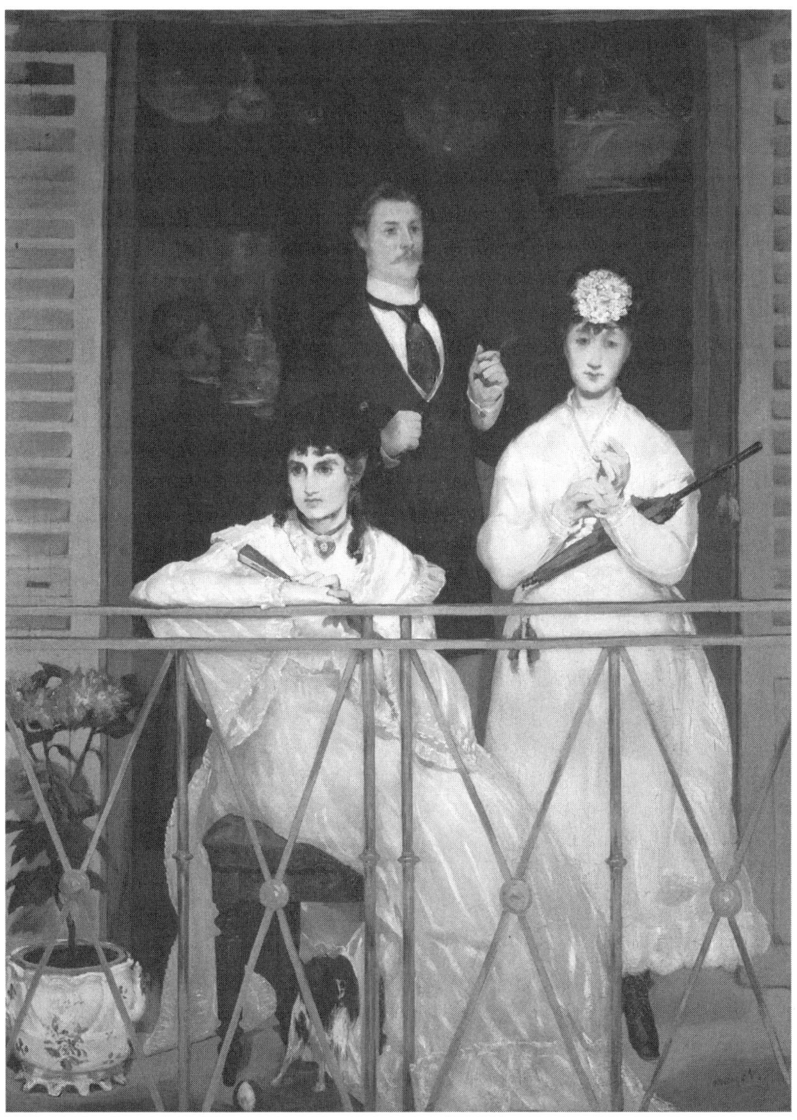

Figure 20. Edouard Manet, *The Balcony* (1868). Oil on canvas. Musée d'Orsay, Paris. Erich Lessing/Art Resource, NY.

fully articulated than the other figures in *The Balcony.* Her more explicitly described form implies that she has a particular significance for the artist both within and outside the painting. Yet the pictorial ambiguities do not add up, so in the end Morisot hangs precariously between meaning and unmeaning. Castagnary is right when he claims that Morisot is seated on the balcony so that she may enjoy the view *of* the street, but I would also argue that she is seated so as to be seen *from* the street as well. More clearly defined than the other figures in the composition, Morisot is not simply the viewer but also the viewed. Claus cradles her parasol as she fiddles with her glove, while the landscape painter Antoine Guillemet, cigarette in hand, strides purposefully onto the balcony. He is followed by the adumbrated image of a boy carrying a tray, posed for by Léon Leenhoff, Manet's presumably illegitimate child with Suzanne Leenhoff.[11] Each looks in a different direction, Morisot intensely to the left, Guillemet to the right, and Claus, ironically, directly at the viewer. The active engagement of the three subsidiary figures in *The Balcony* simply throws into relief the more static image of Morisot. This oppositional fixity is further reinforced by the energetic dog that plays with a ball beneath her chair and by the hydrangeas that bloom to the far left.

The clothing of the women, particularly of Morisot, indexes the degree to which Manet invests his picture with a specific time, place, and class. Like the models in so many of her own images of women in interiors, Morisot wears the dress of a proper bourgeoise at home.[12] Yet Manet's interpretation of this standard summer dress exploits the transparent potentials of the fabric as he allows Morisot's skin to peek through the lacy sleeves, lending the picture a kind of erotic yet not really scandalous frisson.

In a letter to her sister, Edma, Morisot described her reaction to *The Balcony* when it was exhibited at the Salon of 1869. "I am more strange than ugly," she wrote.[13] What is depicted in *The Balcony* must have seemed strange to Morisot, either because it did not correspond with what she knew of herself, or because it disrupted her notion of herself, or because it revealed to her some unknown aspects of herself. Like Sigmund Freud's later formulation of the idea of the uncanny, in which the familiar is seen in an unfamiliar light, Morisot's semblance is masked by that which is unfamiliar, or with Manet's conception of her.[14] Of course, the fact that the image appeared strange to her is also precisely the effect of its being a representation, always a mediated interpretation.

Veils, Ribbons, and Furs

The fundamental consequences of Manet's depictions of Morisot lie in this continual shifting of her identity: she looks different from canvas to canvas. While not overtly disguised in the manner of Victorine, Morisot is still cast and recast in each of the eleven paintings and prints, her image variously manipulated, masked, and veiled. In each of his portrayals of her, Manet incorporates fans, veils, ribbons, and furs that often compete with the paint to disrupt the visual semblance of Morisot. Even the pigment used to fabricate her presence on the canvas, especially in the pictures from the 1870s, becomes so thick and dense that the mechanisms of representation are called into question. Manet's choices of objects and formal strategies in these particular paintings combine to construct a particularly obtuse pictorial vocabulary, one that can best be unpicked using the terms of displacement and conflicted impulses. His pictures of Morisot with fans and veils and ribbons and furs chronicle not so much Morisot's adherence to the dictates of fashion, even though all of these accessories were certainly worn by the upper-class woman of the time, as Manet's fascination with Morisot and his sense of artistic competition.[15]

It is well known that Manet frequently received negative criticism at the Salon and Salon des refusés, where *Olympia,* for example, was deemed indecent, ugly, and repulsive.[16] Morisot's mother, in a letter of May 23, 1869, conveyed her perception of Manet's reaction to the Salon: "Manet was laughing heartily. This made him feel better, poor boy, because his lack of success saddens him. He tells you . . . that he meets people who avoid him in order not to have to talk about his painting, and as a result he no longer has the courage to ask anyone to pose for him."[17] Morisot herself wrote: "Poor man; he is sad. . . . he said that I had brought him luck. . . . I wish for his sake that this were true."[18] As an artist whose own work had been either ignored or relatively well reviewed and as a woman, Morisot must have represented some threat to the ill-received Manet. While Morisot intrigued Manet as an artist, she jeopardized his control over the space of representation, reinforcing for him his own lack of contemporary critical acclaim. Thus, the use of certain objects such as veils and fans and ribbons and furs occludes Morisot's threat by making less frightening the desired object: Morisot herself. On a purely practical level, by painting her so frequently, Manet often took her away from her own work for long periods of time between 1868 and 1874. Although to some degree complicit in the arrangement, agreeing as she did to sit for him, Morisot inactively posed while Manet busily produced.

Morisot's difficulty in finding the time to finish her own work for submission to the Salon is articulated in a letter to Edma regarding the hasty completion of *The Mother and Sister of the Artist* (Figure 21) in 1869–70: "I shall regret very much if this picture is not finished for the exhibition," she admitted.[19] Manet generously offered to "help" Morisot "finish" the painting. She wrote to Edma what Manet had said:

> "Tomorrow, after I have sent off my pictures, I shall come to see yours, and you may put yourself in my hands. I shall tell you what needs to be done." The next day . . . he came at about one o'clock; he found it very good, except for the lower part of the dress. He took the brushes and put in a few accents that looked very well. . . . That is where my misfortunes began. Once started, nothing could stop him; from the skirt he went to the bust, from the bust to the head, from the head to the background. He cracked a thousand jokes, laughed like a madman, handed me the palette, took it back; finally by five o'clock in the afternoon we had made the prettiest caricature that was ever seen. The carter was waiting to take it away; he made me put it on the hand-cart. . . . And now I am left confounded. My only hope is that I shall be rejected. My mother thinks this episode funny, but I find it agonizing.[20]

While "corrections" to a woman artist's canvas by a male colleague were not necessarily uncommon, the detection of another artist's hand, especially in the work of a woman artist, could be grounds for rejection at the Salon or could determine the placement of a picture there.[21] A letter from Morisot's mother to Edma illustrates the extent to which this episode affected Berthe's physical and emotional health:

> Yesterday she looked like a person about to faint; she grieves and worries me; her despair and discontent were so great that they could be ascribed only to a morbid condition; moreover she tells me every minute that she is going to fall ill. She overworked herself to such a point on the last day that she really could not see any more, and it seems that I made matters worse by telling her that the improvements Manet made on my head seemed to me atrocious. When I saw her in this state, and when she kept telling me that she would rather be at the bottom of the river than learn that her picture had been accepted, I thought I was doing the right thing to ask for its return.[22]

One way of interpreting Manet's presumptuous act is to say that he, probably not overtly, wished not only for Morisot's rejection at the Salon but also to invade her space of representation. For by painting her so many times, Manet was able to push *his* construction of Morisot into circulation, thus maintaining some measure of control over her public identity and her ability to produce. His assault of her canvas, his layers of paint effectively veiling her paint, may be seen as a similarly proprietary effort, as

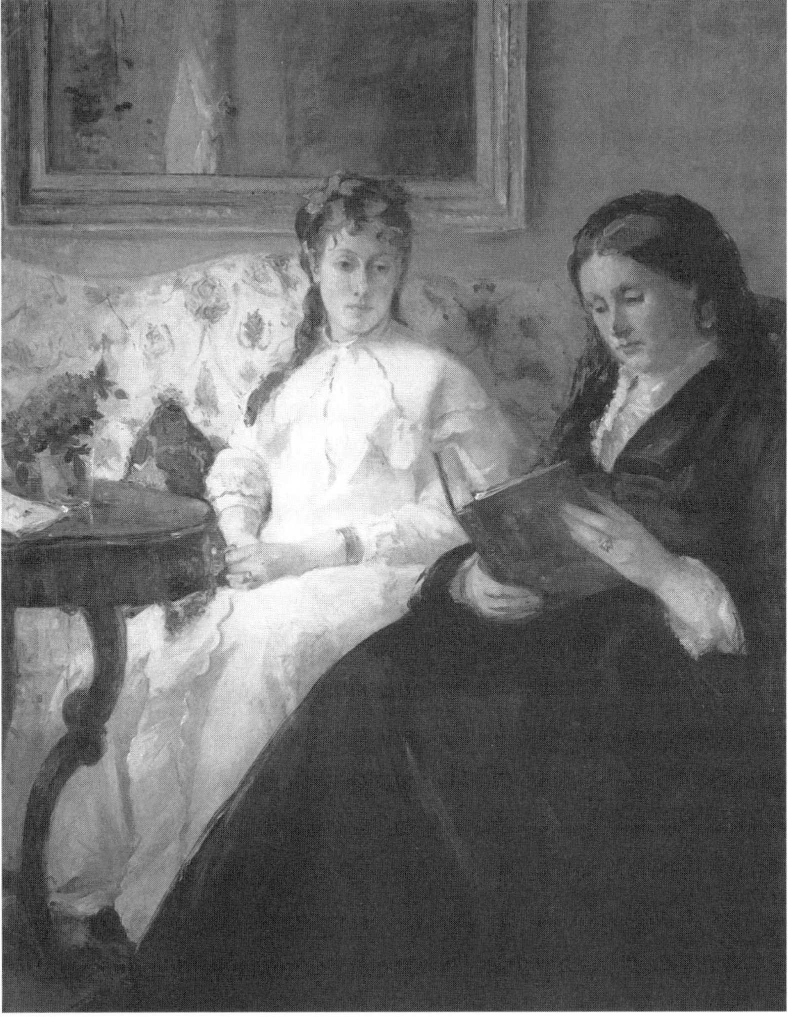

Figure 21. Berthe Morisot, *The Mother and Sister of the Artist* (1869–70). Oil on canvas. National Gallery of Art, Washington, D.C. Chester Dale Collection.

his way of claiming Morisot's space of production and not necessarily as an artistic collaboration.

In fact, the compositional similarities between Morisot's *The Mother and Sister of the Artist* and Manet's *Le repos (Portrait of Berthe Morisot)* (Figure 22), completed a year later, are illustrative of Manet's appropriative behavior in relation to Morisot.[23] In each, a fragmented and framed image hangs above the protagonist's head, and an overstuffed sofa, on which a woman sits, is partly represented. The inclusion of objects such as a lace handkerchief, a fan, and a neck ribbon in *Le repos,* all charged objects within the late nineteenth-century vocabulary of femininity, only reinforces my point about the ways in which Manet's pictures of Morisot function within a gendered language of artistic rivalry. He marks his pictures with these specific objects because their presence renders Morisot's image safer and more familiar to him, for she is depicted not as an artist but as a well-brought-up young woman sitting inactively, not engaged in work.[24] When he painted Eva Gonzalès, who was actually his only student, he showed her twice in the act of painting; yet he never showed Morisot, a better-known and more accomplished painter, as an active producer of art.[25]

The pose of *Le repos* is also indicative of the kinds of devices that Manet used in order to ensure that Morisot is not identifiable as an artist. Morisot's daughter, Julie, later conveyed that her mother "had bad memories of the sittings, that her left leg, half drawn back under the skirt, used to stiffen painfully, but Manet would not allow her to move, lest the skirt be disarranged."[26] The result of the pose, aside from the physical discomfort for the sitter, is the visual obliteration of Morisot's left leg. All we see poking out from beneath the mass of white skirt is her right leg, whose length is carefully articulated by the skirt that gathers around it. The absence of Morisot's left leg is strangely disturbing, especially since Manet calls such direct attention to the one that remains by using saturated white to indicate her stocking. The disparity between where Morisot's hip should be, based on anatomical location, and the placement of it in the painting further perplexes. Manet even elongates the distance between her waist and her foot in order to emphasize Morisot's long line of leg. By highlighting her one ankle, by making it the pivot on which the painting turns, Manet subtly yet sufficiently eroticizes Morisot, fastening our attention to the body of Morisot and not to her body of work.

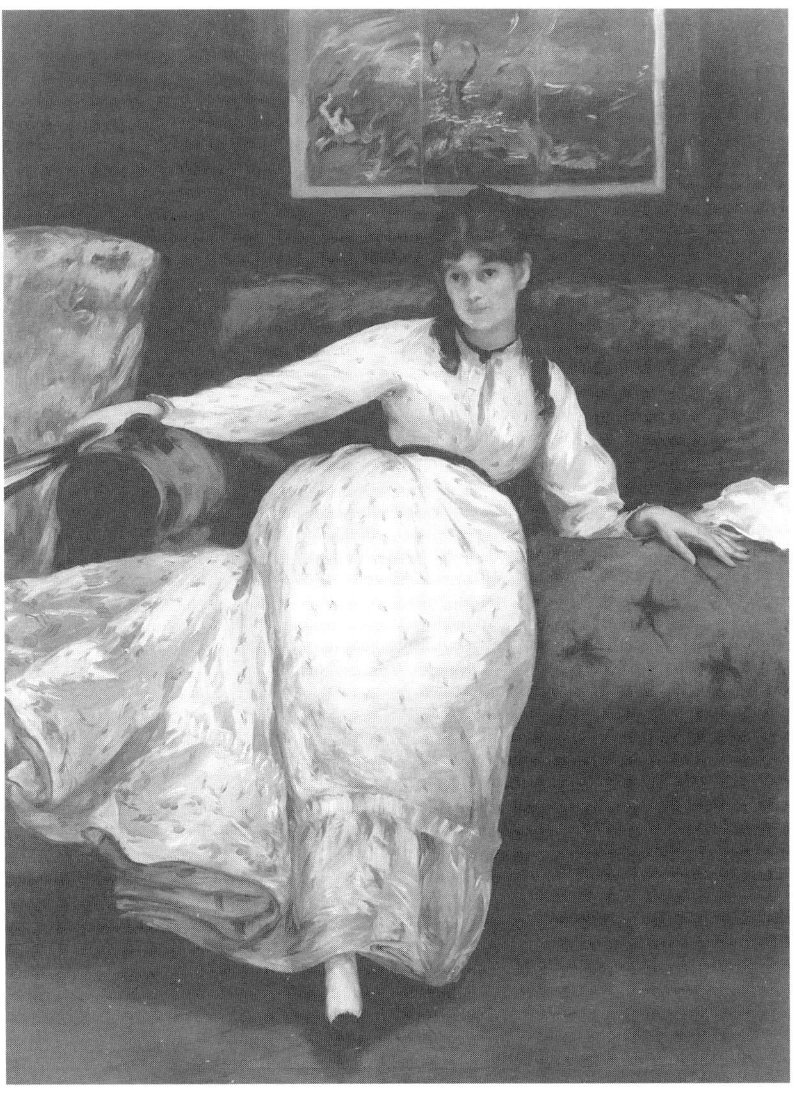

Figure 22. Edouard Manet, *Le repos (Portrait of Berthe Morisot)* (1870). Oil on canvas, 58¼ × 43¾ inches. Museum of Art, Rhode Island School of Design, Providence, Rhode Island. Bequest of the Estate of Edith Stuyvesant Vanderbilt Gerry.

Violets, Fans, and Pink Shoes

Perhaps one of the most reproduced of Manet's paintings of Morisot is *Berthe Morisot with Black Hat,* of 1872 (Figure 23).[27] We may not even notice the violets, the purple paint now mellowed by age, that make this image anything but a simple portrait of a woman with flowers pinned to her garment. What could be taken as an inconsequential prop, a clutch of violets included in order to fill a space or perhaps to add color to a painting that is dominated by rich blacks, is charged with meaning that would have been obvious to a late nineteenth-century viewer and certainly to Morisot herself. For contemporary literary texts were filled with the exchange of violets as a gesture between lovers. Even the violet-toned echoes in the background, which reads simultaneously as a wall and a window, emphasize the importance of the little purple flowers secured at the base of Morisot's plunging neckline.

Writing in 1932, the poet Paul Valéry, Morisot's nephew by marriage, noticed other equally charged elements of this, his favorite, painting. He wrote:

> Before all else, the Black, the absolute black, the black of a mourning hat, and the little hat's ribbons mingling with the chestnut locks and their rosy highlights . . . It is held by a broad black band, passing behind the left ear, encircling and confining the neck; and the black cape over the shoulders reveals a glimpse of fair skin at the parting of a white linen collar. These luminous deep black areas frame and present a face with eyes black and too large, and expression rather distant and abstracted. . . . The full power of these blacks, the cool simple background, the clear pink-and-white skin, the strange silhouette of the hat, in the "latest fashion" . . . the tangle of locks, ties, and ribbon encroaching on the face; those eyes, vaguely gazing in profound big abstraction, and offering, as it were, a presence of absence.[28]

Ribbons wind around Morisot's neck, almost disembodying, choking it with a thick layer of black paint. Valéry picks up on the visual tension produced by the juxtaposition of these black ribbons with Morisot's pale skin and her wild chestnut hair and how they all combine to translate what could be a perfectly straightforward image, a portrait in fact, into something quite different, an absence of a presence.

Like *The Balcony,* this picture clearly undermines convention, for it is not a static rendition of a proper woman simply sitting for her portrait.

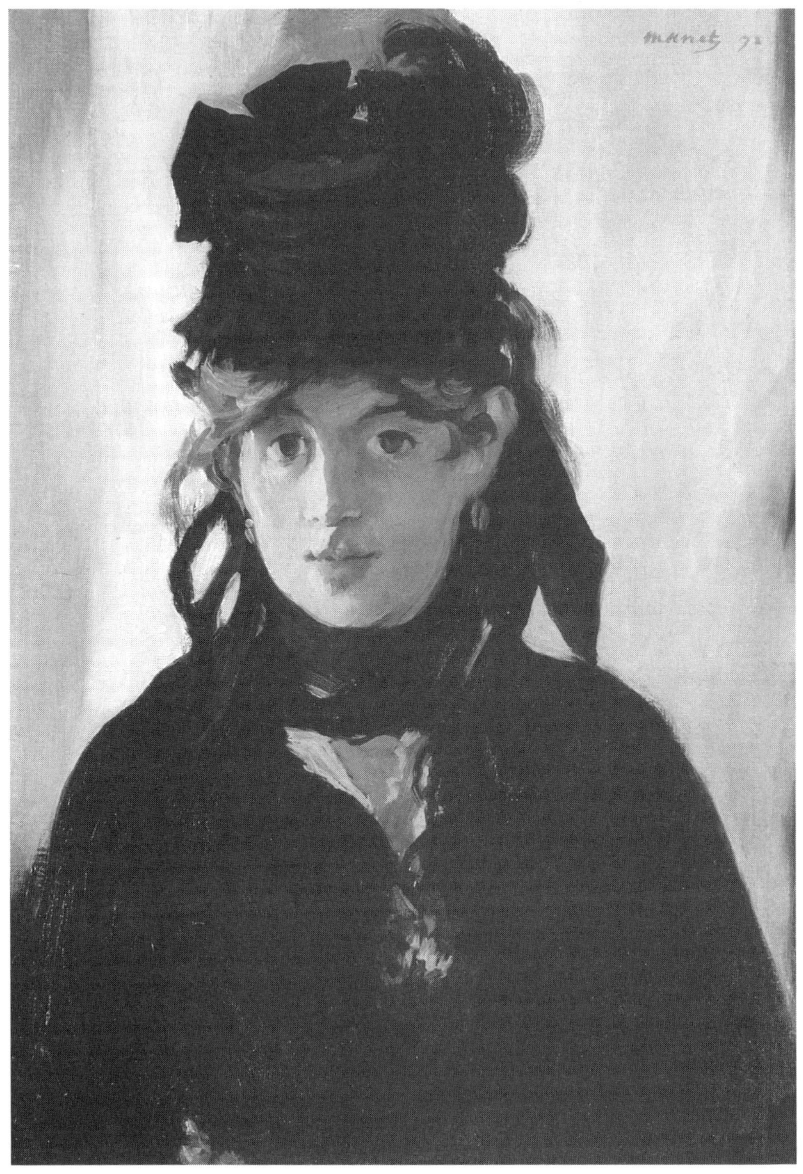

Figure 23. Edouard Manet, *Berthe Morisot with Black Hat* (1872). Oil on canvas. Private collection, Paris. Bridgeman-Giraudon/Art Resource, NY.

Morisot's head is turned to her right, enabling a shadow to mark off the left side of her face, essentially splitting it into two parts. In order to indicate the presence of light on her right cheek, basically an unmodulated expanse of lighter tan, Manet draws a white line down the side of Morisot's nose. He blurs her right eye socket, he drags the outline of her lips into inexplicable shadow, he allows stray hairs to escape from an ornate hat.

Manet based two lithographs and an etching on this painting, reconstituting Morisot's identity multiple times, now in the form of the more reproducible medium of prints. Whereas the lithographs more closely follow the mood and appearance of the painting, the etching (Figure 24), particularly the second state, alters what is already embedded in the painting to produce something far more disturbing and strange. Manet takes certain technical risks in these prints, risks that have the effect of conveying some part of the power of his feelings toward Morisot.[29] Her hat is tilted, and her left cheek is exaggerated by a series of lines and marks. Her hair flies about in seeming disarray. Heavy vertical strokes and deep shadows impart a quality so dark, disturbing, and powerful that it is difficult to believe that this print represents the same person who appears in the oil version on which it is presumably based. Like an image from a nightmare, this version of Morisot breaks out of any sustainable structure of respectability and friendship.

Stéphane Mallarmé's biographer described the effect Morisot had on both Mallarmé and Manet. He wrote: "[T]he artist [Manet] and the poet [Mallarmé] very much love her [Morisot's] authoritative intelligence, her distinguished savagery, and the nervous disorder of her brown hair."[30] Phrases like "distinguished savagery" and "nervous disorder" serve only to reiterate the difficulties, tensions, and complexities Manet built into the pictorial fabrics of his depictions of Morisot, which are so physically embodied in the etching. The evolution of the painting into the etching exemplifies the ways in which an underlying signification, below the surface in the first version, may manifest itself in an explosion of unpredictable and unmanageable lines in a later variant. In other words, what is already present in the prototype, or the oil painting—Manet's feelings for and rivalry with Morisot—has become amplified in subsequent interpretations.

To complete the trajectory begun in 1872 by the image of Morisot with a bunch of violets, Manet gave her *The Bunch of Violets* (Figure 25), regarded by most scholars as Manet's token of thanks to Morisot for posing for *Berthe Morisot with Black Hat.* The violets, a version of the ones pinned

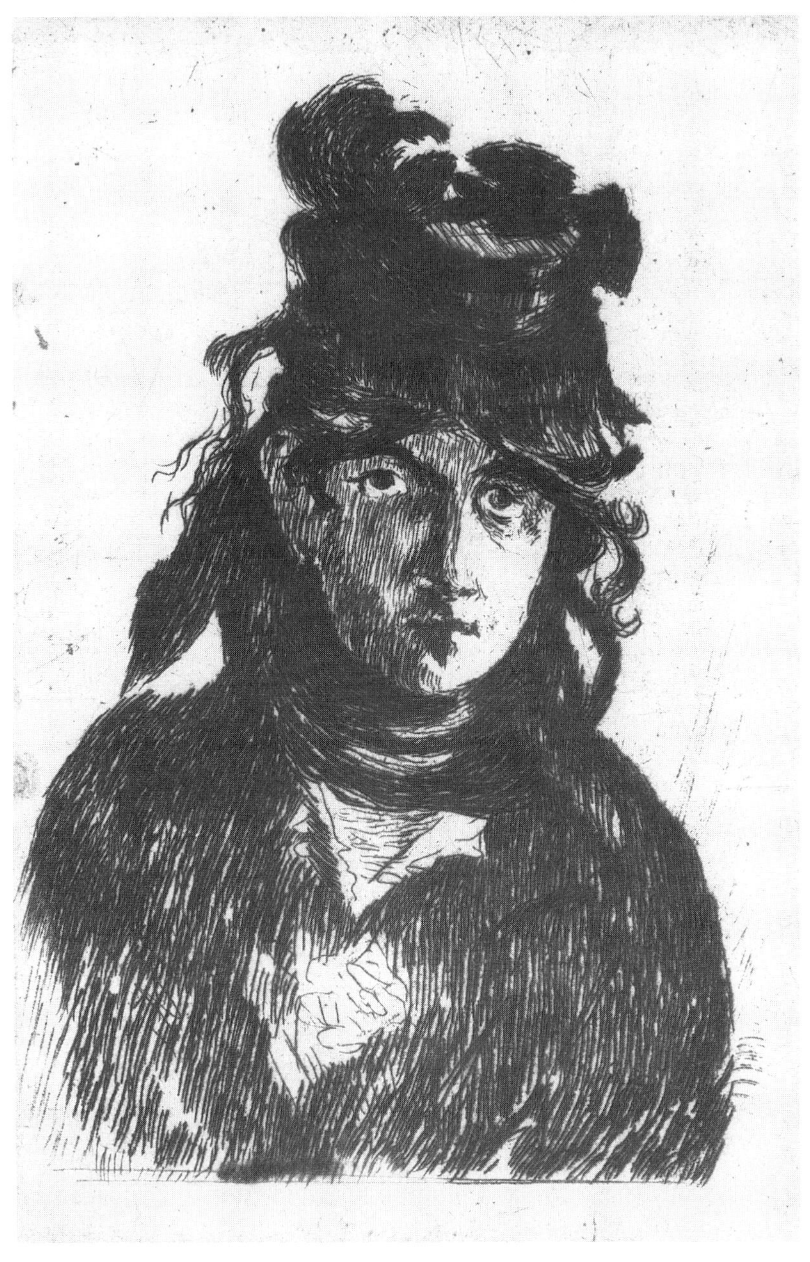

Figure 24. Edouard Manet, *Portrait of Berthe Morisot* (1872). Etching, second state. Philadelphia Museum of Art.

at Morisot's neck in the larger painting, are now captured in close-up view next to the fan that she held in *The Balcony.* Viscerally thick pigments shape the fresh green stems and leaves of the violet bunch, while purples, to which Manet added increments of white, become the flowers. If we follow Elaine Scarry's reasoning in her evocative essay "Imagining Flowers: Perceptual Mimesis (Particularly Delphinium)," these flowers exert a particular power, a power that cannot be contained in a representation of, say, a human face. For Scarry, "[f]lowers, unlike the face of human beings, appear to be the perfect size for imagining."[31] She goes on to argue that the small scale of the flower, along with its intensity of surface and color, makes it an especially salient object with which the author or artist may articulate a vividity of thought. The flower, she claims, is able to enter our imagination and fields of vision in a way in which larger objects and places simply are not. Her logic provides a new lens with which to analyze this painting of flowers, which we can now see as an even more potent consolidation of Manet's complex feelings, as his deepest expression of thought.

Manet's use of the color of the violets to dramatic effect throughout this small canvas further corroborates their crackle and pungency both

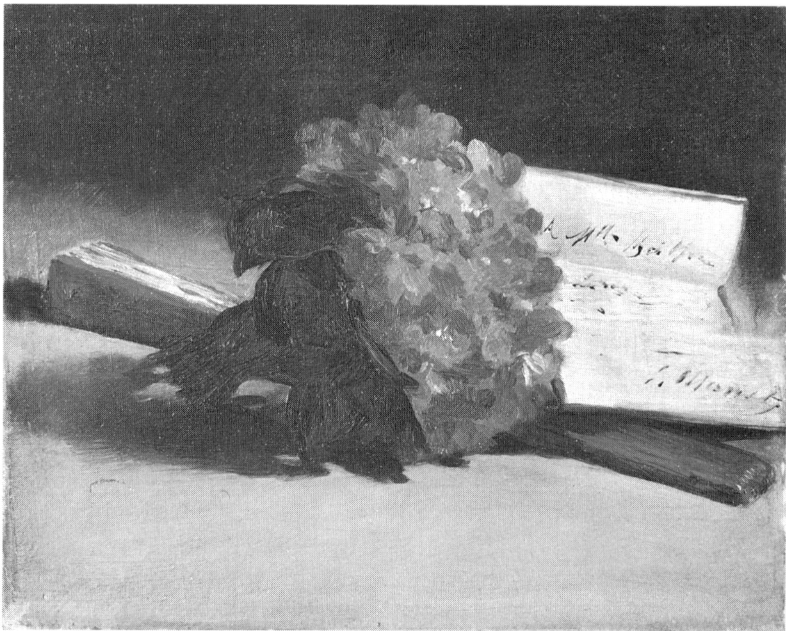

Figure 25. Edouard Manet, *The Bunch of Violets* (1872). Oil on canvas, 22 × 27 cm. Private collection, Paris. Erich Lessing/Art Resource, NY.

for the artist and for their intended viewer—Morisot. Even the white of the paper on which Manet placed the only decipherable words, "A Mlle Berthe . . . E. Manet," is rendered with a heavily loaded brush and haphazardly outlined in the purple used for the violets. The juxtaposition of the only legible words on the letter—the names of the subject and the object—begs to be interpreted in connection with the violets, especially since Manet uses related colors to bring them together formally. And if the closed fan suggests an implied folding of the open letter, already previously creased in three parts, then one can imagine that, when refolded, the names of Morisot and Manet would lie on top of each other.

Propriety stood in the way of anything more than a friendly flirtation. However, this respect for class etiquette did not inhibit the jealousy inspired in Morisot by Manet's relationship with Eva Gonzalès. Morisot's mother exacerbated the situation by playing on Berthe's insecurities in relation to Manet when, on seeing Manet while Berthe was away visiting her sister in Lorient, she wrote to Berthe: "He [Manet] asked how you were, and I answered that I was going to report how unfeeling he is. He has forgotten about you for the time being. Mademoiselle G[onzalès] has all the virtues, all the charms, she is an accomplished woman."[32] In an effort to convince herself of her own worth as an artist, Morisot wrote to Edma in 1879: "Manet lectures me, and holds up that eternal Mademoiselle Gonzalès as an example; she has poise, perseverance, she is able to carry an undertaking to a successful issue, whereas I am not capable of anything."[33] However, later she asserted, "[I]t seems that what I do is decidedly better than Eva Gonzalès," displaying an almost uncharacteristic degree of self-confidence.[34]

In *Berthe Morisot with a Fan,* painted in 1872 (Figure 26), these mechanisms of rivalry and competition, so much a part of the relationship between Morisot and Manet, generate a particularly mysterious and seductive image. It is not surprising that Morisot should be dressed in Spanish costume, since Manet always had a fondness for Spanish art and culture.[35] What is surprising is the virtual obliteration of Morisot's face by an open fan. According to Charles Blanc, "Regardless of the climate, the fan is chiefly an accessory of the toilet, affording an excuse for graceful movements under the pretext of agitating the air to refresh it."[36] Far from operating as an accessory of the toilette or as an opportunity for graceful movement, this fan actually functions to *undo* the very possibility for grace. Air remains stagnant, all action is halted. No longer simply article of the toilette, the ornamental object displaces the sitter, rendering Morisot's identity

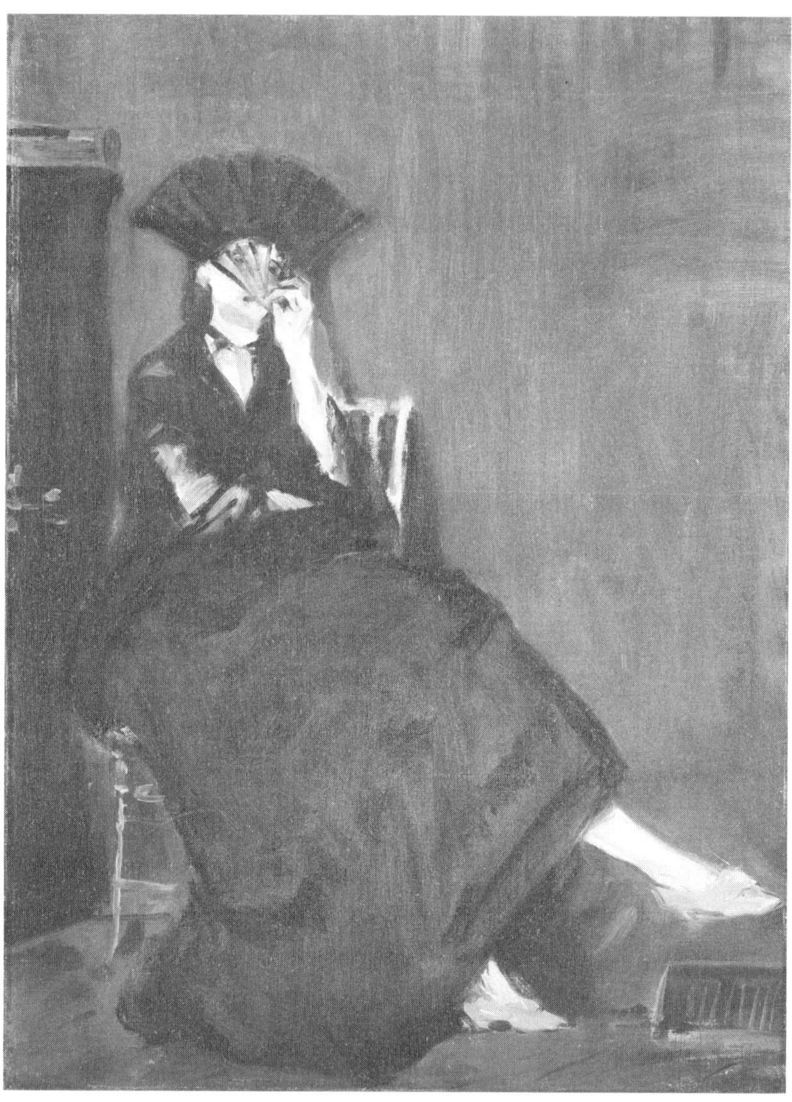

Figure 26. Edouard Manet, *Berthe Morisot with a Fan* (1872). Oil on canvas. Musée d'Orsay, Paris. Erich Lessing/Art Resource, NY.

indecipherable. Her singularity is erased by the object, which now, by occluding Morisot's face, essentially covers over her threat to Manet the painter. The fan thus veils and unfixes meaning, calling increased attention to that which we cannot see. It simultaneously frees Morisot's image from the constraints of bourgeois respectability and masks her identity as an artist.

Ironically, this fan may also be interpreted as a gesture toward propriety, since it ensures that the mystery woman remains unidentifiable. Still, by foregrounding the fan, Manet also heightens the signs of Morisot's sexuality, for he would have known the fan's role in the process of seduction in Spanish culture.[37] Like the veil, the fan can be instrument of both seduction and decorum. Manet thus uses the layered language of the fan in order to enact an erotics of looking in which the looked at is not actually seen. In this way he is able to play out his feelings for Morisot without having to look directly at or touch her, without actually transgressing societal expectations. Yet by painting her and by positioning the fan over her face, he is, in effect, touching her. When understood within the rubric of Spanish culture then, this painting is a kind of secret in which Manet marks out his feelings toward Morisot, not only on the canvas, but also on her body.

In contrast to Manet's use of the fan to produce what may be considered a subversion and sexualization of Morisot's identity is Morisot's own incorporation of the fan as a sign of propriety and beauty in *At the Ball*, of 1875. Working in synchrony with the woman's elaborate gown, silk gloves, and floral corsage, Morisot's highly decorated fan helps to specify this woman's position in French society rather than charge the picture with erotic intent. While this image may have been painted in Morisot's house, she tried to establish the setting of a public ball by creating a tactful balance between the woman's clothing and the background flower arrangement. The fan, colored by sketchy strokes of dense pigments that suggest a picture, also serves as a counterpoint for the woman's less adorned face, which is gently averted and only subtly made-up.

Manet does not situate his painting of Morisot behind a fan at a ball or in a social situation; rather, he isolates this baffling creature without a face, Morisot, in an austere room with only a chair, the edge of an armoire, and a vent, the last of which dramatically reinforces the detachment of the fan from its possible functions, to cool off or to decorate. Instead, it becomes a mask, an object at once adorning and concealing. Morisot peeks through the spokes of the bottom part while the open, circular portion rises above her head, like an unusual headdress. Having little to do with its supposed purpose, this fan has become at once playful, erotic, and disturbing.

Surprisingly, Morisot's face, which we expect to see, is obscured, while her leg, which contemporary propriety dictated that we should not see, is bared. In a painting about covering up and veiling over, Morisot's bare leg and ankle, and the attention lavished on her pink shoe, are indicative of Manet's intense fascination with her body.[38] Her foot points daintily toward the vent at the lower right of the canvas, setting up the expected narrative between the circulation of air via the vent and the fan. Yet the circle is never completed. On a purely formal level, the vent cleverly fills an empty part of the picture, and the gaps in the vent echo the fan slats. However, on a functional level, the vent and the fan, far from working together, end up in tension with one another. The result is a bizarre juxtaposition of things that seem to serve no purpose within the painting itself. Between this curious focus on a pink shoe and the little eyes that peek through the slats of an open fan, a scene of seduction, not function, is enacted, the players created and staged by Manet himself, agreed to by Morisot. To be sure, both artists participate in the realization of this confusing tableau, in which a bourgeois woman assumes a pose of impropriety in order to dismantle, if only visually, the pretense of respectability.

Effacing

It is probably not coincidental that as his brother Eugène began to court Morisot seriously, Manet's images of her grow increasingly perplexing, the facture coating the surface of the canvases in such complex patterns that straightforward visibility becomes almost an impossibility. And while Manet's oeuvre in general is marked by an intense attention to the material quality of paint and to the exposure of the underlying strategies of representation, I would argue that he formulated a particular visual vocabulary for his representations of Morisot, a language that could contain and preserve some of the intricacies of their relationship. It would seem that he had to continue to assert his control over Morisot, even if not consciously, while his brother gradually won her affections. On the surface, Manet maintains the veneer of propriety, but in the end, through the invention of an elaborate pictorial lexicon, he is nevertheless able to enact his sexual effects on her.[39]

In *Berthe Morisot with a Veil,* of 1872 (Figure 27), the veil, certainly prefigured by the fans, hats, and ribbons of Manet's earlier pictures of her, is activated in such a way as to seem to embody the ambiguity of their relationship. Although more of her face is visible here than in *Berthe Morisot with a Fan,* the very constitution of the veil of paint limits the legibility of the image and marks the face as the site of the process of deindividualization. Again, Manet has masked and obstructed. A bizarre and irregular configuration of black netting, in places speckled with dots, this veil complicates the topography of Morisot's face so much that her eyes are merely asymmetrical dots of thickly applied black paint and her mouth is almost indecipherable. At the same time, the grotesque inversion of the bottom of the veil produces the unexpected effect of revealing the infrastructure of Morisot's face, stray strokes of paint epitomizing bones meeting to form the framework of a chin. This veil hangs at the bottom and the sides of Morisot's face in folds of such heavy vertical slashes that the black, gray, and white that Manet used to compose the veil ultimately fight to decompose it, along with the skin underneath. Manet painted this veil so that it reads as several things at once—as lace, a skull, and, yes, even a beard, one that calls to mind the beard Manet himself wore. A kind of displaced self-portrait, perhaps, this image of Morisot with a veil bends gender and addresses the very means through which artistic identities are formulated. And yet this painting on some level still conforms, though in a backhanded, even irreverent, way, to standards of bourgeois fashionability.

An illustration for an 1872 issue of *La mode illustrée, journal de la famille* (Figure 28) shows a veil remarkably similar in style to the one worn by Morisot in the painting of the same year. Both spotted black veils are edged in scalloped lace and are pulled up at the sides and to the back of a hat that is ornamented with ostrich feathers. The dots in the veil in the illustration are regularly dispersed across the model's face, highlighting her perfect features. Compared with the flow of the veil in the illustration, the veritable invisibility of the veil across the middle of Morisot's face in the painting is especially inexplicable. And while the scratchy texture of her cheeks and nose indicates that they are seen as if through a veil, the actual fabric of the veil, which is supposed to hang over her face, seems to end above the eyes and return below the nose. Manet is careful to rouge her cheeks, to suggest the tip of a nose, and even to begin to formulate an ear, but curiously, he leaves this face apparently unveiled and in a state of incompletion. And while the whole painting foregrounds process through its

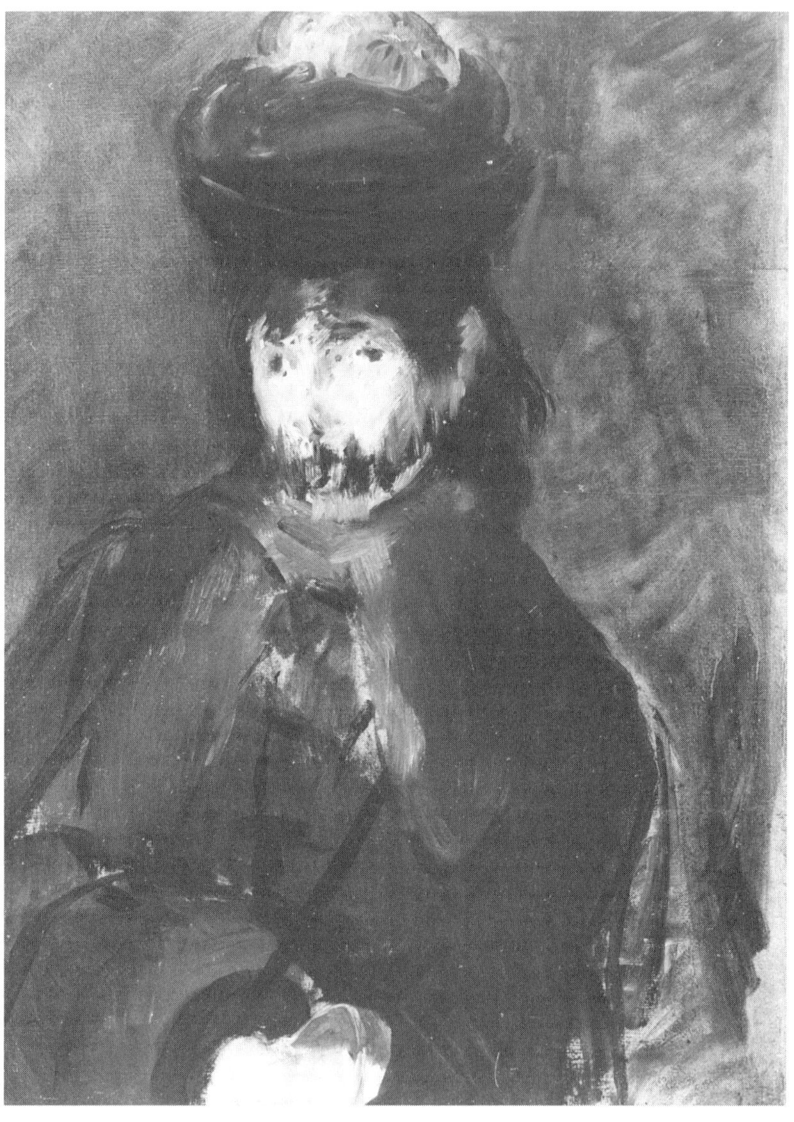

Figure 27. Edouard Manet, *Berthe Morisot with a Veil* (1872). Oil on canvas. Musée du Petit Palais, Geneva. Photograph by Studio Monique Bernaz, Geneva.

actively applied browns and blacks and flesh tones, it is here, in this passage—in this part of the face left virtually uncovered—that something significant has been left undone.

Not only are the face and veil seemingly unfinished, but the broadly brushed and scumbled background further emphasizes the haziness that would indicate that something has been seen through a veil. Morisot's cape and muff are also irregularly handled. The red tie at her neck is so summarily rendered that it dissolves into an indecipherable blotch of dry red paint. The swirl of white feathers at the top of Morisot's hat, made up of an equally open set of white, gray, and black strokes, reiterates the sense of a dispersed view. However, it is the way in which Manet uses the weave

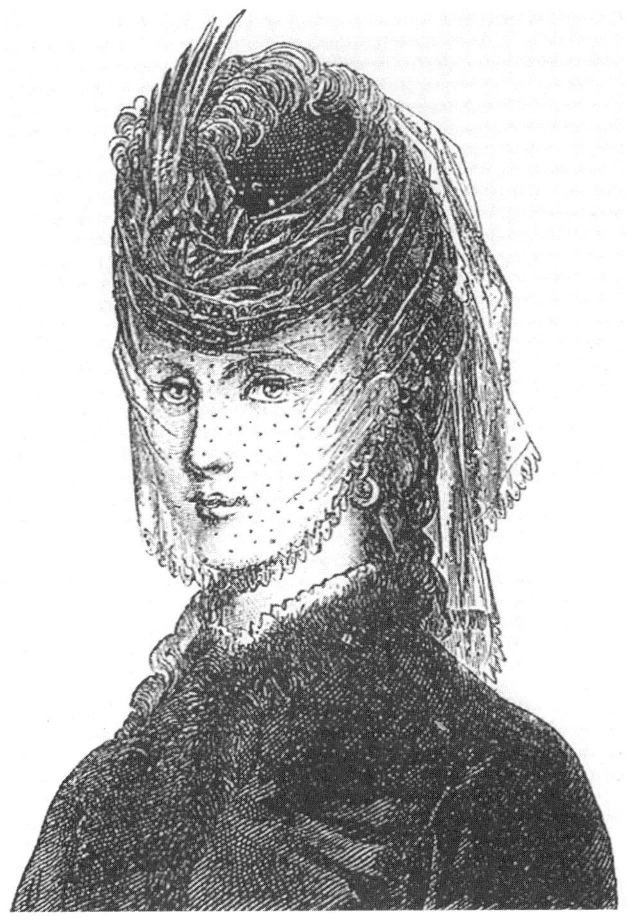

Figure 28. *La mode illustrée, journal de la famille* 15 (April 14, 1872): 117. Engraving. Bibliothèque nationale, Paris.

of the canvas, especially in the background and at Morisot's neckline, that most mimics the presence of a veil. Thus, where there is no pictorial representation of a veil, there is nonetheless the perception that we are seeing this image of Morisot through a veil.

Ordinarily a veil has the effect of seeming to be both there and not, both translucent and opaque, thus inviting interpretation on multiple levels. On the one hand, we may analyze the painted veil's surface, acknowledging its presence and tangibility. On the other hand, we may look below the surface of the veil, to the face, in order to uncover what lies below. It follows, then, that the veil both brings Manet closer to Morisot's image and distances him from it. Without the presence of the veil, Manet's threat, his desire for Morisot and his jealousy of her as artist, would have to be faced, but because the veil is there, the threat is somewhat effaced, rendered simultaneously more manageable for Manet but more complicated for the viewer. The veil mediates, controls, and articulates in visual terms Manet's simultaneous infatuation with and jealousy of Morisot.

Manet's fascination with Morisot virtually implodes in *Berthe Morisot in Mourning,* of 1874 (Figure 29). Several scholars have tried to explain the disconcerting quality of the image, citing Morisot's grief at her father's death as its driving force. I would argue, however, that the canvas's conflict is motivated less by a crisis in Morisot's life than by one in Manet's, for by this time, Morisot was engaged to marry Manet's brother. Labeled a "friendly medusa" by Mallarmé and "easily, dangerously silent" by Valéry, this particular depiction of Morisot is insufficiently explicated in anything but the terms of a displacement of Manet's desire and the sense of impending loss onto the formal terms of painting practice.

With the veil cast aside, part of Morisot's face is now obscured by the hand on which she leans and by the very paint that constitutes her face. Violent slashes and swirls of flesh-colored tones violated by pure white insist on the sculptural possibilities of paint and render the face masklike. The facture both visually dematerializes form and forces our attention to what is behind it. So, although a veil is not represented across her face in this particular painting, one is metaphorically conjured by the physical presence of pigment on canvas, which effectively asserts itself as a veil through which we must try to exhume the semblance of Morisot.

The way Manet executes Morisot's face actually subverts the possibility for anatomical accuracy, for modeling, in an unexpected twist, both disfigures and configures. In fact, the intensely agitated *matière* declares itself as being almost dialectically opposed to representation. Morisot's left eye is essentially a sloppy daub of brown; the right, a neater circle; the effect, a wild asymmetry. The mouth and nose are merged by a thick stroke of brown, a shadow, and the chin is imprecise and strangely pointed. Her left cheek is sculpted by strips of brown and tan that overlap with what could eventually materialize as an ear. Then there is the curious curl of beige that follows the shape of the hand on which Morisot's face rests, producing the miraculously disturbing effect of rendering both cheeks almost symmetrical in their anatomical impossibility. If in *Berthe Morisot with a Veil*

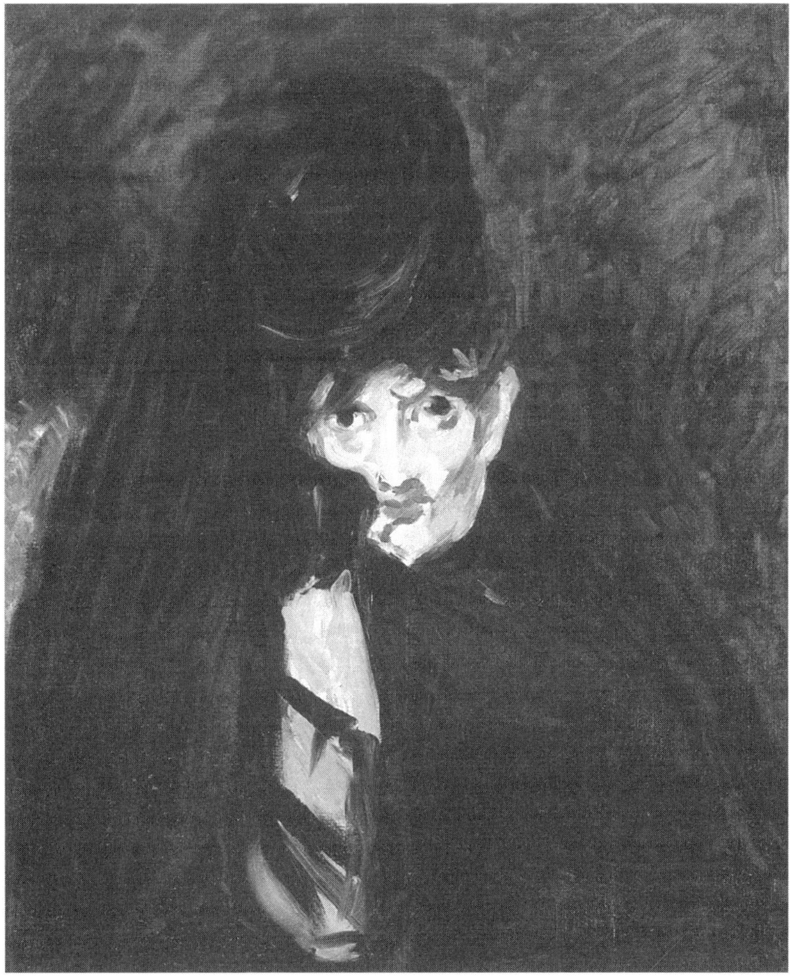

Figure 29. Edouard Manet, *Berthe Morisot in Mourning* (1874). Oil on canvas. Private collection.

Manet made Morisot's face seem skull-like, then this picture comes even closer to conjuring one physically in its emphasis on hollows and bone structure.

So much else about this work is visually confounding. Morisot's arm is composed of stray flesh-toned strokes that lap over a black glove. A fierce strip of black winds its way around this arm, breaking it apart, dismembering it from itself and from the body through ferocious gestures of the artist's brush. Manet fixated on the surface of this painting, working it and reworking it, aggressively endangering its legibility. Facture here fights at once to be what it represents and to disrupt the very conditions of its representation. Morisot's form threatens simultaneously to disintegrate and to tear itself from the canvas, every inch of which is clearly marked by Manet's hand partly dismantling his own construction.

One could even argue that Manet has finally achieved in this, his last portrait of Morisot, what he set out to accomplish when he first "reworked" her own painting of her mother and her sister in 1869. For in each, a kind of veiling of Morisot's subjectivity has taken place. In the one case, Manet effectively veiled Morisot's paint with his own, his brushstrokes covering hers, his construction undermining her subjectivity as an artist; and in his pictures of her, he also veiled her image, with paints that metaphorically constitute veils and masks. He did not paint her again after she married his brother. What started in *The Balcony,* which cast Morisot as mysterious seductress, and followed through with the increasingly built-up surfaces of his subsequent images of her, ended rather abruptly.

Veiling Her Own Subjectivity, or Morisot's Self-Portraits

Perhaps it is precisely because Manet painted her so often and so forcefully that there are no existing self-portraits by Morisot painted before 1885. In fact, she destroyed all but about twenty-four of the paintings she executed before she was thirty, some of which, given the impediment to women artists in finding willing and socially acceptable models, may very well have been self-portraits.[40] We know from letters that she found it difficult to justify her choice of a career as an artist at a time when social pressures dictated that a woman of her class marry and have children. For example, Berthe wrote to Edma, her constant companion until Edma's own marriage in 1869:

> If we go on this way, my dear Edma, we shall no longer be good for anything. You cry on receiving my letters, and I did just the same this morning. . . . But, I repeat, this sort of thing is unhealthy. It is making us lose whatever remains of our youth and beauty. For me this is of no importance, but for you it is different. . . . This painting, this that you mourn for, is the cause of many griefs and many troubles. . . . The lot you have chosen is not the worst one. You have a serious attachment and a man's heart devoted to you. Do not revile your fate. Remember that it is sad to be alone; despite anything that might be said or done, a woman has an immense need of affection.[41]

Although Morisot did have financial, moral, and emotional support from her family, this support was not unwavering. Her mother wrote to Edma in 1870: "I am earnestly imploring Berthe not to be disdainful. Everyone thinks that it is better to marry, even making some concessions, than to remain independent in a position that is not really one. We must consider that in a few more years she will be more alone, she will have fewer ties than now; her youth will fade."[42] Morisot was well aware of the consequences associated with her choice to be an artist and not to marry until her thirties. That she continued to paint at all is really quite remarkable, given the expectations for any woman of her position.

When she did paint her self-portrait, some of these conflicts seem to be embedded in the pictorial fabric. In *Self-Portrait with Julie Manet*, of 1885 (Figure 30), Morisot foregrounds the very problem of the subject as an epistemological construct. One could say that her fragmented representations of herself and her daughter recognize both that completion in self-portraiture is always an impossibility and that career and motherhood are simultaneously conflictual and interconnected. As in so much of her work, Morisot here unfixes more traditional, academic modes of representation by making the facture obvious, by allowing the canvas to show. In effect, she uses her technique to undermine convention and to declare her working process, representing the uncertainties and difficulties of image making through those multiple scissions, reiterations, and asymmetries.[43]

In this picture, Morisot articulates the borders of her form and of her daughter's using quick, scratchy, and dry strokes of black. Her own image is constituted both by paint and by blank canvas, for the semblance of the body emerges where the paint is absent. A network of marks with the canvas constantly showing through, her self-portrait announces the difficulty of portraying oneself. Her face, perhaps the most fully realized part of the painting, reads as white and brown hatchwork, tempered by hazy reddish tones. A tiny dab of gleaming white at the eye intensifies Morisot's gaze. And yet she is careful to smudge the edges of her eyes, each asymmetrical, seemingly unrelated, and totally unidealized. She cleverly takes the red that she uses for her mouth and wipes the brush across two parts of her cheek, one ear, and the side of her nose—just the kind of trick that both unifies and fragments a composition. Her face is framed by a shock of hair, each section of which is composed of both carefully integrated and strikingly separate thick strokes of brown or white or tan.

Her pose declares an assuredness that is emphasized by the bravado of open brushwork. And still so much about this picture is tentative. Little Julie is a transitory gesture across an unfilled canvas. Her face is a simple outline irregularly filled in with chalky white, and her clothing is barely indicated. Yet, despite the sketchy adumbration of her form, Julie functions as an anchor for the composition, as a marker that forces our eye to look at Morisot, and also as a reminder of what social conventions would have considered her other accomplishment to be. By choosing to marry and

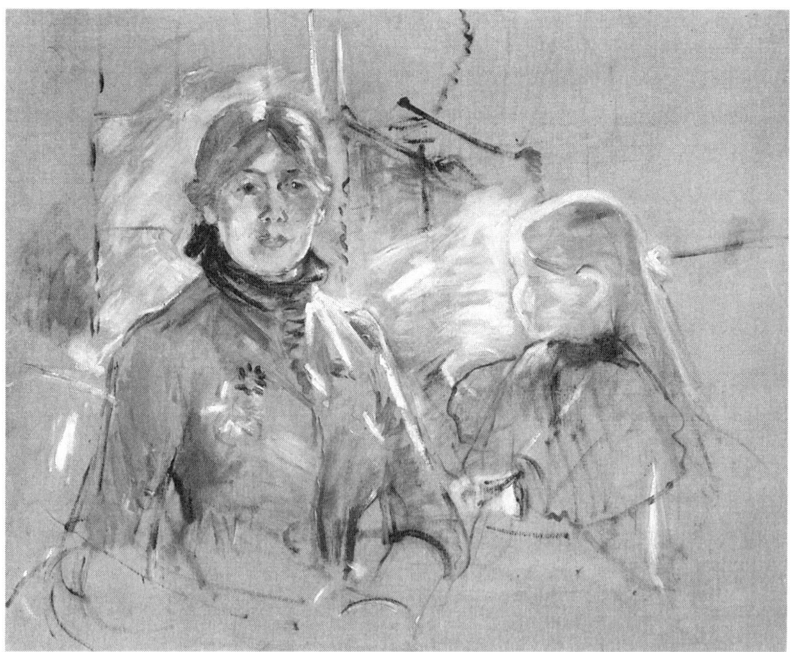

Figure 30. Berthe Morisot, *Self-Portrait with Julie Manet* (1885). Oil on unprimed canvas. Private collection.

have a child, Morisot was finally able to reconcile her art with certain cultural imperatives.

A pastel self-portrait done around 1885 (Figure 31), this one without Julie, seems less self-assured. A blurry flexus of diagonal pastel at once fabricates and threatens to undo the subject. Morisot works over her face with dense and scratchy white and gray. Her eyes are two uneven, ovoid smudges of black rimmed with red. For all of the thick applications of

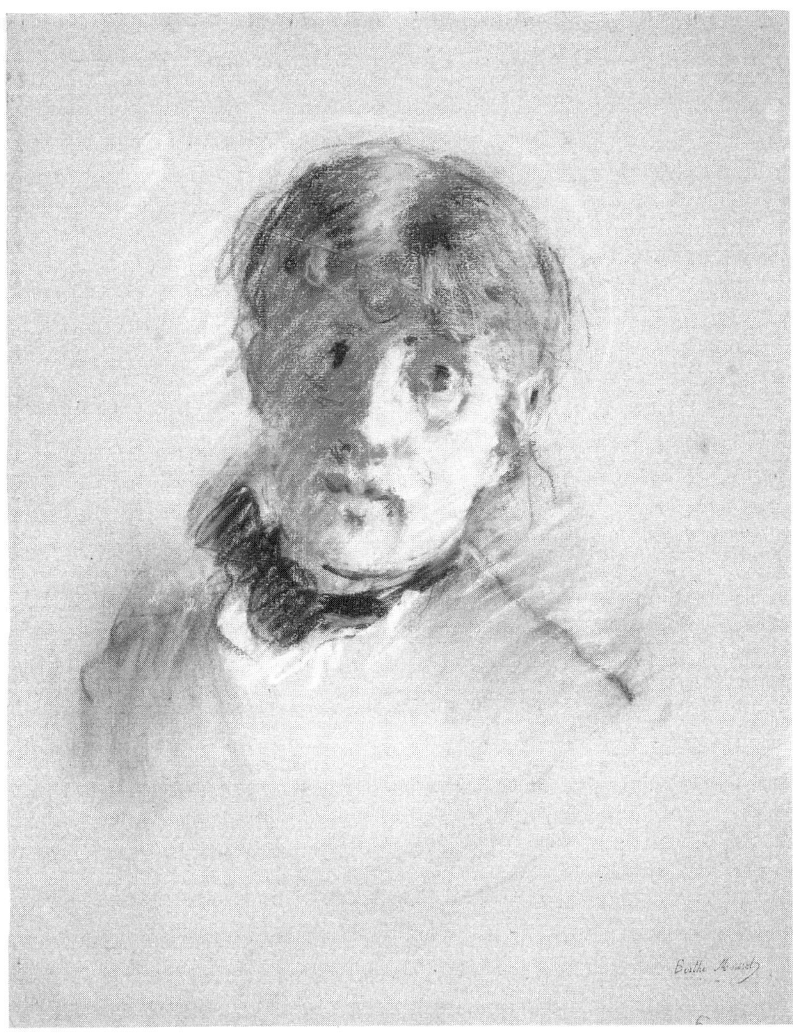

Figure 31. Berthe Morisot, *Self-Portrait* (c. 1885). Pastel with stumping, on gray laid paper with blue fibers, 48 × 38 cm. Helen Regenstein Collection, The Art Institute of Chicago. Photograph copyright The Art Institute of Chicago.

material, her face almost disintegrates into itself. The pastel works at points with the grain of the paper to epitomize the pattern that would be created by a veil. Refiguring perhaps some of Manet's veiling of her face, this self-portrait helps to expose certain other points about the difficulties associated with the act of looking at and portraying oneself. The marks across her face, the crosshatched strains of white, gray, and yellow, signify that one may never truly penetrate below the veil.

Self-portraiture is not necessarily about the way one looks, nor is it necessarily about how one wishes to be seen.[44] We have in Morisot's self-portraits, in their emphasis on process and blank spaces, the assertion of the presence of the author who wants to inscribe her canvas with the essential fracture that must occur in self-portraiture—the division of the subject and the object. The spaces of the paper or of the canvas may be signs of the challenges of simultaneously posing and painting, of being at once object and maker, seer and seen, artist and mother.

When she represents herself in the act of painting, in another self-portrait done in 1885 (Figure 32), Morisot uses the passage in the lower left-hand corner of the canvas in order to comment on her painting practice.[45] Here, the merest suggestion of an artist's palette virtually disintegrates into circular strokes of brown and white paint. While the picture itself is created by open, flat, and textural applications of pigment, the section in the left-hand corner is, oddly enough, even more broadly handled. Morisot reduces the very mode with which she produces art to its minimal means.

Morisot highlights her represented self both by articulating her form in a less approximated technique than she employed for the palette and by using vivid strokes of paint to energize the figure, taupe and lilac-colored paint radiating from her body in lengthened and spiky swirls. Scumbled and impastoed, these pigments activate the figure of Morisot. She is here the active maker of art, assertively gazing out at the viewer. Her face, a thickly modeled mixture of whites, purples, browns, and grays, is vigorous and challenging. Even her posture indicates a level of confidence.

Morisot's self-portraits may be seen as visual documents of a particularly contested position—that of the working mother in late nineteenth-century Paris. They are also inflected by Manet's representations of her. I would argue that Morisot's ways of describing herself are rewritings of Manet's versions of her; they are correctives, so to speak.[46] In her self-portraits, Morisot responded to Manet's elaborately built-up and covered-over surfaces by taking paint away, by baring the unprimed canvas, by

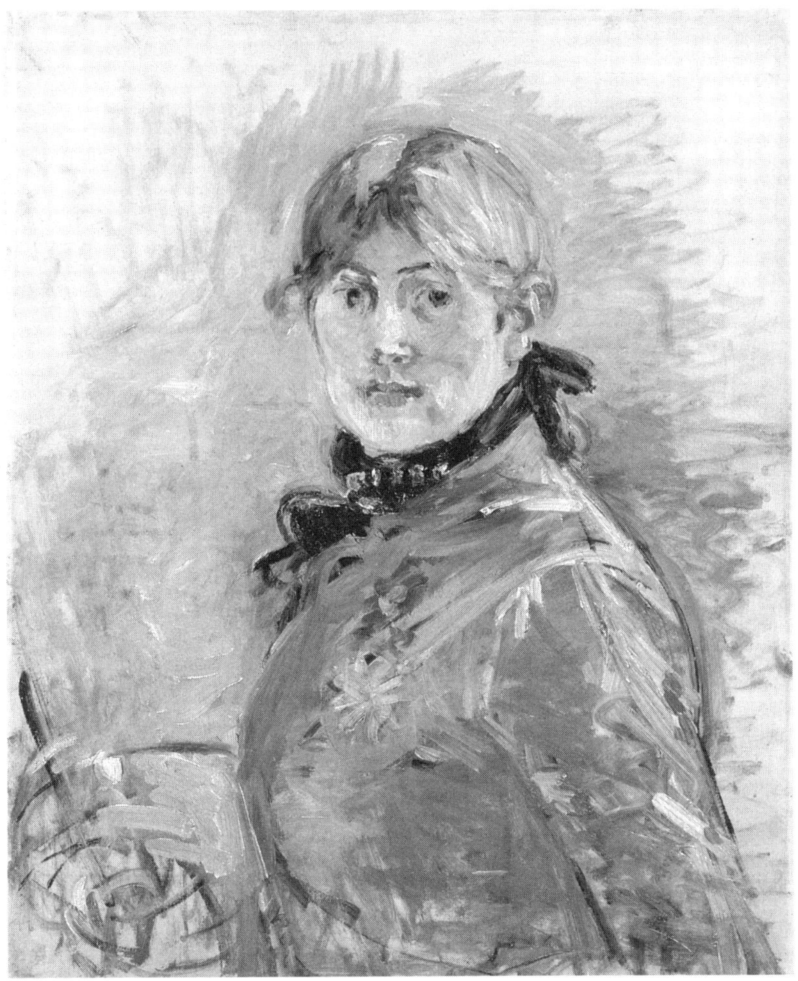

Figure 32. Berthe Morisot, *Self-Portrait* (1885). Oil on canvas. Musée Marmottan–Claude Monet, Paris. Bridgeman-Giraudon/Art Resource, NY.

leaving the paper bare. She cleaned away the excess *matière,* she allowed the fabrication to show through, and in the end she removed some of the veils. Her visual vocabulary, like Manet's, is complex and layered, contrived and artificial, and always filled with deference to bourgeois propriety. Any attempt to unveil Morisot's subjectivity, indeed to read images of her, must factor her self-portraits into the equation. For that is where she is her own construction, however veiled, mediated, and complicated, and not someone else's.

4

The Other Side of the Veil

Face-to-Face: Both Sides of the Loom

My focus thus far has been on the French veil and its specific relationship to various social, historical, and cultural formations in Paris during the Second Empire and into the beginning of the Third Republic. The veil—as object, metaphor, and visual representation—signified the complexity of the position of the proper woman within the urban and, in the case of Manet's representations of Morisot, domestic/professional fabric. But the veil that was worn in Paris at this time was also intimately linked to issues that far exceeded the physical geography of France. Indeed, the connection between the French veil and the Muslim veil of the French colonies in North Africa (mainly Algeria and Morocco) resonated deeply in Paris, even if no one was consciously aware of it or cared to admit it. Not only did Parisian women confront the idea of the Muslim veil in department stores, where Orientalized displays were meant to entice, at the universal exhibitions, where displays were intended to convey a "reality" about the colonies, and in travel journals, periodicals, and fictional literature, but they also encountered it as they donned their own veils each day. In this chapter, I show how the French veil was inscribed by its corollary. Different in design and purpose, the Muslim and French veils came together in unexpected and rich ways that reveal more than they conceal. I begin to explore that intersection as it occurred at the Universal Exhibition of 1889 by looking closely at the June 22, 1889, cover of the periodical *L'Exposition de Paris de 1889.*

This illustration (Figure 33) depicts three Algerian women, two seated and weaving, while a man, also dressed in indigenous garb, stands at the edge of the loom on which they work. A crowd of Parisians led by a dapper gentleman in a bowler hat, striped pants, and polka-dotted vest files past the display. The most notable aspect of the image surprisingly is not the oppositional coupling of the Muslim man covered in flowing white robes and his European counterpart, who looks askance at him, exemplifying one possible set of the circuit of gazes that were acceptable at the universal exhibitions. Nor is it the other men in the picture, who freely survey the weaving women on display. Rather, it is the two Parisian women staring at the Muslim women, their colonial analogues, on the other side of the loom who interject into this otherwise ordinary picture the problematics not just of French imperialism in North Africa but also of the urban female gaze. For this is the East and the West coming face-to-face, peering at each other through the veil.[1]

It is here, at the *expositions universelles,* that the French female gaze was allowed, even encouraged, to exist. At a time when women's vision was somewhat determined by social limitations, the universal exhibitions were unique in that they were powerful sites of licit female gazing, giving the bourgeoise a space of sanctioned and often pleasurable viewing. The engraving makes the circuit of gazes especially clear, for the two most obvious European women bend down to get a closer look. Aside from the male figures at the right and left edges of the loom, who glance at various parts of the display, the other men in the picture are indicated by tilted top hats that progress back into space, offering no evidence of where they are looking. This lack of emphasis on a mobilized male gaze only throws into relief the more serious viewership engaged in by the Parisiennes. They stare down at their colonial analogues so that they may scrutinize them from the other side of the loom. One could even say that in some ways the politics of French colonialism actually endorsed the hegemonic looking of Western women in the "virtual city" of the universal exhibition, whereas their gaze was actively discouraged in the urban environment, or the real city.

This particular allowance of women's gazes, however, both supported and subverted established conditions. On the one hand, I would argue that

L'EXPOSITION DE PARIS
DE 1889

Prix du numero : 50 centimes.	Journal hebdomadaire. — 22 juin 1889.	Prix du numéro : 50 centimes.
ABONNEMENTS. — PARIS ET DÉPARTEMENTS : 20 FR.	N° 17	LA PUBLICATION SERA COMPLÈTE EN 40 NUMÉROS.
Adresser les mandats à l'ordre de l'Administrateur.	BUREAUX : 8, RUE SAINT-JOSEPH. — PARIS	*Adresser les mandats à l'ordre de l'Administrateur.*

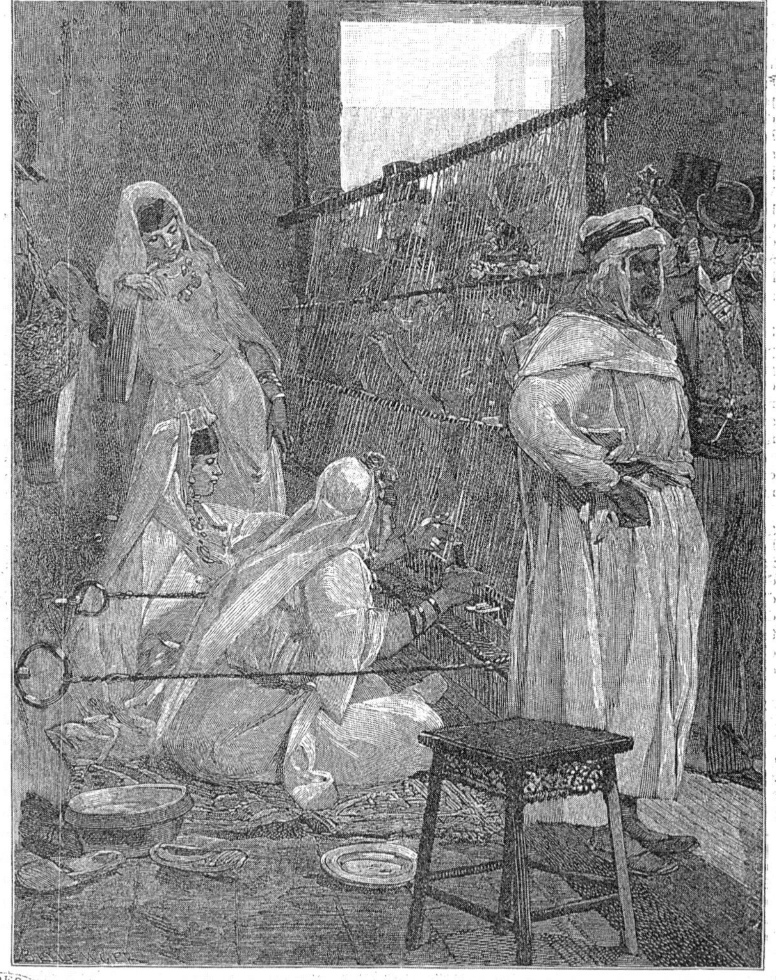

LES TISSEUSES KABYLES A L'ESPLANADE DES INVALIDES.

Figure 33. *L'Exposition de Paris de 1889* 17 (June 22, 1889). Engraving. Bibliothèque des arts décoratifs, Paris.

this looking at the Other was restrictive to Parisian women, since the colonial displays may have been construed by contemporaries as models for proper submissive behavior for the French women who viewed them. Still, it would also be appropriate to consider what happened at the universal exhibitions in terms of a Parisian female authority and dominance over women of colonial cultures and therefore a means of empowering French women at the expense of the women who had been transported from their homes in the French colonies to playact for a European audience.

The textual and visual rhetoric of the universal exhibitions advertised them as being scientific, anthropological, and truthful, suggesting that somehow these constructions of colonial buildings and displayed people were tantamount to the real thing. This "authenticity factor" gives a special charge to the act of the Parisian women looking so closely and carefully at the women in this depiction of the Kabyle display. These Parisiennes are not simply observing what would have been considered an insignificant or theatrical moment. "Nothing is better able to give the impression of Arab manners than this Kabyle interior, reproduced by our print," wrote the architect and cultural critic Frantz Jourdain in the text that accompanies this illustration.[2] Jourdain admits that the picture is a reproduction, but he argues that, despite its status as a representation, it is perfectly able to convey some inherent truth about Arab manners, a truth he sees epitomized by the Kabyle interior on display. The circumscription of some women's vision in the modern city, the entitlement of the bourgeois women to look at the universal exhibitions, and the authority contemporaries accorded the virtual presentations at the exhibitions combined to produce the world's fairs as significant places of allowable bourgeois female gazing.

And yet this particular pictorial story is also told from the perspective of the Algerian women, for the artist has chosen to capture the scene from a viewpoint on the colonial side of the loom.[3] We are in their space and our view of them is relatively unobstructed, though we see two of the women in varying degrees of profile. However, we, and by extension the three women performing their jobs, see the Parisians through the warp of the loom, which essentially forms a visual border between the East and the West. In an ironic manipulation of expectations, it is the Parisians who are veiled by the loom and the colonial women who are not. And if we imagine a narrative that allows the weavers to make actual progress on their work, the loom would gradually become filled, and the carpet or textile they are creating would completely block both their and our view of the Parisians. We would then see that the Algerian women have some control, albeit minor, over how visible they are to the West and how much of the West is visible to them.[4] Thus, the question of who is surveying whom and who is on display constantly oscillates. For each sees and is, in turn, seen through the loom.

Still, the space between the weft and the top of the loom is sufficient, at least at the moment depicted, for the Parisian women to be able to look through the warp filling that space. By bending down to get a view through the warp strings, the women are able to circumvent the obfuscatory work of the loom, whereas, because of their distance from it, the seated Algerian women must see the French women on the other side of the loom as if they were looking through a veil. The weavers may view one another unveiled, but their status does not allow them to be the ones to come close to the border, the loom, and look through so as to observe those who watch them without interference. The way in which the artist uses the loom to describe space in the picture is also similar to the function of the bars and grids in some late nineteenth-century photographs of fictional harem scenes.[5] In the context of representations of the East, bars—the formal equivalent of the warp in this picture—become a trope for, among other things, the seclusion and separation associated with life in the harem.[6] They are the shorthand means for indicating that the person behind or before the bars is simultaneously inaccessible and desirable.

Not one of the Algerian women behind the loom in the illustration looks up at the Parisiennes. This refusal of eye contact did not go unnoticed by contemporaries. Jourdain wrote, describing the scene itself: "[T]he women crouching on their heels are working at weaving cloth in a primitive technique. These *fellahs* carry out their work with regularity and without lifting their eyes to the curious faces of the crowd that surrounds them."[7] Each woman carefully performs her task from within the confines of her section of floor, which is demarcated by the ropes that anchor the loom to the wall. Even the man, whose posture and placement almost suggest that he is guarding the working women, does not look back at the Europeans, who freely observe him. The object of fascination remains, then, the colonial man and women, brought to Paris and displayed as representatives not only of French imperial conquest but also of cultural difference.

Jourdain especially picked up on the ways in which the form and content of the picture assert social differences. He remarked that these weavers use a working method that he called "*primitif,*" probably because their technique was different from what he knew of European weaving practices. The Parisian women, in their active gazing, are really the ones who ironically end up facilitating that arrangement of power, which positions the Algerians as Other to a more civilized France.[8] When seen in specific relation to their Eastern counterparts, the Parisian women have some form of vision, some form of power. Within this particular matrix, they are not the merely viewed but are instead the viewers, at least temporarily.

While I argued in chapter 1 that the bourgeoise's view was shaped by the veil she was encouraged to wear, I want here to suggest that there may be gaps in that veil. For even though the act of looking through a loom marks the Parisian women's vision as patrolled, it also simultaneously shows that it was possible to evade the related regulations, at least in connection with the colonial Other. The French woman's gaze vis-à-vis the colonial woman may even be read as an appropriation of the kind of unobstructed looking typically associated with the masculine in late nineteenth-century French culture. Some scholars have pointed out that the department store was one of the few spaces in modern Paris that legitimated female vision.[9] I want to expand that space of licit female viewing to include the universal exhibitions, which, like the department store, also engaged with issues of consumerism, commodity, pleasure, and voyeurism. And still some form of mediation is in the picture—the veil, the loom—a mediation that calls attention to gender and cultural differences, circumscribes ocular experience, and potentially proposes alternative and appropriate ways of being acceptably feminine.

This illustration also represents one of the means by which France constructed its colonies in visual terms for a specifically European audience. Several levels of interactions and splits occur both within and outside the bounds of this image. Internally, the loom overtly separates the East from the West, Algerian female from Parisian male, Algerian female from Parisian female. This segregation conversely brings together those seemingly opposite entities by facilitating comparisons that emphasize the degree to which the French construction of an Orient was based on strict binarisms. Externally, the French artist, presumably male, depicts both French and Algerian men and women. And a French architect, Frantz Jourdain, provides his own interpretation to accompany the image. On yet another level, the actual displays at the exhibition were also responsible for conveying still more aspects of the Western version of the East. These internal and external constructions worked together in order to perpetuate and further solidify

French conceptions not only of Algeria but also, by extension, of the other French colonies as well. For the seated Muslim women represented in this illustration and in other visual and textual accounts of the universal exhibition displays are positioned as deferential, passive, and different from the people who look at them from the other side of the loom.

To take this opposition further, the carpet or textile that the Algerian women are creating on the loom will probably be bought by a Parisian and end up the object of fascination in a bourgeois home, a tangible confluence of colonialism, women's labor, and French consumerism. It will thus always contain the narrative of the Algerian women workers' "primitive" technique. Like the veil, which is a more public consolidation of cultural similarity and dissimilarity, the carpet will become the possessible manifestation of the East within the privacy of the French interior.

Cross-Cultural Dressings

This confrontation between the West and the East, more specifically between France and its established or potential colonies or both, may be seen in microcosmic form as having played itself out across and through veils—the Muslim one and the fashionable Parisian one.[10] When considered in connection with French imperialism at the time, both veils may become topoi for representing not just territory and boundaries but also vision, surveillance, and difference. In terms of their physical makeup, they emblematize divisions and dissections, geographical markings and ownership. It is in these senses that the persistent fashionability of the French veil was actually an integral part of the structure of imperialism itself, and therefore a subtle mechanism of international politics taking place on a local and quotidian level. Indeed, the rising popularity of the Parisian veil from the 1850s to the 1880s coincides with the government's struggle for the expansion and maintenance of the French Empire in North Africa as it confronted the dwindling of public support for many imperialistic practices.[11]

The coincident timing of governmental efforts to win public backing with the explosion of visual and textual representations of the Orient, especially of veiled harem women, along with an overall increase in the popularity of the veil in French fashion, leads me to speculate that these issues are far from mutually exclusive of each other. Given the historical and political contexts and the source of inquiry and fascination that the veil in Islam had become by then for many Europeans, the contemporary French veil would have had to be inflected with meaning from its discursive Other. In other words, some of the implications of the veil in Paris at this time are actually contingent on the currency of the Muslim veil. This French veil must, therefore, be seen as having been constructed both in relation to and in complete contradiction to the Muslim veil.

In truth, no laws in Muslim doctrine have actually dictated that women wear veils. It has only recommended that women cover their faces in order to protect themselves from unwanted recognition. The thirty-third Sura says, "'O prophet, say to thy wives, and thy daughters, and the womenfolks of the believers, that they let down their mantles over them; that is more suitable for their being recognized and not insulted'" (33:59).[12] The donning of veils by women in ancient Islam was a gesture of modesty and self-protection. Originally, the veil was regarded as a way of controlling not just unwanted sexual advances toward women but also female sexuality in general, for it was thought to protect women from the gaze of men.[13] In many parts of the ancient East the veil also served to distinguish among classes, for only free women had the right to wear veils. Yet in most Muslim countries by the nineteenth century, women could not leave the home or the harem without a veil. The veil in public came to signify that the woman, whether in public or in private, is enclosed, kept apart, visually inaccessible.

As Fatima Mernissi has pointed out, the *hijab,* which she translates as "curtain," served as both a boundary and a form of protection. She writes:

> The concept of the word *hijab* is three-dimensional, and the three dimensions often blend into one another. The first dimension is a visual one: to hide something from sight. The root of the verb *hajaba* means "to hide." The second dimension is spatial: to separate, to mark a border, to establish a threshold. And finally, the third dimension is ethical: it belongs to the realm of the forbidden. . . . A space hidden by a *hijab* is a forbidden space.[14]

The veil is a border, a division between the licit and the illicit in Muslim culture. Its transcription into French fashion could not have erased these extracultural meanings. In fact, I would argue that the Western veil became popular in Paris during the Second Empire in part *because* of its irrefutable reference to its Other and the multitude of issues that the Muslim veil contains: gender, class, and sexual differences, mystery, the forbidden, vision, colonialism, and power. This French veil, then, came to signify certain social, cultural, and political fantasies. The veiled Parisian woman's face became a site for several levels of imperial mastery, for not only was her appearance a reminder of the inhibitions imposed on colonial women, but it also represented her own status as "colonized" being within France. In the broadest sense, the late nineteenth-century French woman was, like her Muslim counterpart, subjected to rules and authority that were externally determined. And in effect, she was made into her colonial counterpart by the very veil across her face.

The two kinds of veils are quite different in terms of both appearance and function. The Muslim veil typically conceals the entire body and face, usually leaving the eyes, though sometimes only one, uncovered. A depiction of a standard Algerian costume that dates from between around 1870 and 1890 (Figure 34) gives us an indication of some versions of this veil. In this studio portrait intended for a European audience, a model stands in front of a highly artificial-looking backdrop. Her legs are encased in billowing white pantaloons, over which floats a long white veil decorated with thick horizontal stripes. We see only her eyes and a bit of forehead, the top of which is crowned by a jeweled headband. The triangle of exposed flesh and eyes inverts the triangle of fabric created by the way the veil closes around the woman's face, generating an interesting counterpoint between covered and not. Indeed, the absolute encasement of this sitter's body renders her uncovered eyes even more present and forceful.

A studio image of a woman of either North African or Middle Eastern descent, created between around 1860 and 1890 and inscribed simply with the number 14, offers yet another illustration of the types of representations of the Orient—and the many varieties of veils—that made their way into Europe during the second half of the nineteenth century (Figure 35). In this image, one of the model's bare feet perches on a frayed footstool and the other on the floor. She rests a hand on a rustic-looking jug, and the other elbow, the wrist of which is adorned with two bangle bracelets, is poised on a wornout carpet that has been placed over a rectangular object. The woman is sharply silhouetted against an artificially black backdrop, the pitch of which has clearly been intensified through hand coloring. The floor in the foreground is tiled, while the back has been painted a deeper shade of uniform gray. The sitter wears a black gauzy veil over a checked garment, parts of which are discernible through the veil itself and along her lower arms. The edge and middle of the part of the veil that covers her face are decorated with rows of gold coins, which have been stitched on in perfect regularity. A hard cylindrical object connects the upper and lower portions of the veil, bridging the gap between them, extending down the woman's furrowed brow and between her kohl-lined, intensely staring eyes. Her appearance would have shocked and intrigued a late nineteenth-century viewer more accustomed to French veils and less complicated Muslim ones. While a veil and headdress of this type were

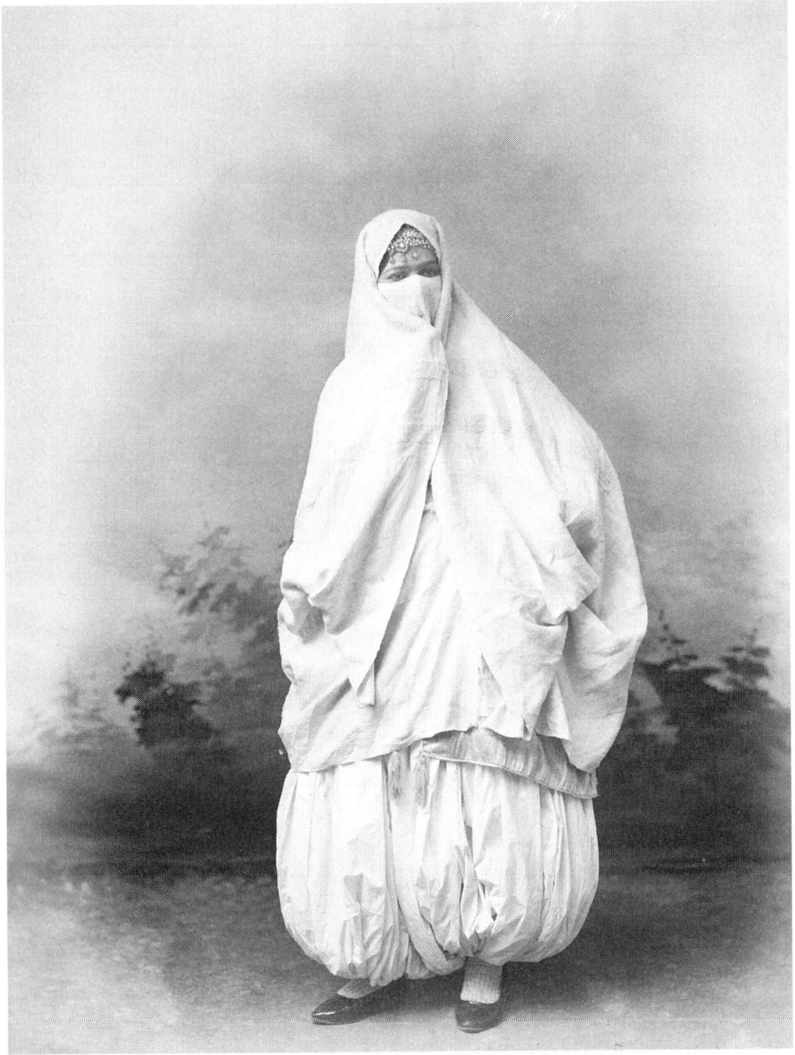

Figure 34. Photograph (c. 1870–90) from "Views of Algeria and Algerians" Collection, Research Library, The Getty Research Institute, Los Angeles (95.R.14).

less often represented in the European-produced visual culture of the Orient, many examples of them exist, and they were certainly fabricated for the benefit of a curious and Other-seeking European audience.

Another powerful illustration of the visual ramifications of the elaborately covered Muslim body is a *carte-de-visite* of three Algerian women, dating from around 1860 to 1890 (Figure 36). Here, one woman remains unveiled, though clothed in ballooning white pantaloons, a jeweled headpiece, and gold necklace. She is flanked by two veiled women, one of whom

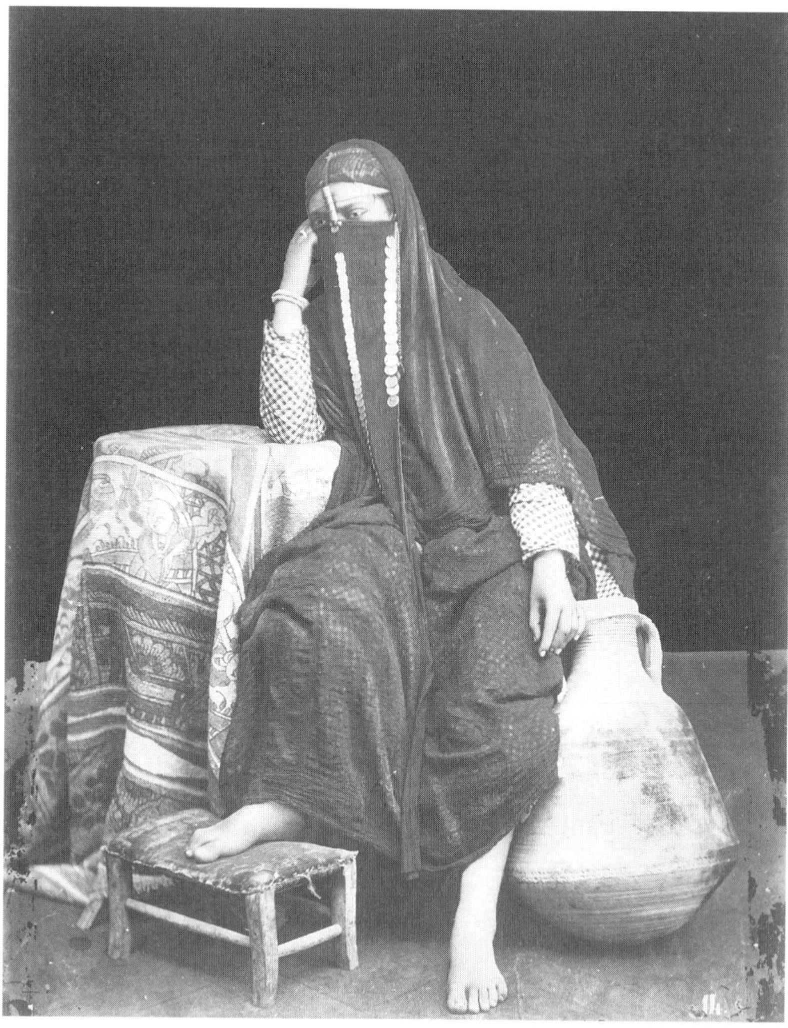

Figure 35. Photograph (c. 1860–90) from "Middle Eastern and North African Portraits" Collection, Research Library, The Getty Research Institute, Los Angeles (93.R.31).

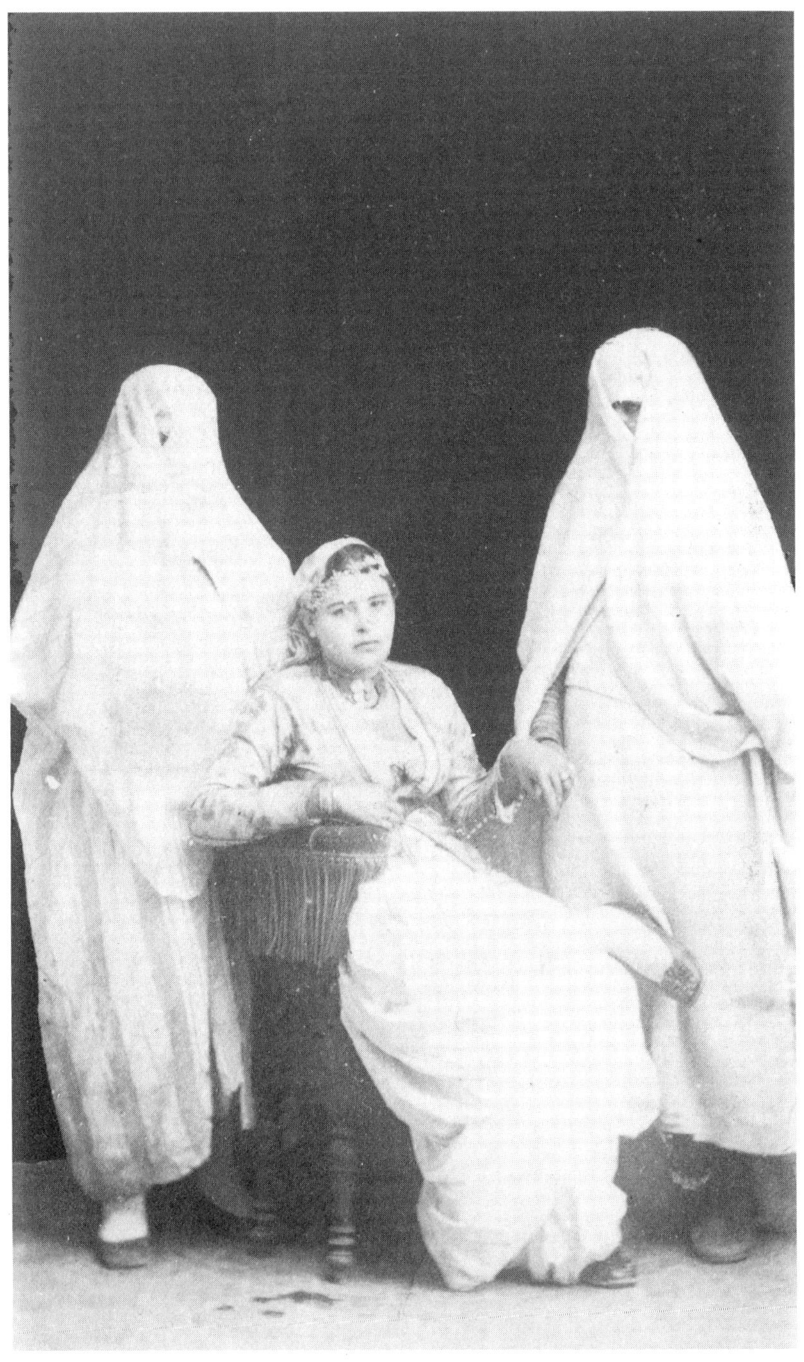

Figure 36. Photograph (c. 1860–90) from "Algerian Types—Cartes-de-Visite" Collection, Research Library, The Getty Research Institute, Los Angeles (93.R.123-134).

has only a tiny gap through which to see, while the other has a slightly larger one. Using the binary language of veiled and unveiled, this photographer represents some of the ways in which Muslim women's vision could be compromised by the veil. The photographer has also chosen to have the unveiled woman cross her legs, a somewhat powerful and perhaps masculine gesture in relation to her standing veiled counterparts. In comparison, however, the French veil and its many incarnations always cover the eyes and all or part of the face and neck. Whatever the possible social implications of such dualities, one thing remains clear: the Muslim woman has vision, but limited visibility, while the veiled bourgeoise, although bodily visible, has more limited vision, since what she sees is filtered through the grid of her veil.

A plate in the *Magasin des demoiselles* from March 10, 1889, of two Parisian women at the Universal Exhibition of 1889 (Figure 37) demonstrates what a typically fashionable French veil of the time looked like. A caricatured drawing of the controversial Eiffel Tower, built for the 1889 exhibition, rises in the distance as two stylish women walk and converse in the foreground. The simplified criss-crossing girders of the tower reiterate the basic structure of the veil worn by the woman on the right side of the illustration and align her with one of the most modern and inventive aspects of the exhibition, the Eiffel Tower, which was to represent the epitome of French technological and architectural advancements. The looming form of what was considered at the time to be the antithesis of a building mimics the upright posture of the veiled Parisienne in the picture, even further connecting them.

If we imagine the women in this fashion plate actually climbing the tower behind them, the power dynamic would again shift, and this association between the veiled woman and French technology would decrease. An engraving in *L'Exposition de Paris de 1889* (Figure 38) also explores this potential. Four people, three women and a man, cautiously negotiate the curving stairs of the Eiffel Tower. The veiled woman in the lower right corner of the picture symbolizes both technological advancement and its gendered ramifications. Careful yet poised, she lags behind the others, perhaps because she has the added nuisance of having to see through her black veil in making her way safely up the stairs. When considered in relation to this engraving, the visual connection forged between the veiled woman and the Eiffel Tower in the fashion plate becomes something of a mockery, for within French culture these women are not associated with power and advancement.

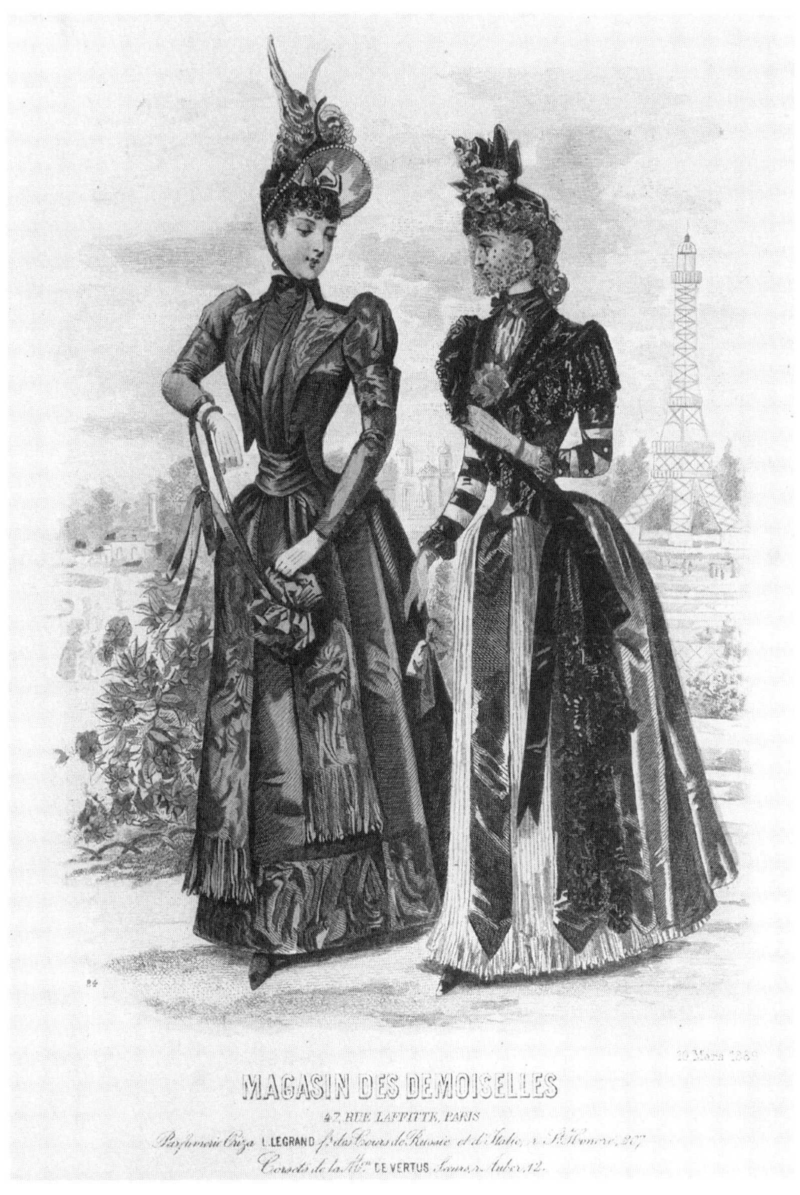

Figure 37. *Magasin des demoiselles* 84 (1889). Engraving. Musée de la mode et du costume, Paris.

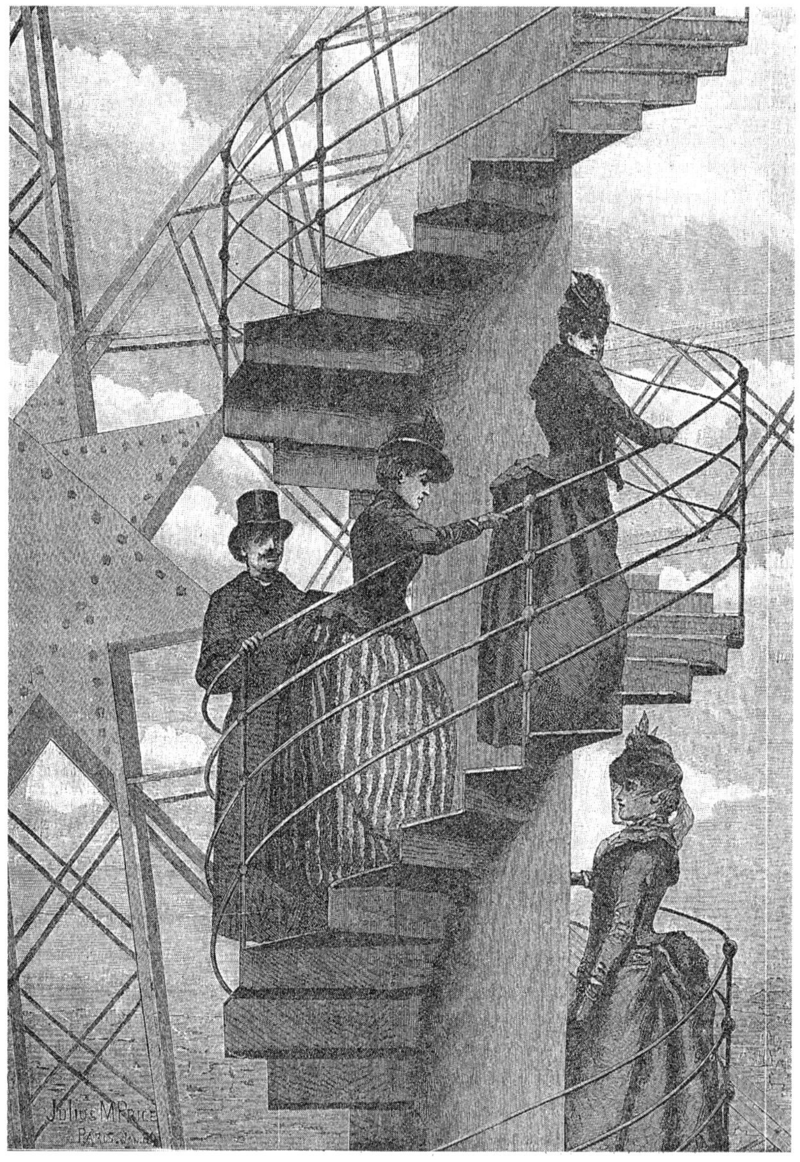

UNE ASCENSION DANS LA TOUR EIFFEL.

Figure 38. *L'Exposition de Paris de 1889* 8 (April 1, 1889). Engraving. Bibliothèque des arts décoratifs, Paris.

Still, once again, the Parisiennes have power in relation to the colonies. Lodged between the two women in the fashion plate, the schematic rendition of a reproduction of a building type that would have been found in a French colony, perhaps Algeria or Morocco or maybe Tunisia, is decipherable. For the Universal Exhibition of 1889, the Champ de Mars was lined with just such colonial edifices, all populated by indigenous people, which sightseers at the exhibitions visited in droves. Caught in the pictorial vise of the heavily corseted French women and appearing in miniature form so far behind, this colonial building and the people whom we can presume are on display inside are also caught in the imperial gaze. The women in the foreground of the print formally frame the colonial building, marking out territory, asserting cultural difference and European authority. Since fashion journals like this one were widely read, we must understand the far-reaching consequences of such images, for they, like so many other forms of visual culture, contributed to the establishment and reinforcement of hierarchies between France and its colonies, between what was perceived as French advancement and its opposite, colonial stagnation.

Yet there is a borrowing between France and its colonies, a cross-dressing between cultures, which occurs not only because the Muslim and Parisian veils are similar but also because they resist one another. It is just this gray area, this intersection between the Eastern and Western veils, that interests me, for here is where cultural parameters are simultaneously mapped out and challenged. In this space between veils, vision, or lack of vision, is located. Whereas the veiled Muslim woman is able to see, for her eyes are left uncovered, her body cannot be seen. She is encased in vast and densely woven fabrics that make an unmediated view of her form virtually impossible. This is her veil. It seems somewhat incongruous to call the more diaphanous and widely woven structure that hangs over the bourgeoise's face by the same name, since the two are so disparate. Yet by looking at them in relation to one another, especially since the two were called by the same word in French, *le voile,* a more nuanced version of each may emerge. And if we consider the veil to be a paradigm for some of the complexities of French imperialism, then, looking through these double veils may facilitate an understanding of the ways in which veiling Parisian women was actually a part of the circuit of colonialism. For, as I have been arguing, the French veil, by virtue of its formal relationship to its colonial counterpart, would undoubtedly have been inscribed by some of the meanings that were associated with the other veil.

French-imported images of veiled Turkish women from around the 1870s reveal that some Turkish veils were more closely related formally to what was popular in France at the time than the North African veils were. "Femme turque voilée," a bust-length photograph by the firm G. Lekeoian and Cie (Figure 39), represents a dark-haired, dark-eyed woman wearing a filmy white veil over her head, across her nose and mouth, and down to her chest. She looks wistfully off to the right of the picture, the forcefulness

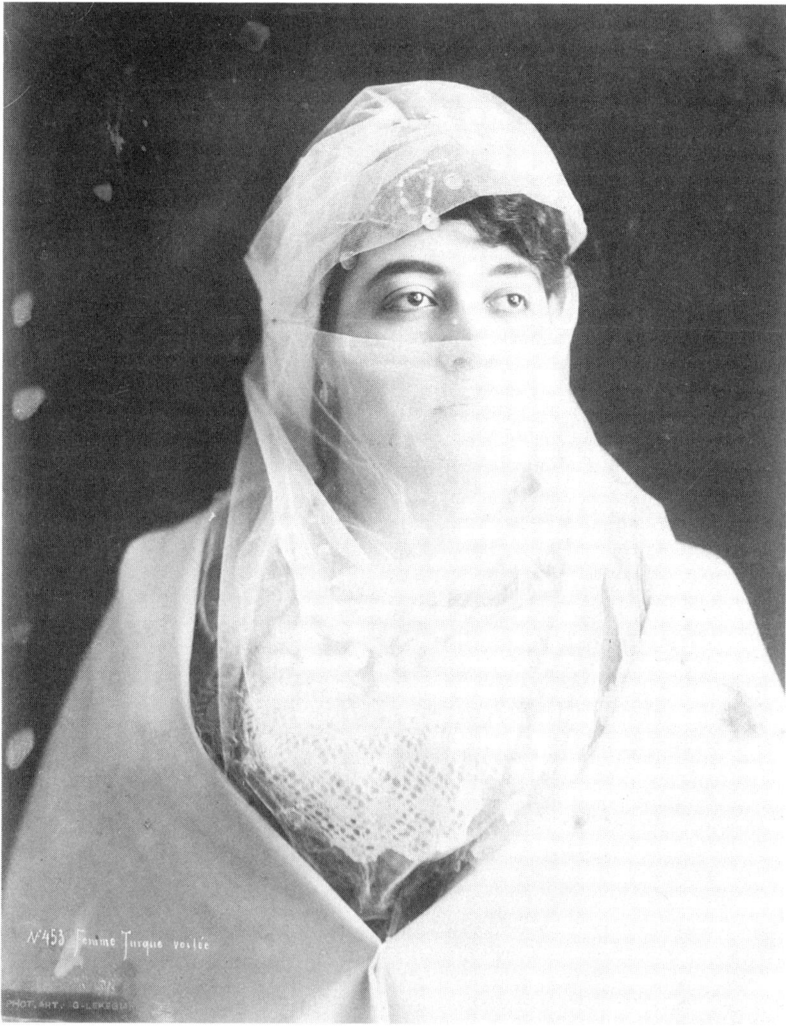

Figure 39. G. Lekeoian and Cie, "Femme turque voilée." Photograph from The Pierre de Gigord Collection, box 88, Research Library, The Getty Research Institute, Los Angeles (96.R.14).

of her look punctuated by the curve of her dark eyebrows. She has on a more densely woven white garment across her shoulders, which may very well reach to the ground, but all we get in this picture is a kind of close-up of the woman's face. In fact, we are so close to the image that we can distinctly see the weave of the veil that passes over her right cheek, creating a perfect gridlike pattern that is interrupted by only a few soft folds. The slight turn of the woman's head generates the optical effect of blurring the right edge of her mouth. This veil filters our view of the lower half of the model's face in a way that is reminiscent of the Parisian veil but also in a way that is quite different, for this Turkish woman's eyes look unfettered out of the picture plane.

Another image executed during the 1870s further expands the category of what was popular, this time connecting veiled women to and pitting them against animals. "Voiture de promenade (Campagne)" depicts four veiled Turkish women in a carriage drawn by two oxen that are led by a man (Figure 40). The consequences of the models' status as veiled are surprisingly highlighted by their ostensible opposities, the bare-faced animals. Yet, this connection is qualified, since the oxen are, in fact, controlled in another sense by the harnesses yoked around their necks. Like

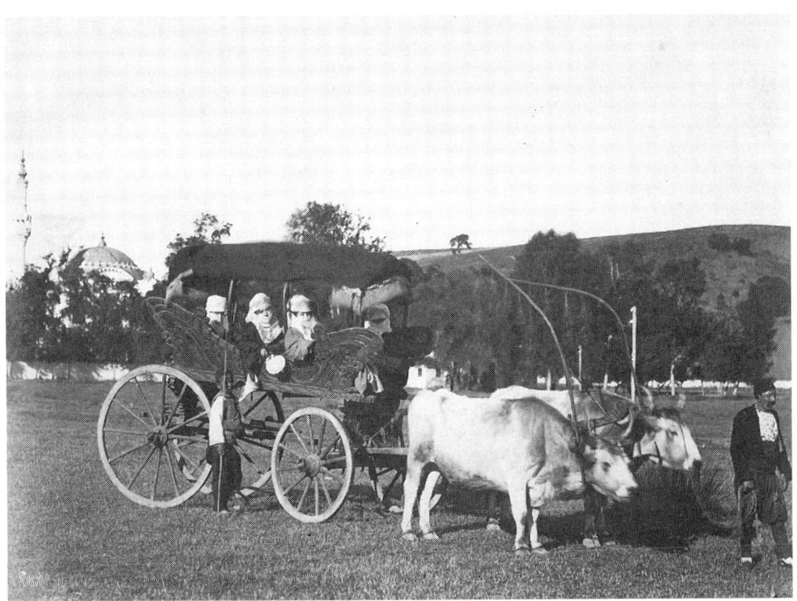

Figure 40. "Voiture de promenade (Campagne)." Photograph from The Pierre de Gigord Collection, box 88, Research Library, The Getty Research Institute, Los Angeles (96.R.14).

the oxen, the women are restrained, but unlike the boy who leans on the right side of the carriage and the man who leads the animals, these women do not have the freedom to move about unhindered. On the one hand, we can interpret them as being privileged, carried as they are by carriage; on the other hand, the free and open expanse of the countryside around them—not to mention the especially melancholy, even pleading, look of the woman who is second from left—reinforces their containment.

An image by a photographer named Abdullah, dated 1865, and titled "Famille turque en promenade" (Figure 41) may likely be seen as a companion piece to "Voiture de promenade." It is as if the women in the carriage in "Voiture de promenade" have arrived at their destination, been left by the man and the boy, and are now settled into enjoying an afternoon by a body of water in the countryside. In this picture, two women and a little girl sit on a rug that has been placed on the ground while another woman poses in profile on a stool that is beside the rug; a dog lies to her right. All the women wear thin white veils across their heads and

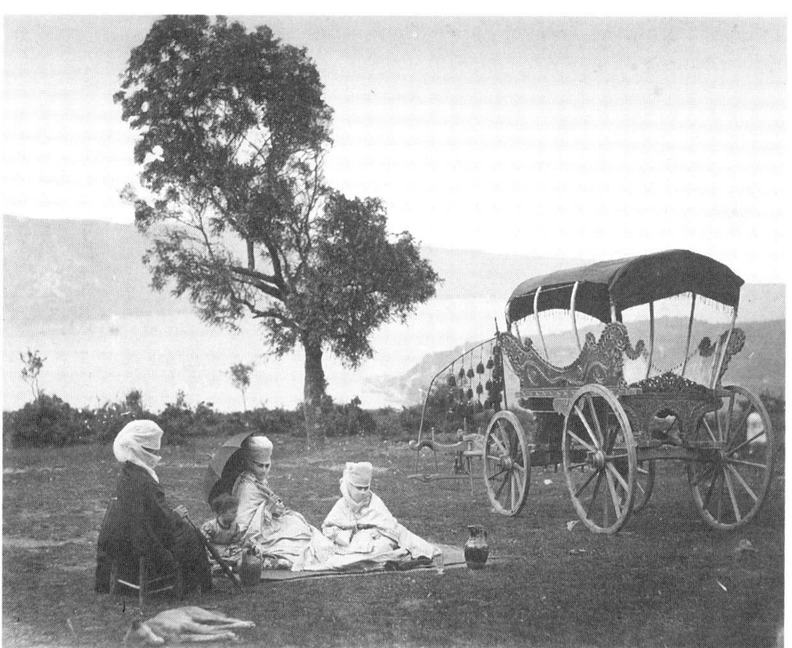

Figure 41. Abdullah, "Famille turque en promenade" (1865). Photograph from The Pierre de Gigord Collection, box 12, Research Library, The Getty Research Institute, Los Angeles (96.R.14).

faces, though their eyes, small dark pupils peeking out from between slices of light white fabric, are exposed. Not one looks out at the viewer. They all gaze to the right side of the picture at some unknown person or thing. One woman holds an open parasol behind her. A jug weighs down either end of the front of the rug, and an empty glass and closed parasol lie undisturbed slightly more toward the foreground. Their carriage sits abandoned to the right, its ornate curves an inverse formal echo of the profile created by the grouping of the women at the left. There are remarkably striking similarities between this image and some contemporaneous French paintings, suggesting its creation for a European viewership. A kind of Turkish version of Manet's *Le déjeuner sur l'herbe* perhaps, this picture even resembles in formal terms some of Claude Monet's seaside scenes.

Fabricating an Orient

An intense interest in the East, fueled in part by expansionist desires and facilitated by technological advancements, developed precipitously in France during the nineteenth century. The establishment of a steamer line between Marseilles and Alexandria in 1835 made safer travel from France to Egypt possible, but it was probably the political climate in Paris at the time that most catalyzed the French pursuit of knowledge about the Orient. The politics of the Second Empire especially helped to set the scene for this kind of inquiry through its emphatic insistence on renovation and discovery. Additionally, as urban life became more complicated and as international travel was made easier and faster, the desire to learn about other places unsurprisingly escalated.

Information about Muslim customs and laws arrived in France through a variety of venues, mainly in highly mediated and aestheticized form.[15] Although interest in the East had existed prior to Napoleon I's Egyptian expedition of 1798, this particular trip was a watershed in terms of French ambitions in those places considered to constitute the Orient, mainly North Africa and parts of what are now the Near and Middle East.[16] Starting in 1810 and ending in 1828, even after the emperor's downfall in 1815, the members of Napoleon's government conveyed their experiences in Egypt to the French public through their publication of *Description de l'Égypte,* a twenty-two volume series of books containing the accounts of the artists, writers, scientists, cartographers, and scholars who accompanied the emperor on his military campaign. As Timothy Mitchell has pointed out, this work actually inspired other artists and writers to travel to the East or to write about it or both, thus helping to perpetuate and feed the appetite for knowing more about what was then considered to be France's Other. European fascination with Oriental cultures continued with, to cite just a few popular examples, Victor Hugo's *Les Orientales,* which was published in 1829, Bizet's *Djamileh,* composed in 1871, and Gustave Flaubert and photographer Maxime du Camp's obsessively written and photographed account of their trip through Egypt between 1849 and 1851.[17]

Edward William Lane, in his book *An Account of the Manners and Customs of the Modern Egyptians: Written in Egypt during the Years 1833–1838,* read in translation by many French people, also participated in defining the terms of an Orientalized culture for the West by articulating some commonly held fantasies about Egypt, a long desired but never acquired colony for France. Lane is noted as having said of his first vision of Egypt, "As I approached the shore, I felt like an Eastern bridegroom, about to lift the veil of his bride, and to see, for the first time, the features that were to charm, or disappoint, or disgust him."[18] Lane's use of the metaphor of the veil as the means through and by which he, as a privileged looker, could interpret Egypt is representative of a Western notion of the veil as both a barrier to and a facilitator of knowledge. Like the bridegroom's newly acquired access to the previously forbidden harem, Lane's status as Westerner entitles him to think he can infiltrate the mystery that Egypt represents. Within this framework of cultural expectations, the harem and Egypt become the spaces not simply of desire but also of conquest. The harem for the bridegroom and Egypt for a British traveler like Lane are each separated from their Other by veils that both distance and fascinate.

When Lane actually comments on the Muslim veil, it still serves as a symbol for cultural differences and borders, though not as overtly as it did when he compared seeing Egypt for the first time to an unveiling, as a privilege to sexual desire. He claims that the veil

> is extremely inconvenient as a walking attire. Viewing it as a disguise for whatever is attractive or graceful in the person and adornments of the wearer, we should not find fault with it for being itself deficient in grace. We must remark, however, that in one respect it fails in accomplishing its main purpose—displaying the eyes, which are almost always beautiful; making them to appear still more so by concealing the other features, which are seldom of equal beauty, and often causing the stranger to imagine a defective face perfectly charming.[19]

No longer in the position of sanctioned looking, Lane recognizes that the veil conceals and disguises at the same time that it calls increased attention to that which is not veiled—the eyes. He notes that the veil is able, mostly through trickery, to render a defective face perfectly charming. The advantages of the veil were various, but this aspect, its ability to make something imperfect appear to be perfect, had considerable appeal to a French public that was concerned with maintaining particular standards of beauty and agelessness.

The representation of the veil in travelogues and in writing about the universal exhibitions was one of the primary textual ways in which France fabricated an Orient for itself. Travel journals such as Lane's, published and read widely throughout Paris, were one of the many popular means through which information and details regarding the colonies and potential colonies were distributed to European audiences. While accounts of British women who visited the Orient were not uncommon, those of French women were rarer.[20] The words of Louise Vallory, a French woman who visited Algeria in 1862, are therefore crucial for establishing a European woman's perspective regarding her colonial counterpart. On observing what she could of the everyday life of an Algerian woman, Vallory wrote, "She does not leave [the house/the harem] alone, probably; she does not have permission to raise her veil in the streets, to show her face to a stranger."[21] Vallory, as a European visitor and a woman, had a certain freedom and viewpoint. In relation to the harem woman, she had a colonial gaze that allowed her to notice the absolute effacement and otherness of the Algerian woman out in public, who is set apart from women like Vallory and from men because she is accompanied and because she is veiled. Unlike Lane's desire to lift the veil to reveal some hidden sexual desire, Vallory's efforts are aimed more toward understanding the veil, its significance, and how it inflects Algerian women's everyday experience. She hints at a link between the harem and the veil, for they are mutually dependent on each other. Both the harem and the veil sequester women, one behind an architectural façade, the other behind a façade of fabric. When a woman leaves the harem, the veil becomes the external sign of, or the visual substitute for, the space of seclusion and enclosure she has left. In this way the street may be seen as an extension of the interior.

In noting the confinement of women in Algeria, Vallory is, of course, forging a connection between herself and the colonial women she observes. For she knows that she, too, is subject to limitations of her activities in

France and that it is her status as European that allows her particular freedoms when in Algeria. If the Muslim veil is really a kind of "mobile harem," then the French veil, it would follow, must be similarly inflected by notions of interiority and isolation. In reporting their observations of features of life in the French colonies, Vallory and other French travelers to the colonies who later published their accounts, such as Gautier, Arène, Blanc, Flaubert, du Camp, and Feydeau, contributed, possibly unwittingly, to the production of a nationalized, gendered, and classed discourse about the Orient. One of the common threads in these texts is a focus on the veil as an emblem of not only the differences between France and its colonies but also their similarities.

Discussion of Eastern clothing especially allowed writers of both fiction and nonfiction to exercise their descriptive skills and their imaginations, for so much of what was conveyed was meant to conjure up images of a faraway and clandestine place for both the writer and the reader. Of all the aspects of colonial culture that could be scrutinized and recounted, the veil was one of the major sources of intrigue, perhaps because it referred to an important and popular element of French fashion.[22] In fact, numerous accounts of journeys to the Orient and writings about the universal exhibitions, considered by many Europeans to be as genuine an experience as traveling to the places exhibited, are peppered with detailed commentaries about the Muslim veil.[23] In an illustrated journal that was published monthly before and during the Universal Exhibition of 1867, *L'Exposition universelle de 1867 illustrée,* Ernest Dréolle recounts his observations of the women and their clothing at the colonial displays:

> [T]he Orient for us—it is not the Orient of astronomers or geographers—it is the country where one sleeps, where one dreams. . . . it is the Eden where women, blond with black eyes or brunette with blue eyes, with white and pink flesh, with smiles sprinkled with pearls, live without living, immersed in clouds of perfumes, enveloped in transparent fabrics. . . . the galleries of Morocco, of Tunisia, of Egypt show them to us faithfully in their essentially original costumes. . . . A woman walks by in a long brown coat, her face entirely covered; this is the petite bourgeoise of the Orient; her clothing is more than modest, and one must really guess to discover a supple body, an elegant waist, beneath these great stiff pleats.[24]

Dréolle is aware that what is represented at the exhibitions is a construction that is meant to appeal to a French audience. He opposes the displayed

Orient to a more specific and scientific place that may be located, charted, and explored. These presentations are Edenic, places about which Dréolle dreams. He is obviously fascinated with costume, especially with the transparent fabrics, the veils that envelop the bodies of the women. He notices the color of eyes and hair, the jewels and the perfumes that the women wear. He is particularly taken with one woman, "une femme . . . en long manteau brun, le visage entièrement couvert." He even goes so far as to imagine and suggest the shape of the body underneath her veil. He surmises that her body must be supple and that her clothes must have an elegant fit. One can imagine that Dréolle may have seen a vision not unlike one depicted by J. Mouttet of la rue du Laurier, who specialized in "Photographie africaine" in his image of a veiled woman descending a long outdoor staircase located on the grounds of the 1867 Universal Exhibition in Paris (Figure 42). In this haunting image, we may well not even notice the lone woman who holds her veil closed while making her way down a long flight of stairs to the left of the center of the picture plane. The whiteness of her veil brutally juxtaposes the darkness of the steps. She is a ghostly apparition on this personless staircase, the sides of which are contained by light-colored stone, past which we see patches of dirt and weeds. At the top of the image looms the faded specter of a building (possibly the Mosquée Sidi-Abd-Er-Haman), which produces an unexpected yet perfect visual complement to this mysterious Muslim woman, who is just the sort who would have captured Dréolle's attention.

Dréolle's reaction to the women he encountered at the universal exhibitions is not unique. Other writers and journalists also pontificated on the elegance and mystery of the veiled women on display, so much so that they emerge in these texts as nothing more than objects of intense fascination, scrutiny, and desire. Ernest Feydeau, for example, in his 1862 account of his trip to Algeria, also described his impressions of the appearance and clothing of the Algerian women with specificity and an obvious captivation. He begins with a detailed analysis of an Algerian woman's face:

> [T]he fine skin of her face, this skin that the sun has never bitten with its rays, pinkens at her cheekbones, and draws a marvelous radiance from the beauty spot placed on the temple or on the chin. Finally, she has red lips, very white teeth, and black eyes shadowed by heavy eyelids, with painted eyebrows; in the physiognomy as a whole there is something fearful and resigned that resembles the expression of a wild beast caught in a trap. But this expression softens when she walks into her room.[25]

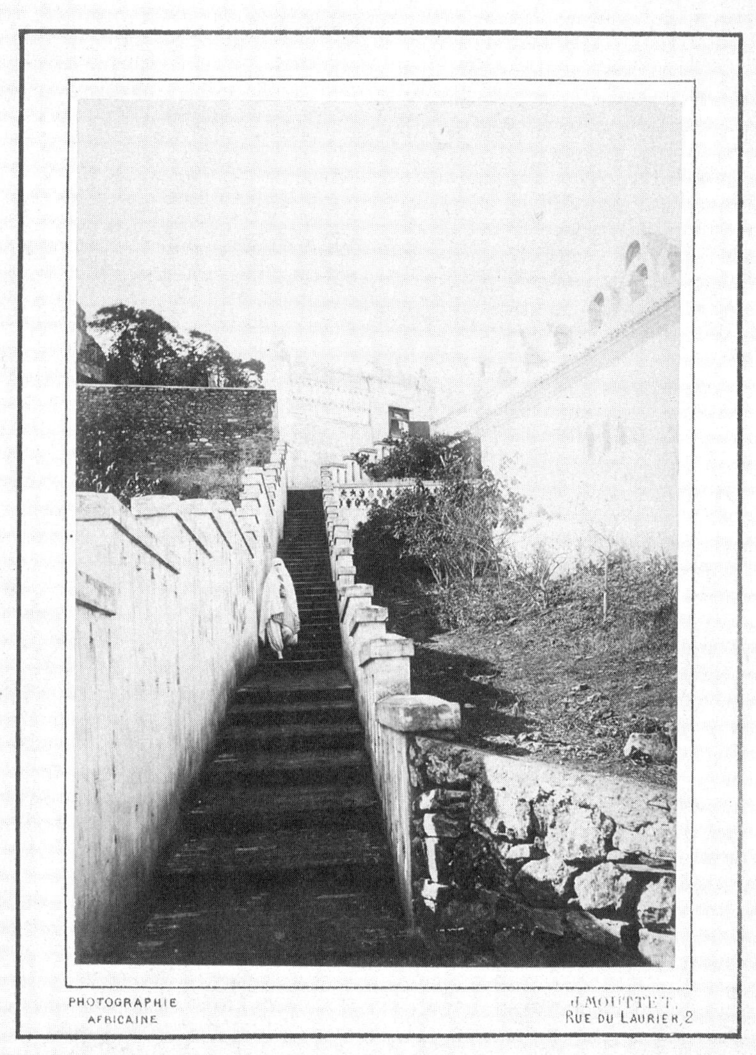

Figure 42. J. Mouttet, "Mosquée Sidi-Abd-Er-Haman" (c. 1870). Photograph from Research Library, The Getty Research Institute, Los Angeles (92.R.49).

Color and makeup play important roles in Feydeau's textual reconstruction of the colonial woman's face. Her lips are red, her teeth, in contrast, white, and her eyes and eyebrows are made-up by powders and liquids. Feydeau wants to believe that this face, and by extension the woman, has never been touched by the sun, that she has somehow been sequestered, presumably in a harem, and veiled on the street. He also likens the woman's expression to that of a wild beast, caught and tamed, possibly because it does not conform to his experience of women's expressions, if one could imagine that there is such a thing as a typical expression. Feydeau's words, however inflected with cultural and imperialistic bias, informed the French reader's sense of what the colonial woman was like. For his writing was, in all of its prejudice, part of a discourse that defined the concept of the female Other for France as something simultaneously highly artificed and associated with an untamed nature.

Later in his account of his trip to Algeria, Feydeau also provides an elaborate description of the veil, further contributing not only to the French understanding of the meaning and uses of it in the colonies but also, by extension, to the currency of the veil in France as well. He writes:

> [S]he completes it [her everyday clothing] so as to disguise herself completely beneath floating veils. A double-folded handkerchief of embroidered batiste is placed over her face, just below her eyes, and the two ends are attached at the top of her head . . . her big eyes resembling brilliant black diamonds that palpate delicately in their frame of eyelashes. . . . When she returns home, she immediately removes her street clothes, raises her mask, wipes her face covered with sweat, readjusts herself.[26]

Feydeau fixates on the uncovered eyes, which are for him two brilliant black diamonds enframed by eyelashes. He describes the fabric that covers the woman's body when she goes out as a floating veil that is embroidered and made to conceal everything but the eyes. Feydeau's assumption that the woman immediately removes the garment of his visual frustration, the veil that disguises completely the person beneath, on reentry to her rooms is significant, for it indicates a belief in the potential satisfaction of his desire to know what is behind the veil. And although Feydeau would in all likelihood have been unable to follow this woman back to her chamber, he is, of course, able to concoct a fantasy of ocular gratification for himself through a narrative that imagines the woman undressed, unveiled.

Not only do the words of Feydeau and his contemporaries evidence the kinds of information that circulated throughout France about the East, but also they demonstrate the extent to which their ideas actually participated in the construction of a complex circuit of knowledge about the Orient. Indeed, these writers were active participants in, not merely reproducers of, a particular colonial ideology, one that maintained authority and certitude over a literally and figuratively veiled colony.

Photography, too, played a significant part in this cycle of stereotyping. Countless photographs, especially in the form of studio cards and *cartes-de-visite,* were produced for and made their way into Europe.[27] An image of an Algerian woman that dates from between around 1860 and 1890 (Figure 43) was clearly produced for a European viewership. Veiled, though not entirely covered, this woman epitomizes the interrelationship between the veiled Muslim woman and her Parisian counterpart. For here, we have a manipulation of the fall of the *hijab,* a change that is so blatantly implemented to appease a European male. Standing in the photographer's studio on la rue Jenina in Algiers, this model wears a long outer veil of tattersall pattern across her head and shoulders and a white veil from just below her eyes to the middle of her chest. She is in partial profile and looks down and out of the right edge of the picture plane. Her arms are bent so that she can place her hands in full view as they linger at what appears to be a golden belt at her waist. She has shockingly pulled aside her outer garment so as to reveal the outline of her breast. But perhaps the most scandalous aspect of this image is the bareness of the woman's lower legs. Her voluminous white pantaloons, which should reach to just above stocking-covered ankles, fall to just below the woman's bare right knee and slightly farther down her left leg. These gestures of indicating the outline of breasts and revealing naked legs very obviously Europeanize the photograph, for a proper Muslim woman would never engage in such overtly sexual behavior (nor would a proper French woman, for that matter), especially in front of a strange man and for the purposes of mass distribution.

Other photographs of Algerians reproduce the more expected stereotype of the completely enveloped body. In two studio cards taken by the firm Vve. Plasse et Oberty, which was based in Constantine, Algeria, and which won an honorable mention at the *Exposition universelle* in Paris in

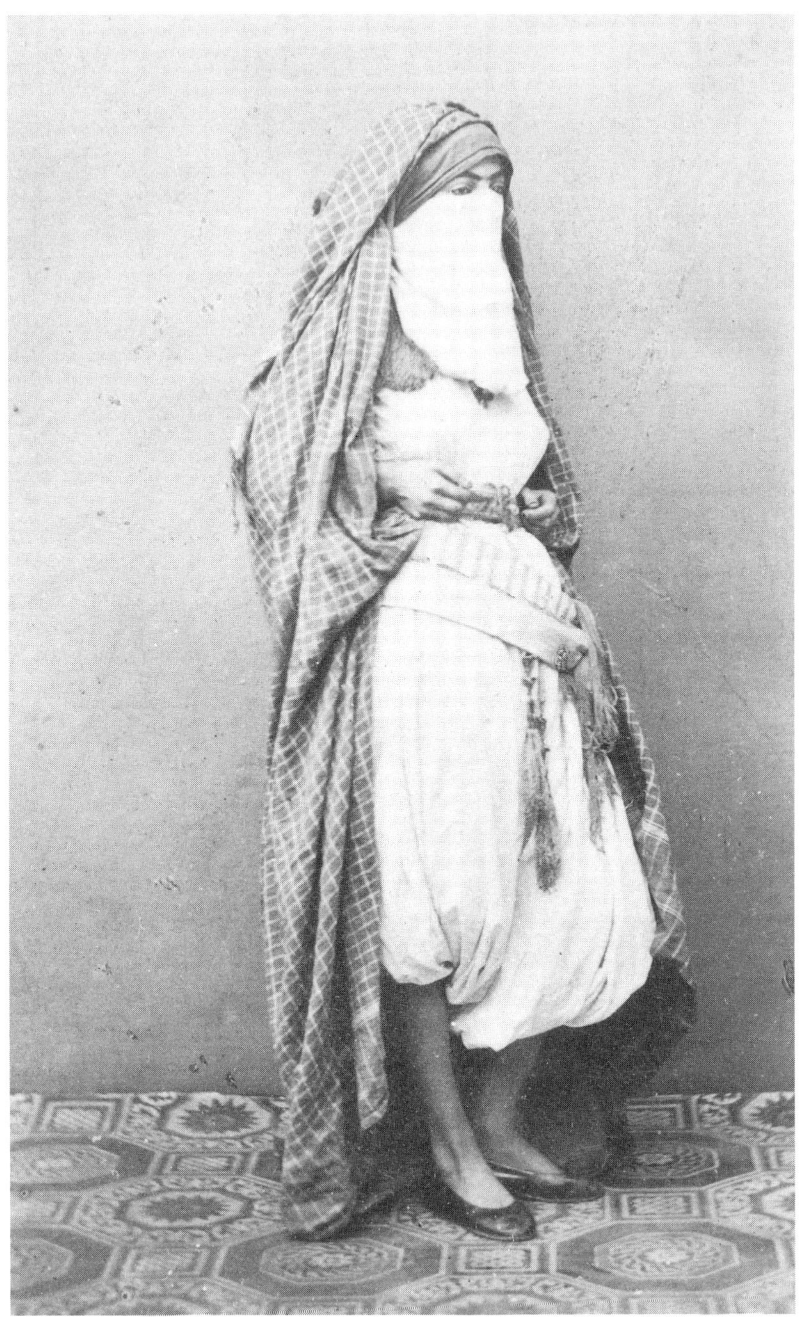

Figure 43. J. Beauchene (c. 1860–90). Photograph from The "Algerian Types—Cartes-de-visite" Collection, Research Library, The Getty Research Institute, Los Angeles (93.R.123).

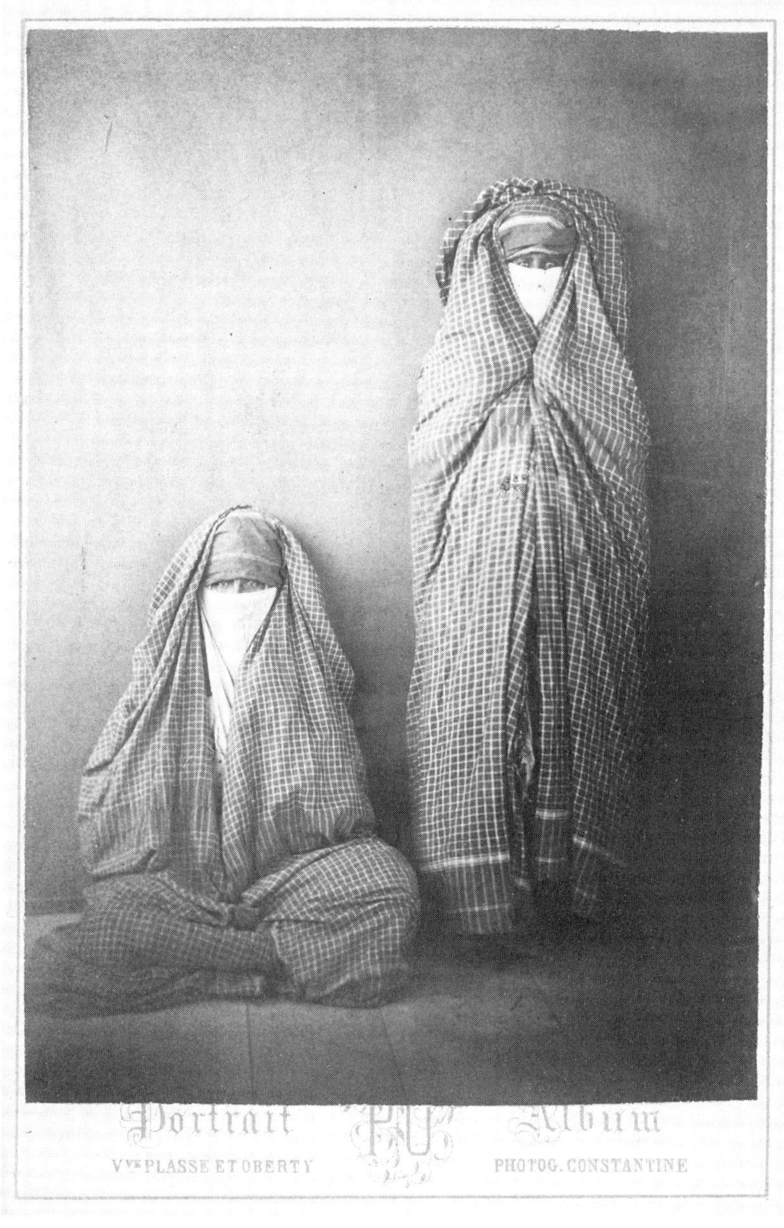

Figure 44. Vve. Plasse et Oberty (1867). Photograph from The "Cities and Sites Cabinet Card Collection," Research Library, The Getty Research Institute, Los Angeles (ZCC2 box 1).

1867, we see barely anything of the bodies of the women who posed for the pictures. In one, the model is swathed in white flowing garments; her sad dark eyes peek out from the slit formed by the meeting of her veils. In the other (Figure 44), two Algerians are fully cloaked in the tattersall-patterned veil that would have indicated their tribal affiliation; white veils begin under their eyes and sweep across their faces. One woman sits cross-legged while the other stands against a dull placeless wall, her side cast in more shadow than the other. Both stare out at the viewer, the standing woman more fervently gazing and clutching her patterned garment tightly around her torso, a look of intensity (or is it horror?) pulsing from her eyes.

Colorized photographs, too, were highly effective at conveying a sense of the vibrant colors contemporaries associated with the Orient. James Robertson, a photographer of Scottish descent who settled in England, went to Algeria, where he used the medium of the salt print layered with watercolor to represent the people he saw there. His images are particularly gripping, for in many he "doubled" the veil by using the watercolor medium as a kind of layer to cover over, even heighten, the surface of the photograph itself.

In his 1850s image of a woman in a voluminous green garment (Figure 45), Robertson thinly washed bright green paint over the merest trace of an image of a woman who poses in profile, head turned to look out at the viewer. She stands on a sandy-colored patch (painted in with Robertson's brush), which could possibly be meant to indicate a beach or desert, one mustard-toned shoe visible, the other hidden from our view. This woman is in a placeless place, the background of which is represented by empty tan paper that conjures up anywhere and everywhere nonurban, non-French. A silvery-white slip of paint highlights the powdery veil across her face and head, the folds of which are outlined in a slightly denser pigment. Her visage—even her eyes, which are not veiled—reads like a ghostly trace below the surface of the paper on which it has been printed. Her mouth is a smudge of an orangey hue and her nose almost disappears beneath the veil that pulls across it. A faint red indicates both the top of the woman's veil and her striped pantaloons, which are seen at points through and below the green garment. Robertson expertly manipulated his medium, constituting an image of a veiled woman using the veiling properties of paint. In other words, we read the photograph—a watery trace of a woman—through diaphanous veils of white, silver, red, and green paint.

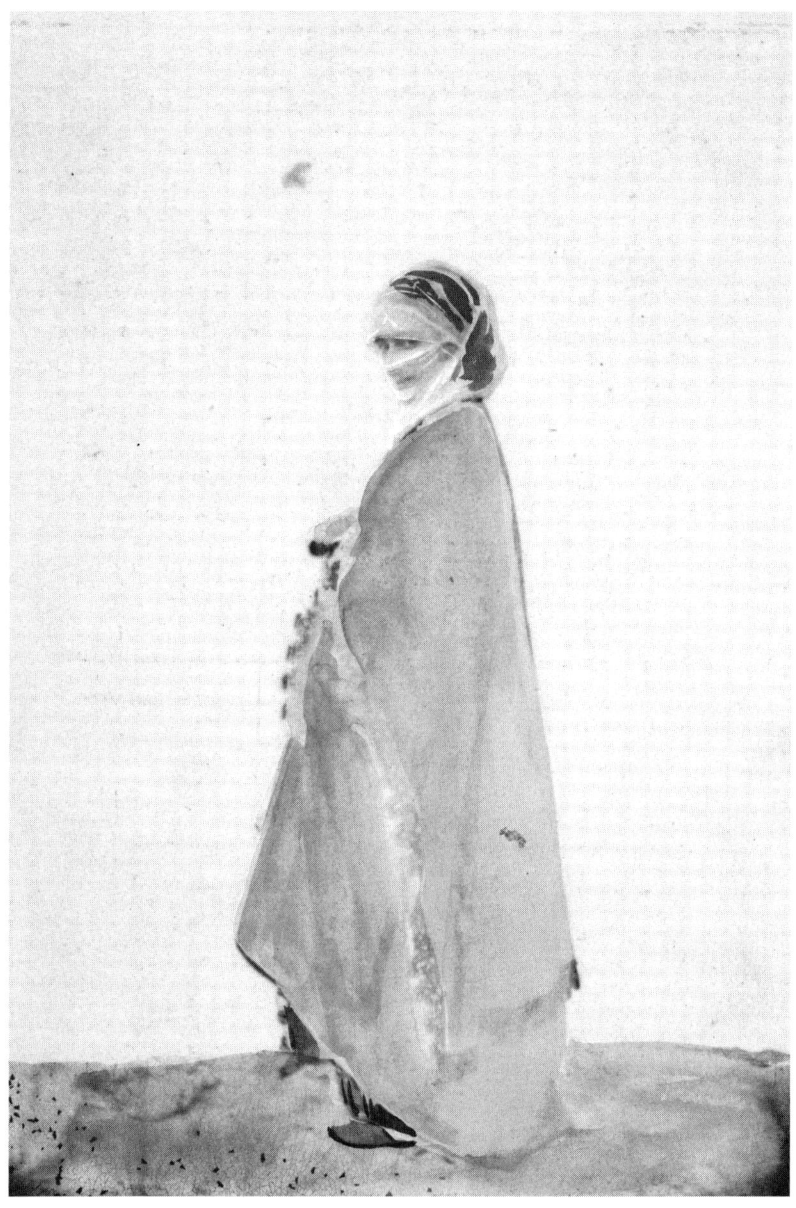

Figure 45. James Robertson. Photograph with watercolor (1850s), from The Pierre de Gigord Collection, box 111, Research Library, The Getty Research Institute, Los Angeles (96.R.14).

At the Universal Exhibitions, on the Streets, and in the Harem

In their groundbreaking essay "Ethnography and Exhibitionism at the *Expositions Universelles*," Zeynep Çelik and Leila Kinney argue that the representation of the colonies at the universal exhibitions was used, in large part, in order to legitimate stereotypes of the Orient.[28] They claim that the architecture and the placement of the pavilions at the exhibitions created both a sense of an "authentic Orient" and a sense of France as a protective father figure presiding over his conquests. Yet, the belly dancer who performed the popular *danse du ventre,* they explain, was especially exploited in order to construct the appearance of an Orient that was defined as feminine, in keeping with more mainstream explanations of Orientalism.[29] Additionally, Çelik and Kinney point out that the dance was actually reformulated so that it would have a greater appeal to the French viewing audiences at the exhibitions. They write that this reinvention of the *danse du ventre* was a way of amplifying "the calculated eroticism in countless orientalist paintings of women by making it more accessible; if anything, they heightened the 'reality effect' of a body of orientalist imagery already legitimized by travelogues and paintings."[30]

While I agree with this argument and acknowledge the importance of the universal exhibitions and the belly dancers on display there in helping to codify some of the terms of French colonial history,[31] these exhibitions occurred only about every ten years and therefore remain somewhat limited in their effect on defining the circumstances of everyday life.[32] And although the ways in which the colonies were presented at the exhibitions helped to determine their subsequent treatment by the colonizer and their representation by Europeans in general, it would seem equally, if not more, compelling to consider the veiling of French women as a quotidian, albeit subtle, means of circulating imperialistic propaganda throughout Paris. In short, the veiling of French women, the significance of which was further sustained by the colonial displays at the universal exhibitions, worked to keep a particular image of the colonies in the minds of the French public in order to contain a growing skepticism toward imperialism and to maintain the concept of the colony under a hegemonic France. Thus, a substantive encounter between East and West did not simply take place every ten years or so at the universal exhibitions, but rather this interaction occurred daily on the streets of Paris, most specifically on and through the faces of veiled Parisian women.

Keeping Parisian women veiled continued the cycle that feminized the Orient, for the sighting of a veiled French woman on the street served as a reminder of this colonial counterpart and thus reinforced an understanding of the Orient as being enigmatic, distant, and seductive. The discrepancies between the French and the Muslim veils, like the discrepancies between the belly dances performed in North Africa and those performed at the universal exhibitions in Paris, point out some of the ways in which the veil in each place is codified to satisfy certain cultural locations and moments. In other words, the veil that became popular in Paris during the second half of the nineteenth century was in part an appropriation of the Muslim veil, reformulated in French terms and infused with cross-cultural meanings, meanings that also had the effect of othering French femininity. Since the Parisian veil is always already referring to what I am claiming is its corollary, the Muslim veil, an encounter with a veiled woman on a Paris street would have been an indirect encounter with French imperialism, a kind of internal colonization. The sighting of a covered face, even on a fashionable Parisian boulevard, may well have summoned up the idea of the colonial Other, for it was widely known—and described ad nauseam by the various venues I have already discussed—that it was Muslim women who wore veils when outside.

The French veil served, then, as an everyday *aide mémoire* of the government's political power in relation to its colonies, and it also simultaneously mediated and became a repository for French fears of the East. Not only were these places in North Africa construed for the French population as exotic, seductive, and passive, but also they were represented at times as being brutal, violent, and irrational.[33] By translating the Muslim veil into French, certain cultural clichés associated with the colonies could be smoothed over and perhaps contained. Unlike its Muslim counterpart, the French version of the veil did not obfuscate the body of the woman wearing it. Nor did the French veil leave the eyes uncovered. Instead, an object that drew on its own history in French culture also incorporated meanings from outside its immediate ethnic affiliation. The French veil could therefore be a means of defining ideals of beauty and aging, of controlling the inhalation of contaminated dusts, of being a marker of the modern in a modern city, but it could also be a vehicle for referring to the colonies in North Africa. Once transposed into French terms, the veil could make the Orient seem more familiar, appealing, and tangible to the local French population.

The Orientalist Trajectory

French fashion was quick to pick up on the fad for Orientalism and exoticism during the second half of the nineteenth century. The reinvention of the veil, the revision of a garment typically associated with colonial culture in order to make it suit modern urban needs, is part of an even more general move toward making the Orient and interest in the Other fashionable.[34] In 1855, a columnist for *Le petit courrier de la mode* claimed, "[F]ashion loves the Orient; it is there that it seeks out its felicitous inspirations. Its nimble and pink fingers scatter myriad pearls and gold on all of our finery."[35] Sparkle and glitz in French clothing were associated with, perhaps even understood to refer to, the Orient, since so many of the details that came to France via travelogues, paintings, photographs, and universal exhibitions fixated on just these aspects of the garments worn in the colonies.

Not only did some French designers incorporate Orientalized themes in their clothes, but also department stores exploited the vivid gleam of Eastern fabrics in their decoration. In *The Ladies' Paradise,* Émile Zola's fictional department store is itself "dressed" *à l'orientale.* The entrance of the store is made to look like an "Oriental saloon" through "harem-like decoration." Inside, colorful carpets and fabrics from places such as Teheran, Mecca, and Daghestan line the walls and ceilings.

> This sumptuous pacha's tent was furnished with divans and arm-chairs, made with camel sacks, some ornamented with many-coloured lozenges, others with primitive roses. Turkey, Arabia, and the Indies were all there. They had emptied the palaces, plundered the mosques and bazaars. A barbarous gold tone prevailed in the weft of the old carpets, the faded tints of which still preserved a sombre warmth. . . . Visions of the East floated beneath the luxury of this barbarous art, amid the strong odour which the old wools had retained of the country of vermin and of the rising sun.[36]

Like the universal exhibitions, the department store could be constituted as a space of difference and accessible exoticism for the French consumer, and that fantasy is achieved mainly through the borrowing of fabrics.

Ornamental colors, gold tones, and faded tints construct the sense that Turkey, Arabia, and the Indies were all there. It is not surprising that veils of muslin and lace are used at the end of the novel to decorate the Ladies' Paradise after its renovation, for the swaths of material help to advertise that there is something desirable beneath them.

> Round the iron columns were twined flounces of white muslin. . . . The staircases were decorated with white drapings, quiltings and dimities alternating along the balustrades, encircling the halls as high as the second story; and this tide of white assumed wings, hurried off and lost itself, like a float of swans. And the white hung from the arches, a fall of down, a snowy sheet of large flakes. . . . long jets of Maltese lace hung across, seeming to suspend swarms of white butterflies; other lace fluttered about on all sides, floating like fleecy clouds in a summer sky, filling the air with their clear breath. And the marvel, the altar of this religion of white was, above the silk counter, in the great hall, a tent formed of white curtains, which fell from the glazed roof. The muslin, the gauze, the lace flowed in light ripples, whilst very richly embroidered tulles, and pieces of oriental silk striped with silver, served as a background to this giant decoration. . . . It made one think of a broad white bed, awaiting in its virginal immensity the white princess, as in the legend, she who was to come one day, all powerful, with the bride's white veil.[37]

The new department store, on its Haussmannized street of whitened edifices, is likened to a virginal bride. It is draped with tulles and muslin and lace that turn the store into a kind of female body. Orientalized almost to the point of misrecognition, this body is both knowable and not, for it is simultaneously all powerful and naive. Yet, it is always kept at a distance, for it is seen only through its elaborate veils.

Connecting Western and Eastern women through clothing and the spaces in which they buy clothing is an effective way of infusing one with meaning from the other. "These gauze veils lend an Oriental sweetness to totally Parisian creations," wrote Julie de Puisieux in her column in *La mode actuelle*, firmly linking an Oriental sweetness to the French veil, and by extension, bridging East and West.[38] Still, there is a fundamental contradiction in the French construction of the Orient, for, even as they defined it as mysterious and impenetrable, writers and painters still endeavored incessantly to describe it in intimate detail. The Orient held a kind of fascination for Europeans; it had a "secret force . . . [an] instinctive power," to use the words of Richard Cortambert in his essay "Promenade d'un fantaisiste: À l'Exposition des beaux-arts de 1861." He continues, "The Orient created the best writers and the most eminent painters of our century,"[39] upholding the widespread cultural belief that using the Orient as subject matter could legitimize one's textual or visual practice.

Visual Cultures

A photograph taken between 1847 and 1853 and titled "Jeunes européennes vêtues à l'orientale" (Figure 46) establishes a direct visual coupling between East and West through the convergence of costume, setting, and fantasy. In the picture, three European women are clothed in flowing dresses and headdresses. One plays a stringed instrument. All three look at the viewer. They are set apart from us by a blank expanse of carpet and a small table on which sit three cups in the right foreground, all held in formally by the palm tree in the left background and by the hanging carpets on the walls. The carpets are horizontally striped and conjure up the bars that artists and photographers often depict in order to create the sense that we are seeing a scene through a harem window. The hookah that we are meant to think these women have been smoking sits in the middle ground and functions as both a barrier and a device that links us to these actresses, each of whom is a French woman pretending to be an inhabitant of a harem.

This picture is a fantasy, a French photographer's dream of the interior of a harem, fabricated and filtered through a complex circuit of props and cultural expectations. The image is created for the pleasure of a Western male viewer and therefore fulfills certain expectations about French practices, but it is also a stereotyped construction of an Eastern interior that is exotic and different from what we know about the late nineteenth-century Western interior.

These kinds of images multiplied during the second half of the nineteenth century. Around 1870, an anonymous Turkish photographer created an image that its Parisian owner called "Int. de harem" (Figure 47). In this photograph, three Turkish women (or are they French?) are contrived to fit the "Oriental formula" perfectly. One reclines on her side and stares wistfully upward while she is serenaded by a woman who plays the lute and another who taps a tambourine. Each is clothed in silky, flowing, embroidered garments, and each wears a decorated hat. The setting abounds with stereotypes. It contains the requisite hookah, bronze tea service, ornamental pillows, Oriental carpet. The difficulty in determining the women's nationality would have made the image even more desirable, familiar though different, to its French viewer.

"Jeunes européennes vêtues à l'orientale" and "Int. de harem" borrow their iconography from a long tradition in French painting of depicting imaginary harem scenes. Ingres's *Odalisque and Slave,* of 1839, in its pairing of overdetermined visual opposites, its inclusion of hookahs, hanging

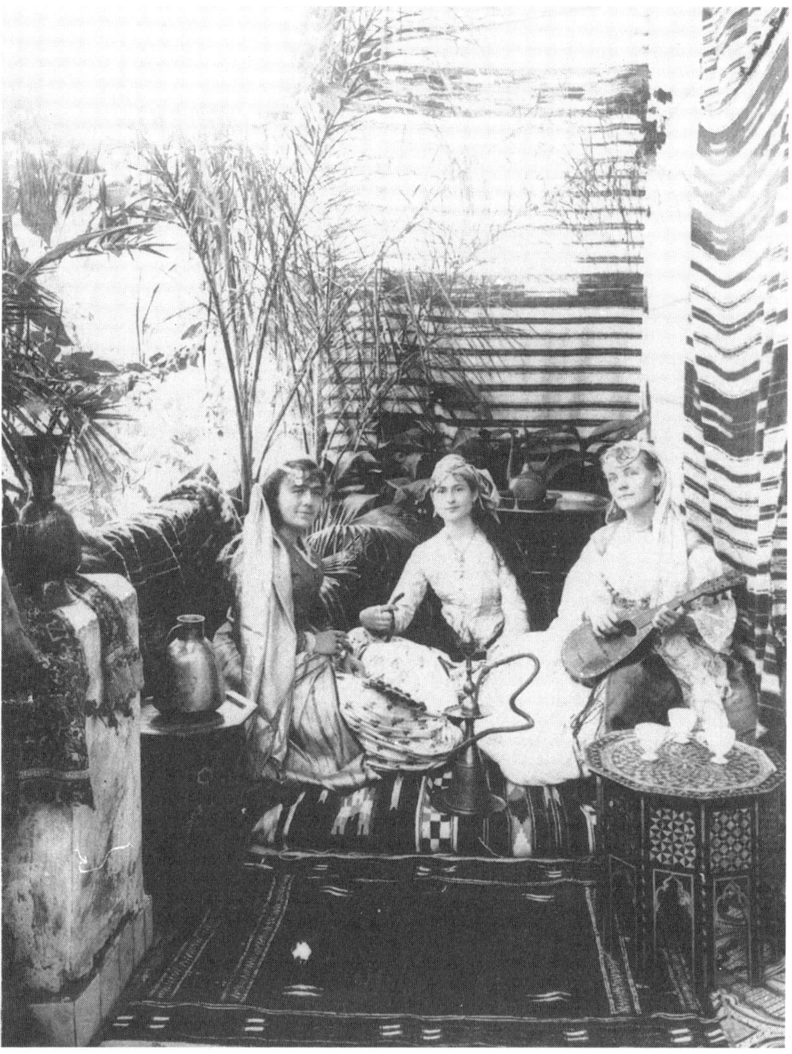

Figure 46. Anonymous, "Jeunes européennes vêtues à l'orientale," *Costumes féminins* (1847–53). Photograph. Cabinet des estampes, Bibliothèque nationale, Paris (Oa 20 [fol.]).

carpets, and colorful flowing drapery, as well as its effort at presenting a stilled and languid moment, is one such type of painting to which these two photographs refer. Ingres's oil painting is part of the visual discourse of Orientalism established by the time the photographers set up their images. By alluding to works such as Ingres's, the photographers assimilated themselves into the legacy of academic Orientalism that was popular in public and at the Salon. This visual reference also allows the photograph greater artistic credibility at a moment when the medium was in the process of becoming a viable and respected means of representation. Obviously, there are dissimilarities between the genres, but the similarities, the incorporation in each of stereotyped topoi and poses, place them at some point on the same late nineteenth-century Orientalist trajectory.

Ingres's *Grande Odalisque*, painted in 1814, has come to occupy one of the most significant spots on this trajectory, in large part because it is one of the best known and most reproduced of his works. Commissioned by Napoleon's sister Caroline Bonaparte Murat, Ingres's version of the harem is a highly fabricated one, constructed not out of any firsthand experience but rather from books and other filtered Western versions of life in the

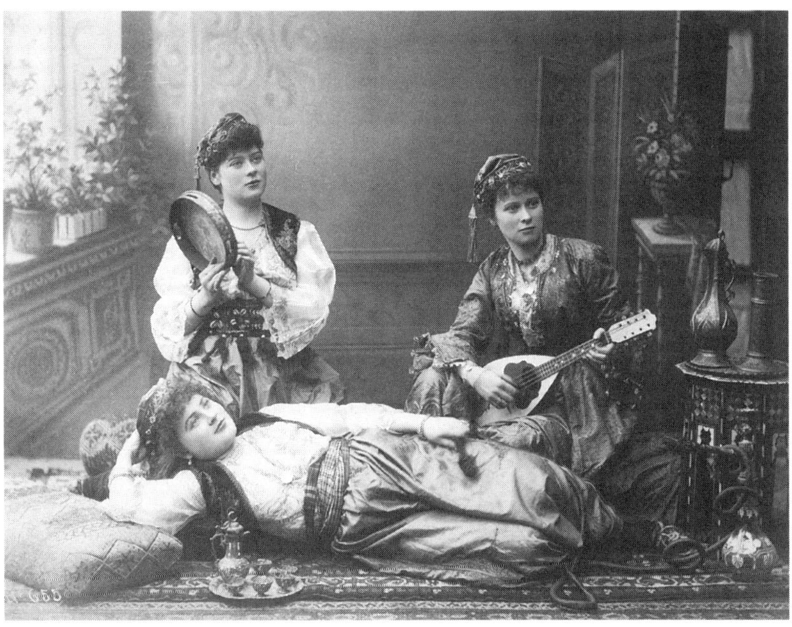

Figure 47. "Int. de harem" (c. 1870). Photograph from The "Algerian Types—Cartes-de-visite" Collection, Research Library, The Getty Research Institute, Los Angeles (93.R.123).

East, most notably Lady Mary Wortley Montagu's letters.[40] In fact, all visions of the harem are always already fictionalized for anyone but its inhabitants and the men who have access to it, since the harem exists, by definition, only for them. Yet, Ingres endeavors to construct an image so seemingly perfect stylistically that it would have been easy for a contemporary viewer, unfamiliar with the traps and lures of academic painting and Orientalist tropes that we more readily recognize today, to forget that this is a representation and not some transparent view of reality.

In her groundbreaking essay "The Imaginary Orient," Linda Nochlin points out that this ability to render absent the sense that an artist's hand was ever implicated in the construction of the picture is one of the aspects of Orientalist painting that makes it most able to function successfully as veristic. She writes:

> Part of the strategy of an Orientalist painter like Gérôme is to make his viewers forget that there was any "bringing into being" at all, to convince them that works like these were simply "reflections," scientific in their exactitude, of a preexisting Oriental reality. . . . A "naturalist" or "authenticist" artist like Gérôme tries to make us forget that his art is really art, both by concealing the evidence of his touch, and, at the same time, by insisting on a plethora of authenticating details.[41]

Nochlin's working explanation of Orientalism in painting situates absence—the absence of the artist's hand, the absence of history, and the absence of the Western presence—as the prerequisite for Orientalism's effectiveness. All of these entities are there, but they are suppressed, present but held below the surface. The hidden or the invisible is, then, the precondition for Orientalism, and it determines the extent to which an image is convincing and acceptable.[42] "The mystery of the East itself [is] a standard topos of Orientalist ideology," Nochlin continues, further reiterating the importance of mystery and the restriction of what is seen for the unqualified acceptance of the Orientalist enterprise.[43] Mystery itself is always connected to what we can and cannot see, what is hidden or kept from our view.

While Edouard Manet's *Young Woman in Oriental Costume,* of 1871 (Figure 48), may not conform precisely to Nochlin's incisive interpretation of successful Orientalist painting, it is connected, in that the picture's goals are analogous to those of Gérôme, to use the same example she uses. Manet's painting is Orientalist in several respects, especially since it is marked with some of the most common trappings of Orientalized imagery. There is a hookah in the right foreground, a colorful pillow to the right, a bed in the background, and the model's face conforms to the type typically associated at the time with women of some nonspecific though clearly non-French origin. She wears a multicolored hat, a double strand of orange beads, and gold earrings, and she holds an unexplained colorful flag, all of which have the effect of highlighting her supposed non-Frenchness.

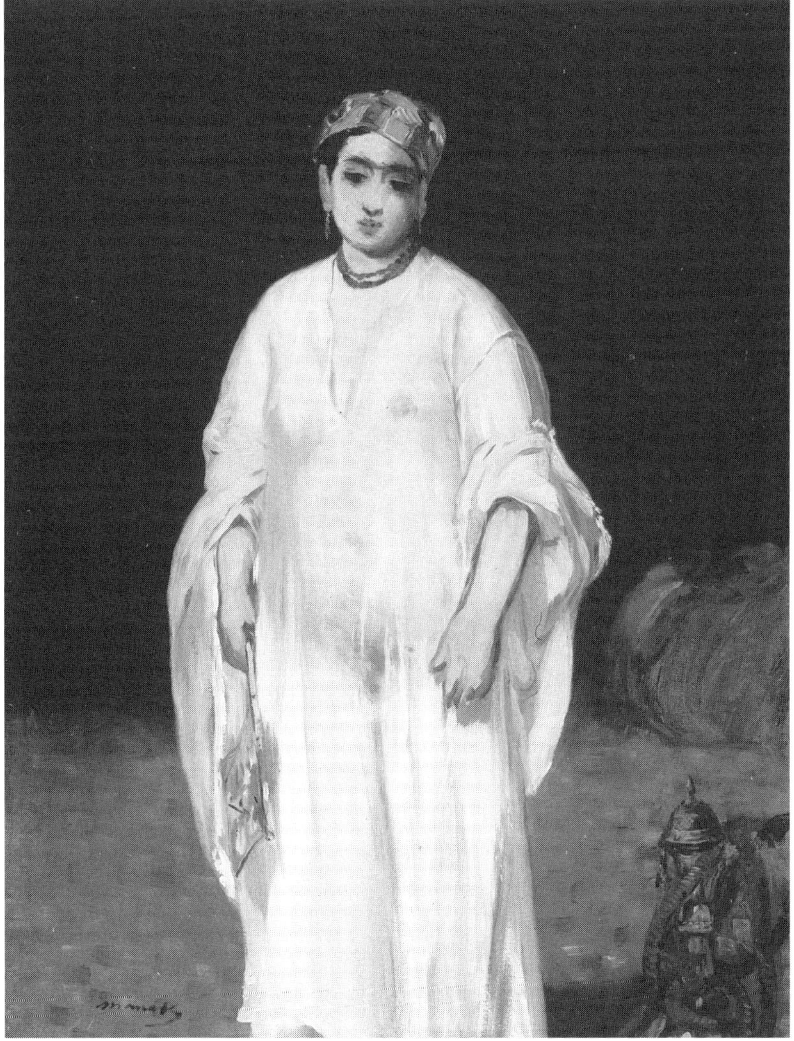

Figure 48. Edouard Manet, *Young Woman in Oriental Costume* (1871). Oil on canvas. Foundation E. G. Bührle Collection, Zurich.

And yet, everywhere his brush touches canvas, Manet makes it clear that this is a representation, that he has been present in the making of this image. The painting is executed with such bravado and broadly handled brushwork that the implication of the artist's touch is always apparent. Unlike the glossy polished surfaces of Gérôme's or Ingres's paintings, Manet's picture is rough, summarized, at times scumbled, and always assertive, an example of what I would term avant-garde (as opposed to academic) Orientalist painting. The sultana's sheath is composed of thin drags of white paint, sharpened by swaths of gray and black.[44] The disclosure of her naked body through the white gown reminds us that the painted body is like canvas beneath pigment—present, a support, but not entirely visible. The billowing arms of the woman's garment are summarized by thicker strokes of grays and whites. Her face and arms are distilled to dense and creamy flesh tones. The bedspread is clotted with horizontal patches of burgundy, red, and milky beige.

Despite Manet's obvious interest in making his working process clear, his sultana is no less mystified than any academic Orientalist's more precisely rendered women. Manet's working method—his avant-garde Orientalism—may even be more able to articulate the ineffable essence of the Other, a concept that is itself fractured, fissured, unfinished, to use Homi Bhabha's notion.[45] Manet's simultaneously thinned and coagulated pigments, laid on in obvious strokes, may actually describe the very reality that it is not possible to represent another culture, that the mystery is always an essential ingredient of the final result. In fact, Manet's sultana may be even more mysterious than Gérôme's *because* Manet actually foregrounds the literal and metaphorical veil of representation. This exposure of the precepts of representational practice is analogized in the painting itself by the muslin sheath, which both covers and uncovers, for it drapes the sultana's body but is sufficiently translucent that one may readily see through to the body beneath it. Here, the body may be read as the canvas on which Manet has placed his veil of paint. The sheath becomes the displaced veil that declares the artifice of the picture and forces us to look even closer. For, behind the sheath, behind the veil, the woman's body is made more obvious. It is both present and not, seen and not seen.

Whereas the green and black veils falling across the face and body of Gérôme's hypersexualized woman in *The Almah,* of 1882 (Figure 49), are perhaps more obviously implicated in the work of a conventional kind of academic Orientalism, the mousseline covering the young woman's body in Manet's painting is equally invested in perpetuating stereotyped standards of an Orient. In some ways the veils, Manet's and Gérôme's, are even similar, for each covers over, rendering that which is behind it mysterious, erotic, desirable, and worthy of more careful scrutiny.

To push this point even further, Manet's sultana's body becomes a version of her face; her breasts correspond to her eyes, her navel to her nose, her genitals to her mouth. In fact, it would seem that Manet actually wants us to make this connection between the face and the body, since

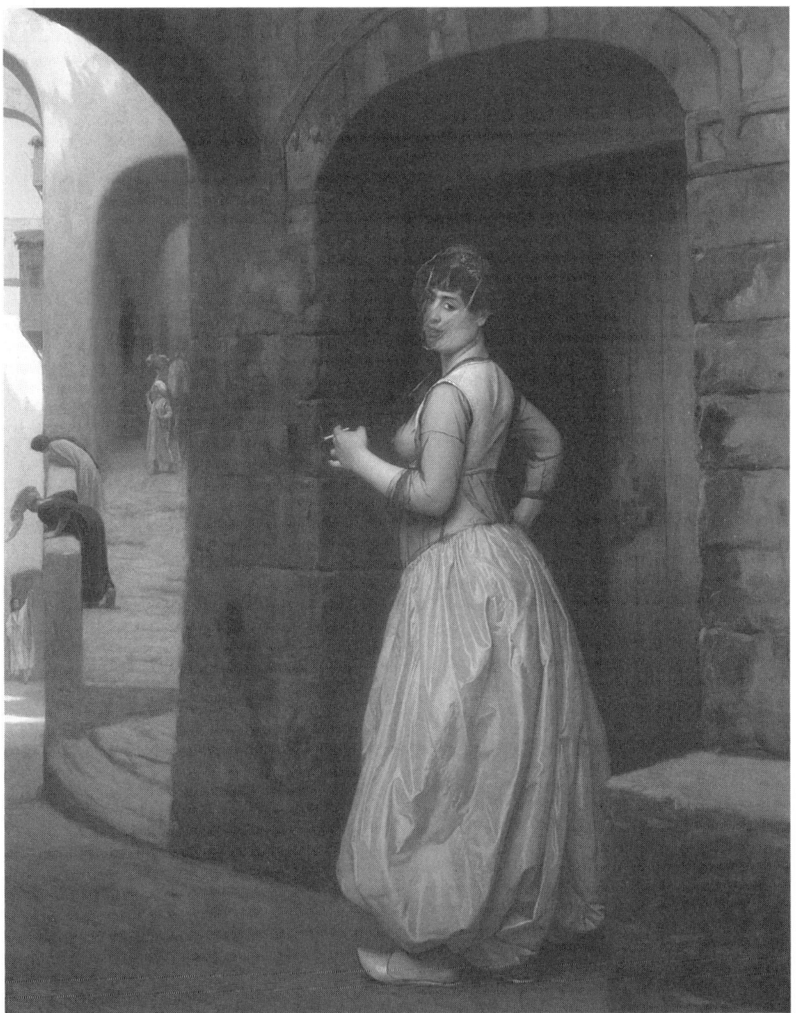

Figure 49. Jean-Léon Gérôme, *The Almah* (1882). Oil on canvas. NAJD Collection. Courtesy Mathaf Gallery, London.

the parallel formal relationships are so startlingly obvious.[46] So, while the woman in the painting is not veiled in any conventional sense, she is veiled in all other senses. Perhaps unknowingly, Manet produces a visual pun here between the French veil, which covers the face, and the Muslim veil, which encases the body. In fact, he conflates the two types of veils on this woman's body, thus calling attention to both the similarities and the differences between them. By using what is most likely a French model to stand for a woman of Eastern origin, the artist further connects East and West, forcing the viewer to see the distinctions and the convergences between the two.

Manet's picture may not hide the artist's touch from view, and it may not pretend to be devoid of history and the Western presence, but, like Gérôme's paintings, its Orientalism establishes and perpetuates stereotypes of the East as being contingent on what is hidden, what is veiled. In fact, Manet's painting may be even more effective in upholding certain of these stereotypes, since its work seems to be less obvious than that of Gérôme. Manet is subtler, in that his picture does not pretend to be anything but a picture, while Gérôme, in hiding his brushwork through more detailed and thinly layered glazes, is trying to cover over the fact that his image is a representation.

In the case of *The Almah,* which is one of many tightly worked paintings Gérôme executed of *almahs* in veils, the slick surface and highly aestheticized pose make the point of the picture almost too glaringly obvious. Whereas the woman in Manet's *Young Woman in Oriental Costume* looks passively and with disinterest out at the viewer, the model in Gérôme's painting casts a seductive gaze over her left shoulder. She holds a lit cigarette in her left hand while her right hand is poised at her hip. We see her from behind and the side, yet remarkably we have a virtually full view of her left breast, made all the more evident by the thin black veiling that impossibly hugs it. Her sexiness is keyed up to an even greater extreme by her formal juxtaposition with the drab niche of the building. Her voluminous red pants, the green of her face veil, and her little yellow vest are made more emphatic because they visually pop against the muddied color that surrounds them. These vibrant hues serve to reinforce one of the most important statements artists and writers articulated about the Orient: that it is colorful. In fact, the intense hues often used in depicting Eastern subjects became crucial elements in the very establishment of the stereotype that the Orient is a place of exoticism, eroticism, and non-Europeanism.

Manet refused to conform to the standards of visual Orientalism practiced by contemporary academic artists, who were experiencing popularity at the salons and in sales.[47] While Gérôme's sexy *almahs* overtly point out the ways in which the Orient is a place of sexuality, otherness, and mystery, Manet is less conspicuous. Indeed, his woman clothed in Orientalized garb in some ways resists those very standards only to reinforce them on other levels. She does not really engage the viewer by her look, and she does not strike a seductive or knowing pose. She simply stands there, arms hanging loosely at her sides, head tilted slightly to her left shoulder. Yet, there is a hookah at her feet, she wears a multicolored hat, and she is clothed, if one can call it that, in what would have been considered by French standards to be a compromising fashion. The visibility of her body beneath the sheath further declares her availability, undermining whatever modesty we may read into her disinterested gaze.

Manet's 1862-68 watercolor, India ink, and gouache depiction of an odalisque (Figure 50), his only other known work with an Orientalized theme (besides the etching version of this, which he created in 1868), is more conventional in its pose, for it is one typically associated with a long tradition of reclining odalisques.[48] This image has also been formally related to *Young Woman Reclining in Spanish Costume*, of 1862 (Figure 51). In fact, Beatrice Farwell has argued that Manet used the same model for

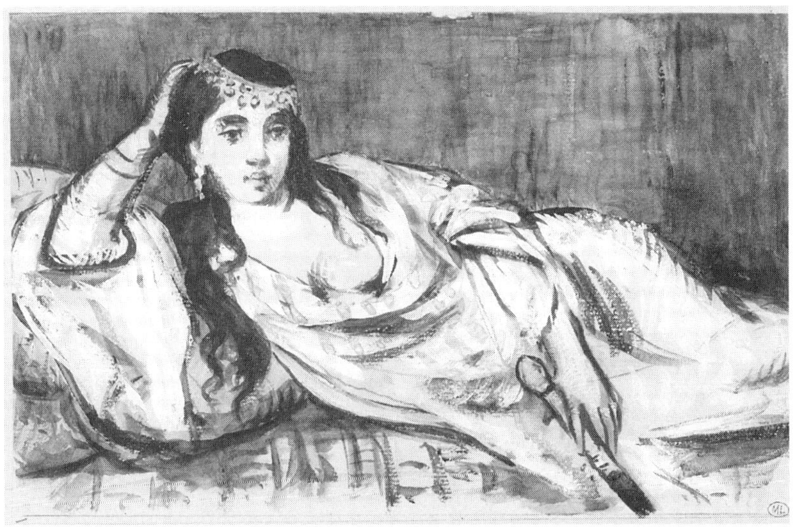

Figure 50. Edouard Manet, *Odalisque* (1862–68). Watercolor, ink, gouache highlights. Musée du Louvre, Paris. C. Jean. Réunion des musées nationaux/Art Resource, NY.

both.[49] Besides the obvious similarity in pose and posture, the two figures resemble each other facially. They both have full lips, dark eyes, and dark hair. Each lifts an arm to her head, a gesture that further heightens the seductive possibilities of her demeanor. The big distinction, other than the differing media of these depictions, is that one of these women, if they were indeed two different models, is supposed to be Spanish and the other is of some unspecified North African nationality.[50]

Manet's treatment of Eastern themes is similar to his depiction of Spanish themes. The same types of dark-haired and sallow-skinned women who populate his Spanish paintings are found in *Young Woman in Oriental Costume* and the reclining odalisque prints and watercolor.[51] He freely interchanges social types and cultures, using dark-haired French models to pose for women of both Spanish and Eastern derivation. Clothing and variously stereotyped accoutrements add to the supposed believability of the images.[52] This imposition of another national affiliation on a French body is what makes these pictures so profoundly filled with cultural clichés. For, in order to establish some sense of national identity through appearance,

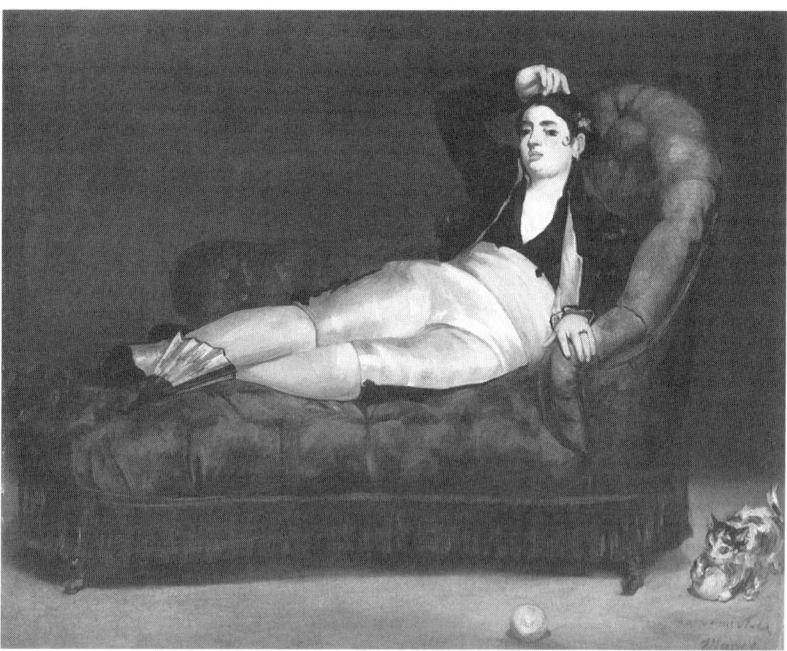

Figure 51. Edouard Manet, *Young Woman Reclining in Spanish Costume* (1862). Oil on canvas. Bequest of Stephen Carlton Clark, B.A. 1903, Yale University Art Gallery, New Haven, Connecticut.

features must be reduced to their basic components. In other words, black hair, dark eyes, and full lips, at least in Manet's Orientalized and Spanish paintings, constitute the non-French.

Auguste Renoir, like Manet, took French models and manipulated facial features, clothing, and setting in order to produce his brand of Orientalist painting. Stylistically different means may have been used, but the props and poses were somewhat standardized. Renoir's *Woman of Algiers,* also called *Odalisque* (Figure 52), was exhibited at the Salon of 1870. Painted in Renoir's studio in the Batignolles quarter of Paris and posed for by Lise Tréhot from Montmartre, this image claims to be a depiction of a woman from Algeria, but it is really simply a Parisian model wearing an Algerian costume, lying sensually across a golden carpet that had been laid on the floor in Renoir's studio.

Lise reclines, her legs slightly splayed, her fingers suggestively curled. Renoir cleverly tilts her head against a pillow, probably so that we can get a good look at her seductive facial expression and piercing gaze. All of the expected visual clichés are in place, for she has dark eyes, long brown hair, olive-toned skin, and her lips are accentuated by bright red lipstick. Her billowy pants, which end just below her knee, are composed of an intricate pattern of red, black, and gold, while her vest is of gold and burgundy. One of her feet half slips out of an ornately feathered mule only to emphasize the high and elegant instep of her right foot. At her waist is a belt of teal and red, and around her neck are multiple strands of black

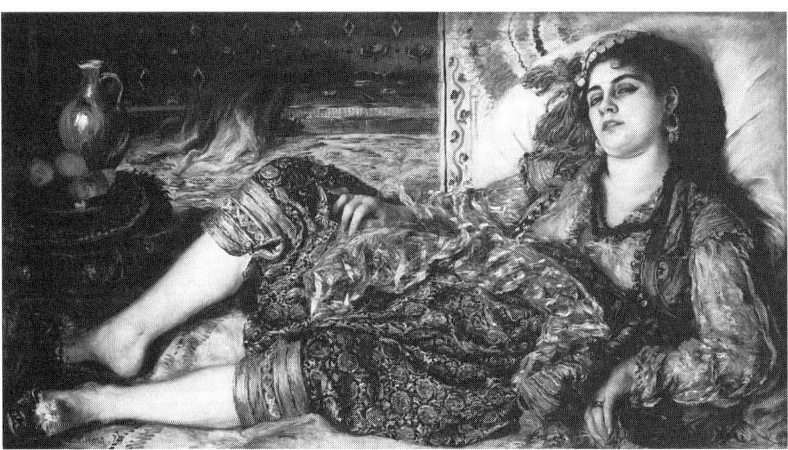

Figure 52. Auguste Renoir, *Odalisque* (1870). Oil on canvas. National Gallery of Art, Washington, D.C.

beads. She wears a headpiece of gold coins and red feathers, as well as large gold earrings. Yet, it is her sheer blouse that is perhaps the most literally and figuratively revealing aspect of her dress, for it barely veils the parts of the body that it covers. Her vest, in fact, falls to the sides of Lise's body in such a way as to follow the form of her breasts, visible from behind the diaphanous blouse.

Like this painting of Lise, Renoir's *Parisian Women in Algerian Dress,* of 1872, submitted to the Salon of 1872 as *Harem,* also borrows some of the conventions of preexisting Orientalist painting in an effort to turn four French women into sultanas in a harem. Drawing on the composition and subject matter of Eugène Delacroix's *Women of Algiers,* of 1834, which had participated in establishing a visual language for depicting the interior of a harem, Renoir has done the unthinkable. He has used a blond-haired Parisian model to stand for an Algerian. Nevertheless, she still represents the epitome of the kind of sexual lasciviousness that the French assigned to women in harems, for her jeweled ankles, golden earrings, bare legs, and gauzy and revealing drapery undermine her non-Eastern coloring in order to convince the viewer that this model is of a type that could have inhabited a harem. Her nude attendant and the brunette sultana in the foreground, along with the Orientalized setting, equally maintain the fantasy of the Orient as a place of sexual promiscuity and availability.

It is not entirely surprising that a blonde could pass as an Algerian, in the nineteenth-century visual sense, since the models of Manet, Gérôme, and Renoir *had* to have recognizable elements of Frenchness (or Europeanness) to be desirable to a French audience. Indeed, the traces of cultural familiarity when veiled by the trappings of Orientalism combined to give these paintings their powerful appeal to their European audiences.

If the veil is a screen on which we may project our desire, and if the veil is the quintessential sign of the Orient, then it is also a necessary element in the construction of our understanding of Orientalism. Just as these artists literally and figuratively veiled their French models in their pictures through clothing and context, the veiled Parisienne on the streets of the new city was also converted into a colonized and sexualized being. If the veil in Islam is, in part, a public sign of the harem, then the veil in Paris is the visual symptom of a colonial convergence that took information about the East and displaced it, albeit in a limited way, onto the French woman. Thus, the popularity of the veil in Parisian fashion is a manifestation not only of imperial ambition but also of desire.

The illustration for the cover of *L'Exposition de Paris de 1889* with which I began this chapter is an appropriate image with which to end. That picture, however modest, describes levels of literal and symbolic veils that are present in popular imagery as well as in academic and less conventional painting practice. In its simplest sense, this illustration shows France and its colonies together at the Universal Exhibition on both sides of the veil. This representation of Parisians and Algerians coming face-to-face through the warp of a loom articulates visual Orientalism as a process of putting on layers, as a view through a veil.

Epilogue

THE VEIL DID NOT, OF COURSE, cease to be fashionable after 1889. Indeed, its popularity continued well into the mid-twentieth century in Europe and America. Fashion photography of the 1950s was especially attracted to the veil, for it was already deeply invested in notions of high style and an ideal of feminine beauty. For example, the photographer Irving Penn often depicted models wearing veils when he or the designer wanted to convey the sense of impeccable taste and fashionability. In "Woman in Balenciaga Coat (Lisa Fonssagrives-Penn)," from 1950, Fonssagrives-Penn's perfectly made-up face is rendered even more idealized by the billowy and frothy veil that floats across it. Like those Second Empire "soft . . . adorable . . . sparkling [and] transparent" veils that Octave Uzanne described, this veil seduces the viewer into seeing only perfection and radiance.

Penn subverted the typically beautifying effect of the veil in a well-known *Vogue* cover of 1950. By representing the most stylized and exaggerated of veils, he was able to call attention to the seams of feminine beauty, the cracks in its façade. In this photograph, a magnified grid of thick black threads knotted at each intersection fragments the face and underscores the virtual impossibility of an unmediated view of or for the woman. The model looks off to the side in a dramatic gesture that further reinforces the degree of artifice involved in creating a paradigm of female beauty and the ways in which the gaze, on both sides, is invested in maintaining it. This veil has clearly been inflected by its nineteenth-century predecessor. And yet, like its earlier manifestations, it moves in a slightly other direction, inscribes new issues for a changing economy of beauty, gender, and capitalism.

The veil that was constructed by the time of the Second Empire and early Third Republic had specific significance, a great deal of which would always be present to varying degrees in later variations. This is not to say that the veil's even earlier incarnations did not have resonance that inscribed the Second Empire version. Surely the purity associated with the white veil in the fourth century was every bit a part of the meanings generated by its nineteenth-century interpretation. And if there is a truly transhistorical property for the veil, it is precisely the veil's place within the discourses of sexuality. The seductive and mysterious aspects of wearing a veil, the ways in which it can generate a surface of fantasized beauty, know no geographic or temporal boundaries.

The veil on which this study has focused is a text that contains the discourse of the spectacular new city. In it we find the strands that help to reconstruct part of the story of life in late nineteenth-century Paris. For this veil is a locus of certain interrelated practices, all of which blended to form a particularly modern identity. Like Barthes's notion of the literary text, my text, and the veil on which it discourses, is variable and permeable. For him, "[t]ext means *Tissue;* but whereas hitherto we have always taken this tissue as a product, a ready-made veil, behind which lies, more or less hidden, meaning (truth), we are now emphasizing, in the tissue, the generative idea that the text is made, is worked out in a perpetual interweaving."[1] Reading these words as a graduate student years ago made quite an impact on me as I wrote the dissertation with which this book began. Barthes's words, though ahistorical—literally disinterested in the exigencies of history and how they propel and define an object or a text—helped me to see more clearly the object about which I was writing, with all of its attendant richness and complexity, even as I knew that one book could hardly capture its many meanings fully. A veil from 1872 (Figure 53), which is made of thin lace and decorated with curious shapes that remind one of musical notes or hieroglyphics, has the look of something that can make and remake itself, move with the wind and become a new semblance, a new text for our analysis, one that is never quite containable. The idea of the text as something that perpetually makes itself has stayed in my mind, resolute in its energetic pull, as a metaphor for the veil, about which I write, and for this text as a whole.

I suspect that painting veils had a similar pull for the artists about whom I have written here, a pull that had to do with the veil's shape and structure but also with its intractable connection to the moment within which they were working. Caillebotte, Degas, and Manet represented veils not only because their formal qualities facilitated the technical experimentation that appealed to these painters but also because veils were idioms

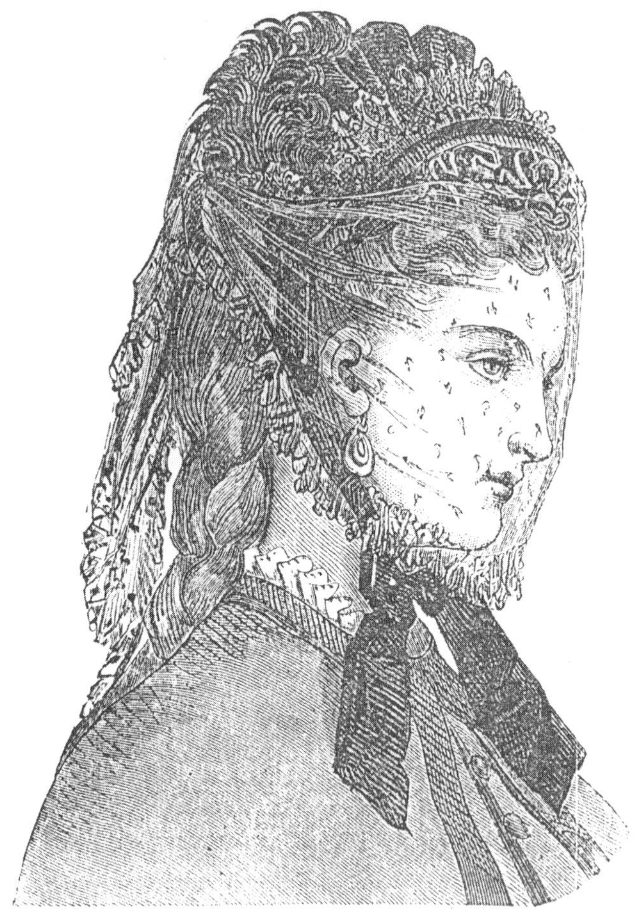

N° 1. CHAPEAU DE CHEZ Mme AUBERT.

Figure 53. *La mode illustrée, journal de la famille* 15 (April 14, 1872): 19. Engraving. Bibliothèque des arts décoratifs, Paris.

of urban contemporaneity. Their preponderance in the periodical literature certainly emphasizes this point. The importance of their being at the height of late nineteenth-century Parisian fashion happened also to intersect with other social formations. When proper women began to wear veils in abundance during the Second Empire, the underlying reasons exceeded the bounds of the fashion journals that helped to popularize them. I have shown that veils were a method of actual and imagined protection from dust and disease, part of a system of maintaining an ideal of youthfulness and beauty, a formal challenge for certain artists, at the same time that they were also entangled in French imperial policies in North Africa. Above all, veils were a means for keeping bourgeois women's vision in check.

This is precisely the issue that Manet inscribes on his canvas *Young Woman in a Round Hat,* of 1877 (Figure 54). In the lively streak of brownish black paint that he spreads over the woman's eyes, Manet epitomizes the visual consequences of the veil. We can imagine that in the moment before he touched his finger or palette knife to the paint, he saw a more straightforward, clearly articulated, speckled voilette covering the model's face. Always ready to experiment, Manet went one step further and instead chose to memorialize in his blur the active play of the voilette across the eyes and how it interrupts the woman's line of vision. We can still see part of an eyebrow and a corner of her eye, but really it is the way in which the veil overtly disrupts this portion of the woman's face that is most striking, most ravishing.

Charles S. Moffett, in his entry for the painting in the Manet retrospective catalog of 1983, noted, "[T]he obscuring effects of the veil and the shadow cast by the brim of the hat suggest that it is not a portrait in the conventional sense."[2] While Moffett is one of the few to remark on the obscuring effects of the veil in this particular picture, his interpretation leaves me wanting more. He uses the curious blur of paint to categorize this as an unconventional portrait, as one of "Manet's pictures of women dressed for particular roles in urban society."[3] This easy system of classification represses what seem to me the most challenging aspects of the image. What Moffett assumes is a shadow from the brim of the hat, I read as the work of the veil, the way it gathers at sections and obscures, the way the assertion of materiality can invoke an immateriality.

This small passage in the painting is indeed confounding, if not nearly impossible to understand in anything but the parameters I have mapped out in this book about veils. This bit of blackened pigment on the canvas

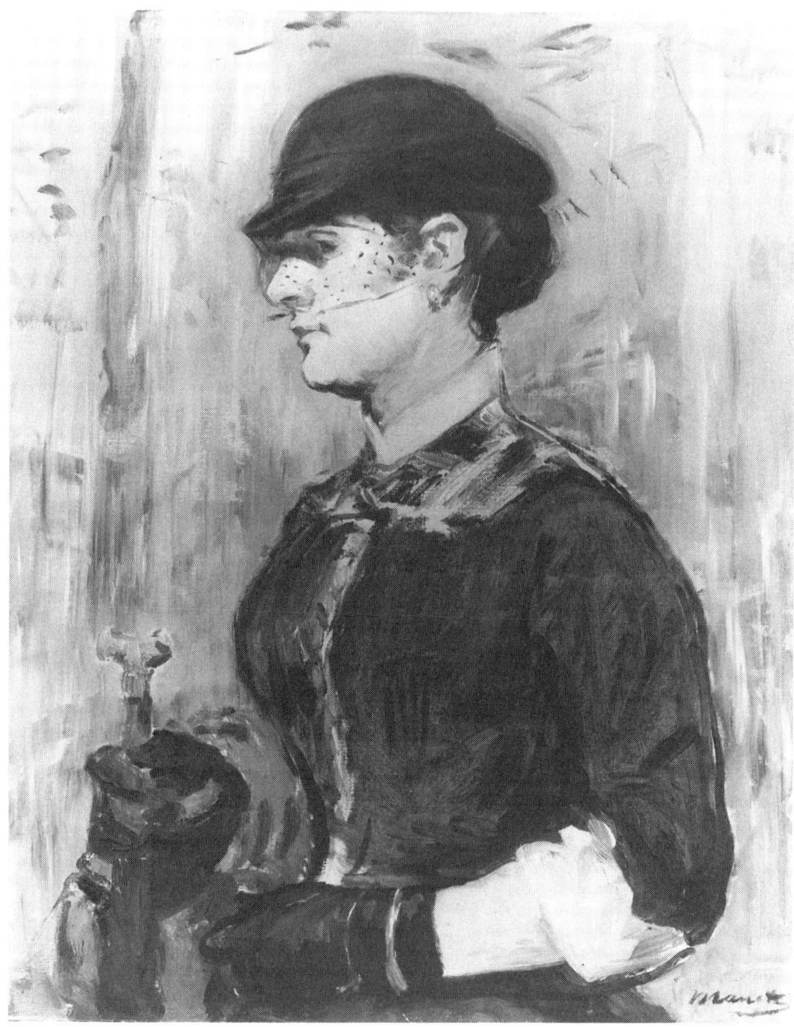

Figure 54. Edouard Manet, *Young Woman in a Round Hat* (1877). Oil on canvas. The Henry and Rose Pearlman Foundation; on long-term loan to the Princeton University Art Museum, Princeton, New Jersey. Photograph by Bruce M. White.

is neither pure nor coincidental. It articulates the circumscription of a modern woman's vision, the way it may be shaped by the veil. Conversely, it demonstrates how our view of the woman may also be limited by the veil. Ultimately, Manet's smudge of paint reminds us of the veil itself, how its fragile filaments infinitely intersect in a web of sheer presence.

Notes

Introduction

1. See, for example, Varnedoe's *Gustave Caillebotte,* and Julia Sagraves's contributions on the painting in the exhibition catalog *Gustave Caillebotte.*

2. See Barthes, *The Fashion System.*

3. The Second Empire lasted from 1852 to 1870; the Third Republic began in 1870 and lasted until 1940.

4. Throughout this book, I use the terms *respectable women, proper women,* and *bourgeoises* interchangeably to describe French women of the second half of the nineteenth century who were not of the lower and working classes.

5. My primary focus is not on academic painting, because I am most interested here in articulating the importance of the veil within the urban environment that was so often represented by artists who resisted academic conventions. To be sure, veils appear often in academic art, though usually in the context of a mythological, biblical, or history painting.

6. Adriani, *Renoir,* 154.

7. For brief histories of the veil, see Kybalova, Herbenova, and Lamarova, *The Pictorial Encyclopedia of Fashion,* 365; and Lester and Oerke, *An Illustrated History of Those Frills and Furbelows of Fashion Which Have Come to Be Known as: Accessories of Dress,* 60–73. While some of the information in these books is helpful, they contain generalizations and inaccuracies, especially in relation to nineteenth-century France. These histories tend also to prioritize the cataloging and aestheticizing of material over close discursive analysis. Some exceptions to this trend are

Philippe Perrot's *Fashioning the Bourgeoisie;* Valerie Steele's *Paris Fashion;* and Ulrich Lehmann's *Tigerpsrung,* all of which are cultural histories of fashion that consider their objects of inquiry within social, material, and historical contexts. Still, none of these authors addresses the importance of the veil in constructing his or her version of French fashion history.

8. Troy, *Couture Culture,* 10.

9. I cite as an example of this ignorance and fear vis-à-vis the Muslim veil the debates and attempts to ban the wearing of it in French public schools over the last few years.

10. For analyses of the Muslim veil and its histories, see particularly Ahmed, *Women and Gender in Islam;* Mernissi, *Women and Islam;* and Mernissi, *Beyond the Veil.* A recent exhibition, cataloged in Bailey and Tawadros, eds., *Veil,* has been the first to explore the historical, political, and cultural complexity of the veil as it is manifest in some contemporary visual culture. As Reina Lewis succinctly summarizes in her preface to the catalog, "Standing as a beacon of tradition or an emblem of progressive modernity, the veiled or unveiled, de-veiled or re-veiled woman has been a feature of divergent struggles over decolonization, nationalism, revolution, Westernisation and anti-Westernisation" (10).

11. *The New Oxford Annotated Bible,* 64.

12. Perhaps one of the most famous biblical veils is that of Veronica; however, since this so-called veil was actually a napkin, I will not address it in detail.

13. See Wilcox, *The Mode in Hats and Headdress,* 10, for a description of the emergence of the veil, which Wilcox calls an "emblem of feminine modesty, submission and respect" in the Mesopotamian Valley.

14. Vogelsang-Eastwood, *For Modesty's Sake?* 20.

15. Herakleides, *Diakatarchos* I, 18 ff., as quoted in Vogelsang-Eastwood, *For Modesty's Sake?* 24.

16. Homer, *The Odyssey,* 35.

17. Challamel, *History of Fashion in France,* 25.

18. Ibid., 25.

19. Harris, *The History of the Hat,* 58.

20. Challamel, *History of Fashion in France,* 32.

21. Ibid., 34.

22. Ibid., 35.

23. Quoted ibid., 86.

24. Beebe, *Lace, Ancient and Modern,* 22–23.

25. Winkel, "Fashion or Fancy?" 59.

26. Challamel, *History of Fashion in France,* 122.

27. The lace trade underwent many changes throughout the centuries. Since my focus here is on the late nineteenth century, I will explain that the industry contracted somewhat during the 1820s and expanded, especially in Belgium, during

the 1840s and on. In fact, Parisian commissions of Belgian lace increased dramatically by this time. Production was, however, still taking place in the French cities of Lille, Caen, Bayeux, Valenciennes, and Chantilly during these years. For an in-depth discussion of lace and its history, see Levey, *Lace.*

28. Beebe, *Lace, Ancient and Modern,* 78–79.

29. Challamel, *History of Fashion in France,* 229.

1. Pathologizing the Second Empire City

1. My understanding of the meaning of dust has been shaped by the writings of Walter Benjamin, who privileged it as both an active force in the production of history and a container for history. See Benjamin, *The Arcades Project,* 102–3; and Buck-Morss, *The Dialectics of Seeing,* 95–96. Building on Benjamin, Carolyn Steedman also writes compellingly of the role of dust both in the archive and as archive and as indicator of class and social change, in *Dust.*

2. While my focus here is specifically on the period of the Second Empire in French history, it is important to note that this kind of gendered social restriction of course predates the early 1850s, when mass production really brought the problem to the fore.

3. Michelet, *La femme,* in *Oeuvres complètes de Michelet,* 18: 413. "Elle ne peut guère sortir le soir; on la prendrait pour une fille. Il est mille endroits où l'on ne voit que des hommes, et si une affaire l'y mène, on s'étonne, on rit sottement. Par exemple, qu'elle se trouve attardée au bout de Paris, qu'elle ait faim, elle n'osera pas entrer chez un restauranteur. Elle y ferait événement, elle y serait un spectacle. Elle aurait constamment tous les yeux fixés sur elle." Unless otherwise indicated, all translations are mine.

4. Morisot, *Berthe Morisot,* 36.

5. Bashkirtseff, *Journals of Marie Bashkirtseff,* 347.

6. Griselda Pollock was one of the first to chart the ways in which the new city was segregated according to gender and class lines. See Pollock, "Modernity and the Spaces of Femininity," in *Vision and Difference,* 50–90. Janet Wolff's seminal essay "The Invisible Flâneuse" launched years of scholarly discussions on the absence of women from the nineteenth-century urban environment and its literature. Recent scholarship, however, has argued that there was fluidity between public and private in the second half of the nineteenth century. See, for example, Janet Wolff's reevaluation of the position of women in the nineteenth-century city in her "Gender and the Haunting of Cities," 68–85; Marcus, *Apartment Stories;* and Johnson, *Boundaries of Acceptability.* Lynda Nead and Jane Rendell write compellingly of the mobility between public and private spaces in nineteenth-century London. See Nead's *Victorian Babylon;* and Rendell's *The Pursuit of Pleasure.* Most recently, the studies in D'Souza and McDonough, eds., *The Invisible Flâneuse?*

Gender, Public Space, and Visual Culture in Nineteenth-Century Paris explore this more inclusive notion of women in the urban environment.

7. The fashion industry in general also promoted this neutralization of women's identities. The Bon Marché, Paris's first department store, which opened in 1852, pioneered the sale of ready-made clothing, the availability of which aided the transgression of class distinctions through dress that had, under the specialized shop and *couturière* system, been a more dependable visual measure of class. Additionally, the sewing machine was patented in 1851, which further accelerated the ability to produce clothing quickly.

8. *Le journal des demoiselles* 4 (April 1863): 124. "Au milieu de ces robes blanches, et de tous ces visages voilés, sa mère elle-même aurait de la peine à la reconnaître."

9. Of course, as many scholars have pointed out, there were also some hidden political purposes behind the renovations. For example, broad boulevards would prevent the building of barricades and enable the swift movement of troops through the city.

10. See Shapiro, "Paris," for an interesting analysis of another aspect of falsity in Haussmann's plan. In this essay, Shapiro argues that the government's attempts to house the working classes were merely, as she puts it, an effort to "normalize" and "placate" a group that was perceived as contagious and seditious.

11. Primarily the poor and working classes were shifted to other areas of the city and certain of its suburbs, such as Clichy and Montreuil. In his unfinished *The Arcades Project,* Walter Benjamin quotes a vivid description of the displacement of the working classes from A. Granveau's *L'ouvrier devant la société:* "Hundreds of thousands of families, who work in the center of the capital, sleep in the outskirts. This movement resembles the tide: in the morning the workers stream into Paris, and in the evening the same wave of people flows out. It is a melancholy image. . . . I would add . . . that it is the first time that humanity has assisted in a spectacle so dispiriting for the people." See Benjamin, *The Arcades Project,* 137.

12. McCabe, *Paris by Sunlight and Gaslight,* 714.

13. Zola, *The Ladies' Paradise,* 87.

14. Uzanne, *La femme et la mode,* 194. "Les nouvelles facilités de la vie produisirent presque aussitôt un abandon général de ce quant à soi qui était la ligne de démarcation de l'existence d'aristocratie sédentaire. Toutes les classes sociales se trouvèrent peu à peu mélangées."

15. Susan Hiner points out the significance of the quality of the cashmere shawl in helping to determine a woman's class during the 1820s and 1830s in Paris in her excellent essay "Lust for *Luxe.*"

16. Zola, *Nana,* 138.

17. "Modes de Paris," *Le journal des demoiselles* 1 (January 1857): 1. "La façon de porter et de mettre un chapeau ou une robe, à Paris, est encore aussi difficile à

saisir. On ne reconnaît un chapeau de Mmes Bricard et Callmann que sur une femme élégante; sur la tête d'une femme vulgaire, il est celui de tout le monde."

18. See Clayson, *Painted Love,* 56; and Corbin, *Women for Hire,* 85. Corbin writes that municipal by-laws prohibited *filles en cartes* (unregistered prostitutes) from circulating while wearing a hat, and Clayson cites police records that stipulated that hats on registered prostitutes had to be of a certain size. While official proscription did not necessarily match social reality, the existence of the rules indicates a widespread anxiety over confusing the proper woman for a prostitute.

19. *Filles en cartes* could be arrested for violating any of the regulations on their behavior and dress. However, because of the difficulty of distinguishing the *fille en carte* from the registered prostitute and even from the bourgeoise, public authorities were ineffectual in their efforts at enforcing these guidelines. Of course, a large segment of the prostitutional population, the unregistered or clandestine prostitutes, remained entirely outside these and other policies.

20. Blanc, *Art in Ornament and Dress,* 115.

21. In the exhibition catalog *Gustave Caillebotte,* 102, Julia Sagraves proposes that the central figures are not traveling together. Like many others, she argues that an unaccompanied woman in the city would have been understood to be a prostitute and that the well-dressed woman on this bridge would have been a high-class courtesan. While I disagree with this interpretation because it does not allow for the ambiguity that is actually built into the painting, it strengthens my point about the ways in which the veil was used to differentiate class. For if a courtesan wanted to hide her profession, she would borrow the veil, a sign of respectability.

22. Zola, *La bête humaine,* 25.

23. Certeau, *The Practice of Everyday Life,* 128.

24. For an overview of Haussmann's architectural changes, see Van Zanten, *Building Paris.*

25. Charles Blanc also understood this analogy between the veil and architectural elements when, in 1877, he wrote of lace: "Thus in this fairy-like architecture, in which the courses of stone are, as it were, linen or silk threads, the solid masonry is represented by the *toilé* and the *mat;* the apertures half by the *grillé,* and half by the openings called *jours.*" Blanc, *Art in Ornament and Dress,* 205.

26. See Callen, *The Spectacular Body,* 185, where she discusses the connection between levels of eye contact and propriety.

27. Though it is difficult to determine, the figure seated on the left side of the carriage in the distance may also be female. Nevertheless, the ambiguity of that blob of black paint calls increased attention to the foregrounded woman's position as the only clearly indicated female presence in the painting.

28. Kirk Varnedoe saw this smoke as serving a purely formal purpose in his essay on the painting. He wrote: "One pylon is totally occluded, rising just beyond the field of view on the right; while the strolling woman, her umbrella, and the

engine steam are all used to obscure the juncture of the road, bridge, and partially visible far pylon." Varnedoe, "Caillebotte's *Pont de l'Europe,*" 10.

29. Zola, *The Ladies' Paradise,* 193.

30. Ibid., 185–86.

31. See La Berge, *Mission and Method,* 3.

32. See Corbin, *Women for Hire,* 133.

33. Robert Nye discusses the link between urban health and morality in his *Crime, Madness, and Politics in Modern France,* 39.

34. See Sartory and Langlais, *Poussière et microbes de l'air,* 41.

35. A distinction was made at this time between public hygiene and private hygiene movements, though both were ultimately dedicated to the betterment of public health. The former was composed of the state's departments that were concerned with illnesses and contagious diseases that affected the public at large. Public hygiene also addressed issues such as street cleaning and the public food supply. Private hygiene complemented public hygiene but dealt with ways in which individuals could avoid contamination in their everyday lives. For more on the studies of public and private hygiene, see Bonnier, *Sciences naturelles et hygiène,* 1.

36. J. H., "L'hygiène et la mortalité à Paris," 636. "Il est incontestable que l'hygiène a fait d'immenses progrès dans ces vingt dernières années, tant au point de vue purement scientifique que sur le terrain des applications; en particulier, l'hygiène urbaine, qui s'est développée parallèlement à la science des microbes, a pris une importance considérable."

37. These same anxieties also led to the modernization of the underground sewer system in Paris in the 1830s.

38. Grandière, *Notions d'hygiène à l'usage des instituteurs et des élèves des écoles normales primaires,* 31–32. "Beaucoup d'affections épidémiques sont contagieuses, et cette contagion peut se faire par les courants d'air, les vents, les vêtements."

39. David S. Barnes, in *The Making of a Social Disease,* points out that, prior to Koch's work, explanations for the spread of tuberculosis were essentialist.

40. I thank Dr. Sherwin Nuland of the Yale University Medical School for pointing out to me the importance of the germ theory in instituting a change in medical models of tuberculosis in the 1880s. Whereas dust was known to be dangerous, a more accurate understanding of contagionism was not achieved until the proponents of the germ theory convinced its opponents and the public in general that it was not the dust per se but rather the contents of the dust that were hazardous.

41. Rochard, *Encyclopédie d'hygiène et de médecine publique,* 685. "Le microbe, agent de la contagion, existe surtout dans les poussières."

42. Bonnier, *Sciences naturelles et hygiène,* 19. "Les poussières de l'air sont surtout dangereuses parce qu'elles renferment des germes vivants, et en particulier des bactéries, qui peuvent transmettre certaines maladies telles que la tuberculose, la diphtérie, la grippe."

43. See note 24.

44. See Stallybrass and White, *The Politics and Poetics of Transgression,* 136: "From the balcony, one could gaze, but not be touched. . . . the bourgeoisie on their balconies could both participate in the banquet of the streets and yet remain separated." Although Stallybrass and White do not relate this practice to an avoidance of germs and disease, the implication is inherent in this statement. Also see Corbin, *Women for Hire,* 227, for a detailed description of the belief that airborne proletariat germs would "threaten the genetic patrimony" of the bourgeoisie.

45. See *Revue d'hygiène et de police sanitaire de médecine* 1 (January 15, 1879): 43–59, for a detailed discussion of sweeping methods.

46. See Nye, *Crime, Madness, and Politics in Modern France,* 39; Jack Ellis, in *The Physician-Legislators of France,* also addresses what he calls the "interplay between medicine and politics" (1). And La Berge, *Mission and Method,* 4, points out that the cholera epidemic of 1832 was a kind of watershed in the active correlation between epidemic disease and environmental and social conditions.

47. Maurice Barenne, *L'hygiène: Journal des familles* 1 (March 10, 1886): 2. "La femme est l'âme ardente de la famille. . . . elle est bienfaisante par instinct. . . . la santé et le bonheur des femmes, c'est la santé et le bonheur de tous les hommes."

48. In fact, the Société de médecine publique et d'hygiène professionnelle de Paris, established in 1877, played an important role not only in the journals of public hygiene and medicine but also in political and social journals.

49. Sartory and Langlais, *Poussière et microbes de l'air,* 9–10.

50. Beaugrand, *L'hygiène ou l'art de conserver la santé,* 123. "[L]e voile blanc ou de couleur . . . garantit le visage du froid pendant l'hiver . . . pendant l'été, préserve les yeux de la poussière et de la lumière trop vive des rayons solaires."

51. Cléophée, "Modes, fashions et causeries," in *Les modes parisiennes* (1854): 1742. "On trouve aussi chez Violard *[sic]* les plus belles dentelles de Chantilly et les plus admirables guipures noires qu'on puisse imaginer, puis les claires voilettes si necessaries pour garantir des brumes de l'autumne."

52. Cléophée, "Modes, fashions et causeries," *Les modes parisiennes* (1855): 1921. "Après les jours de pluie d'une temperature assez douce, la gelée est venue durcir la boue et étendre un glacis sur les rues de Paris; sur ce miroir de l'hiver est tombée une couche blanche de neige; Paris resemble à une ville de Russie: le visage des femmes se dérobe sous des voiles épais."

53. *Les modes parisiennes* (1854): 1802. "Les voilettes les plus aériennes et les plus diaphanes, qui se sont abaissées à l'issue de la séance sûr plus d'un joli visage pour les preserver de la brume du dehors, venaient aussi de la maison Violart." This author, like Cléophée, refers to the "*brume,*" or mist, which I would argue is probably a polite euphemism (this is, after all, a fashion journal) for pollution or dust rather than a reference to a function of the weather.

54. Blanc, *Art in Ornament and Dress,* 116.

55. *La mode illustrée, journal de la famille* 5 (February 2, 1863): 33. "Les voilettes rondes sont toujours à la mode, quoi-qu'elles soient absolument insuffisantes pour garantir le visage. Nous recommandons à nos lectrices le voile (dit loup) dont nous publions le dessin et le patron, il leur rendra des services incontestables, en toute saison."

56. Information regarding health and the spread of contagious disease was published in books, journals, and periodicals intended for a bourgeois audience with expendable incomes, thus maintaining the classed dispersal of crucial knowledge. Furthermore, most working-class women at this time were not literate.

57. Zola, *Nana,* 470.

58. Sartory and Langlais, *Poussière et microbes de l'air,* 103. "Dans les blanchisseries, les poussières sont nombreuses et l'on peut considérer comme dangereux le triage du linge sale qui répand dans les pièces où il s'effectue un nuage de poussières contenant une grande quantité de micro-organismes."

59. This negligence was still in force even as late as 1906. See Bernheim and Roblot, "Tuberculose et blanchisseries." Eunice Lipton also points out in *Looking into Degas,* 130–31, that some ironers actually prepared food, ate it, and slept in the very rooms in which they sorted and cleaned dirty laundry. Émile Zola provides a good fictional illustration of this tendency to eat in the place where laundry is done in *L'assommoir* of 1876 when he describes the women who worked in the facility where the main character, Gervaise, goes to do her family's laundry (which will later become her place of employment). "All round them the wash-house had gone quiet. It was striking eleven. Half the women were perched with one thigh on the edge of their tubs, an open litre of wine on the floor, and were eating sausage sandwiches." Zola, *L'assommoir,* 37.

60. J. B. Dancer quoted in Tyndall, "Poussières et maladies," 239. "Dans diverses professions ou occupations poussiéreuses . . . respirateurs auraient bien leur agrément et constitueraient une utile protection."

61. Those in professions such as construction and street cleaning were also recognized as being vulnerable to epidemic disease because of the amount of dust these types of work produced, yet the mortality rates from tuberculosis and cholera for laundresses remained double that of any other occupation.

62. See Callen's linking of the discourses of science and medicine to a modern form of art production: "The language of science and medicine provided the artist [Degas] with a new vocabulary of visual signs to modernize conventional pictorial codes and give art new representational powers—while simultaneously validating the authority of science" (*The Spectacular Body,* 3).

63. In fact, Degas's interest in science and medicine is well documented. For example, his sculptures and some of his portraits have been linked to physiognomic

studies that were popular during the late nineteenth century. Additionally, he was known to have read the popular science periodical *La nature.*

64. See La Berge, *Mission and Method,* 185.

65. Barnes, *The Making of a Social Disease,* 132.

66. Linda L. Clark points out that the primary school curriculum was expanded during the Second Empire to include not only history and geography but also science and hygiene. See Clark, *Schooling the Daughters of Marianne,* 16.

67. "De l'air . . . impuretés de l'air: Poussières, substances gazeuses, miasmes, virus contagieux, microbes, bactéries."

68. Monin, *La propreté de l'individu et de la maison,* 22. "Les vêtements que nous portons doivent être, tous les jours, soigneusement brossés et débarrassés de leurs souillures."

69. *La mode illustrée, journal de la famille* 14 (April 1, 1860): 106. "Ce voile, d'un genre nouveau, présente quelques avantages sous le rapport de la grâce et des bons offices qu'il rend en préservant complètement le visage du vent et de la poussière."

70. *Les modes parisiennes illustrées* 479 (March 20, 1852): 135. "[L]eurs bonnets plus garnis que jamais, leurs petits visages sont perdus dans un volume de dentelles et de petits rubans."

71. "Contre les voilettes," *La fronde,* n.d., Bibliothèque Marguerite Durand, DOS 391 MOD: Mode 1872–1911. "[V]ient de déclarer la guerre à la voilette. Il affirme qu'elle est funeste à la vue. . . . Les voilettes semées de pois sont, paraît-il les plus dangereuses."

72. Staffe, *Le cabinet de toilette,* 151. "Les voiles, et surtout les voiles à pois, sont très nuisibles à la vue."

73. In London, too, doctors understood the dangers of decorated veils for the women who wore them: "Oculists have often made great and justifiable objections to the use of spotted or figured net in veils," wrote Harry V. Barnett in 1882. He continued, "Advantage was taken of this fact to exhibit veils of wire ground net with an invention attached which should altogether supersede the ugly and unbecoming respirator. It consists of a piece of thin delicate wire gauze introduced into a deep hem at the bottom of the veil. Fastened over the face in the usual way, it comes just before the nose and mouth, and, whilst acting as a respirator, is quite unnoticeable in appearance." Harry V. Barnett, "Fitness and Fashion," *Magazine of Art* (London, Paris, New York) 5 (1882): 339.

74. *Journal des dames et des modes* (1834): 78. "La mode est aux demi-voiles. Les demi-voiles de tulle sont très bien portés avec des chapeaux de demi-toilelle."

75. My reading of vision is, of course, indebted to Michel Foucault's understanding that looking is always an act of power. See especially chapter 3, part 3, "Panopticism," in his *Discipline and Punish,* 195–228.

76. Callen, *The Spectacular Body,* 89.

77. Walter Benjamin's interpretation of Baudelaire's *flâneur* in his chapter "The Paris of the Second Empire in Baudelaire," in *Charles Baudelaire,* is somewhat different from mine in that he argues that the *flâneur*'s vision is actually veiled by the crowd in the city. Benjamin writes: "For the *flâneur* there is a veil over this picture [of the city]. This veil is the mass; it billows in the 'twisting folds of the old metropolises.' . . . Only when this veil tears and reveals to the *flâneur* 'one of the populous squares . . . does he, too, get an unobstructed view of the big city'" (60). Benjamin likens the crowd to a veil and claims that the *flâneur*'s view of Paris is obstructed by this "veil." While I would assert that the *flâneur*'s vision was not really veiled, at least in the ways in which I am arguing the respectable woman's vision was, Benjamin's claim that the *flâneur* experienced a mediated form of vision strengthens my argument nonetheless, since it assumes that a veil, whether real or metaphorical, thwarts vision.

78. Anne Higonnet links a doubling of women in fashion plates to modern marketing strategies. She writes, "What matters is not one person or one image but the infinitely reproducible spectacle of femininity." Higonnet, *Berthe Morisot's Images of Women,* 95.

79. Flaubert, *Madame Bovary,* 63.

2. Making Up the Surface

1. The theories of Gilles Deleuze and Félix Guattari regarding the importance of the face in producing subjectivity and meaning have influenced my reading of this part of the body. For them, the face is always a close-up, a surface marked by wrinkles and cavities, and a social politics. See Deleuze and Guattari, "Year Zero: Faciality," in *A Thousand Plateaus,* 167–91.

2. Solomon-Godeau, "The Legs of the Countess," 80.

3. Here I am assuming that the countess herself chose what to wear and how to look in these photographs, although Solomon-Godeau rightly points out that even if the countess had made those decisions, the social circumstances and expectations of late nineteenth-century France would have conditioned her choices, making them far from objective preferences.

4. Raymond, "Hygiène du visage," 111. "[L]eur principal ennemi, c'est la poussière, qui durcit la peau, qui s'y incruste et s'y installe, de façon à ne pouvoir plus être expulsée si l'on tarde à la combattre. Il faut donc porter constamment un voile quand on sort, se laver le visage fréquemment, soigneusement, et n'y pas manquer le soir avant de se coucher."

5. Michelet, *L'amour,* in *Oeuvres complètes de Michelet,* 194. "Une sévérité cruelle qu'on a pour les femmes, c'est de les juger précisément sur ce qui se fane le plus, le visage."

6. Ibid., 194. "Il n'est pas rare . . . que le corps ait vingt-cinq ans et le visage quarante."

7. *L'express des modes* 32 (January 1, 1867) : 3. "Les dentelles venant trop sur le devant du visage vieillessent. Pour que la dentelle produise tout son charmant effet, et le vaporeux qui est son principal élément, elle doit être disposée de manière à laisser jouer la lumière entre le visage et ses délicats réseaux."

8. Staffe, *Le cabinet de toilette,* 99. "La femme vieillie et fatiguée se trouvera à merveille de couvrir ses cheveux (fussent-ils encore beaux) d'une mantille de dentelle, qui voilera un peu les atteintes de l'âge . . . et encadrera gracieusement celui-ci. Une vieille femme est affreuse tête nue. L'ombre légère de la dentelle dissimule beaucoup les ravages du temps."

9. *Les modes parisiennes* (1854): 1334–35. "Sur un frais visage, ce rouge est comme le duvet qui recouvre un beau fruit. Sur une peau blanche, le blanc de Guerlain s'étend et se confond comme du lait sur de l'albâtre."

10. Rétif de la Bretonne and Vandermode (a pseudonym perhaps), quoted in M. L. J. Larcher, *La femme jugée par les grands écrivains des deux sexes,* and later quoted in "Librairie de Garnier Frères," *Les modes parisiennes* (1854): 1372. "La vraie beauté consiste dans une taille moyenne et bien proportionnée, dans des traits réguliers, nobles et délicats, et dans une belle peau. 'C'est une toile qu'a formée la nature,' dit Vandermonde, 'pour y fondre toutes les variétés du plus beau coloris: tantôt elle y fait éclore les lis et les roses; tantôt on n'y voit que le sombre violette, ou le fruit noir du myrte.'"

11. *Les modes parisiennes* (1854): 1334. "Pour le visage, c'est le lait de fleurs de sureau, la crème de limaçon, l'extrait de benjoin; c'est dans une armoire reserve, les rouges et fards merveilleux: le carmine de Chine, le rouge de la Reine, le rouge de Damas, les extraits de roses pour les lèvres; c'est le blanc de perles, la poudre de lis. Le teint se metamorphose sous ces merveilleuses compositions, la peau fine et satinée exhale une senteur suave."

12. *Dictionnaire des gens,* as quoted in "Maquillage," n.d., DOS 391 BEA, Beauté—articles généraux 1890–présent, Bibliothèque Marguerite Durand. "Le fard est une composition qui a la proprieté de rendre les vieilles femmes un peu plus laides, et les jeunes un peu moins jolies." The French word *fard* does not have an English equivalent. It often suggests not simply makeup but heavy, thick cosmetics, though *fard* is used also to describe powders.

13. Gastou, *Hygiène du visage,* 45. "Les fards abîment très rapidement la peau et la vieillissent, d'où l'obligation de les maintenir appliqués le moins longtemps possible, d'en combattre les mauvais effets dès l'enlèvement par des applications calmantes et adoucissantes (lotions et crèmes)."

14. See Peiss, *Hope in a Jar,* 9–36, for a parallel discussion of the toxic chemicals used in the production of much makeup during the second half of the nineteenth and early part of the twentieth centuries in the United States.

15. Raymond, "Hygiène du visage," 111. "[L]e fard est un poison! . . . Le fard, qui contient de l'arsenic, quelle que soit sa base, antimoine ou blanc de bismuth, agit dans un espace de temps bien court sur l'estomac, dont il trouble les fonctions: des vomissements se produisent, l'haleine devient fétide, les dents se pourrissent."

16. *Les modes parisiennes* (1854): 1323. "Le fard est une poussière fine composé de carbonate de plomb et de chaux, douce et onctueuse au toucher et adhérent facilement à la peau; mais le plomb, absorbé par cette dernière, peut avoir une action délétère."

17. See Lassablière, *Annuaire et guide pratique d'hygiène par un comité d'hygiénistes,* 147, which warned as late as 1911 that makeup manufacturers must start using nontoxic substances and that the use of mercury, iron, zinc, barium, and bismuth in the production of makeup had to end.

18. Vaucaire, *La femme,* 43. "La première et la plus impérieuse est l'abstention de tout maquillage. La surface cutanée doit normalement fonctionner, et la présence de substances étrangères ne pourrait qu'empêcher l'absorption, la sécrétion ou l'excrétion de se produire."

19. Ibid., 52. "Il vaut mieux recouvrir le visage d'une poudre inerte que de le laisser se recouvrir de poussière."

20. "Maquillage" n.d., DOS 391 BEA, Beauté—articles généraux 1890–présent, Bibliothèque Marguerite Durand. "L'actrice doit exagérer ses effets à cause de la distance et des lumières, et la coquette l'imite sottement pour songer qu'au lieu d'attirer les hommes, elle les force à se reculer . . . pour juger de l'effet."

21. See Holden, *The Pearl from Plymouth,* 68, for a more detailed description of Pearl's toilette.

22. Cora Pearl, quoted in Godfrey, "Baudelaire, Gautier, and *une toilette savamment composée,*" 82.

23. Zola, *Nana,* 154–57.

24. Clayson, *Painted Love,* 108.

25. For a discussion of Degas and physiognomy, see Callen, *The Spectacular Body,* 1–31.

26. Raymond, "Hygiène du visage," 111. "En les voyant promener leurs visages peints en blanc et en rouge, leurs sourcils teints, leurs yeux entourés d'un cercle noir, comme ceux des petits chiens King's-Charles, on est saisi de pitié pour le ridicule qu'elles se donnent et pour les maux qu'elles se préparent: ces visages artificiels, ces masques ambulants, indignent en même temps qu'ils font rire; il est impossible de respecter une femme fardée: le mensonge permanent de sa figure semble impliquer d'autres mensonges plus sérieux."

27. See, for example, Adler, *Manet,* 200. Carol Armstrong's essay "Facturing Femininity" also addresses this painting. She reads, as do I, the facture as maquillage. However, we disagree about the woman's status. While acknowledging that the woman is alone at a café and that she is drinking beer, Armstrong claims that

the sitter is probably not available and is instead more likely a *femme honnête.* Armstrong analyzes *Woman Reading* in relation to Manet's *The Plum,* a painting that more overtly classes its subject through pose, facial expression, context, and dress, and she is thus able to find the sitter in *Woman Reading* to be of somewhat respectable standing. Given the significance that makeup held at the time, the excessive presence of it across the woman's face in *Woman Reading* seems to me to be a more compelling factor in the assessment of her status.

28. See Sidlauskas, "Painting Skin," for an excellent discussion of a kind of conflation of skin and makeup in Sargent's painting. In her analysis, Sidlauskas argues that the surface of Mme X's lavender-tinted skin itself betrays the model's "highly aestheticized self-fashioning" (11) at the same time that its formal complexity vexed the artist: "Gautreau's body painting foiled Sargent's painting of her body" (17).

29. For interesting analyses and reproductions of contemporary posters used to advertise cosmetics and perfumes, see the exhibition catalog *Grain de beauté.*

30. The fact that the woman is looking at an illustrated periodical, not at an all-text one, suggests that Manet is deliberately not allowing us to know whether she is literate, which heightens again the possibility that she is not of the bourgeoisie.

31. In her essay on Boucher's *Jeanne-Antoinette Poisson, Marquise de Pompadour,* Melissa Hyde locates the beginnings of this discussion of the correspondence between makeup and painting in Roger de Piles's 1708 treatise *Cours de peinture par principes.* See Hyde, "The 'Make-up' of the Marquise," 455.

32. Deleuze and Guattari, "Year Zero: Faciality," in *A Thousand Plateaus,* 190.

33. I diverge from Deleuze and Guattari's claim that the face collapses into a sameness, a universal, a metaphor for a white wall–black hole system (the wall is significance and the black hole is subjectivity) that has meaning only in relation to itself. There is nothing universal about Meurent's face—or any other face, for that matter.

34. Stewart, *On Longing,* 127.

35. Clay, "Ointments, Makeup, Pollen," 41.

36. Baudelaire, "In Praise of Cosmetics," in *The Painter of Modern Life and Other Essays,* 33.

37. Ibid., 33–34.

38. Solomon-Godeau, "The Legs of the Countess," 74.

39. Roland Barthes would later build on this notion of the tangibility of cosmetics in his quite subtle and evocative reading of Greta Garbo's face in *Queen Christina:* "[T]he make-up has the snowy thickness of a mask: it is not a painted face, but one set in plaster, protected by the surface of the colour, not by its lineaments. Amid all this snow at once fragile and compact, the eyes alone, black like strange soft flesh . . . are two faintly tremulous wounds. In spite of its extreme beauty, this face, not drawn but sculpted in something smooth and friable, that

is, at once perfect and ephemeral, comes to resemble the flour-white complexion of Charlie Chaplin." Barthes, "The Face of Garbo," in *Mythologies,* 56.

40. Baudelaire, "In Praise of Cosmetics," 33.

41. One could also argue that a woman in late nineteenth-century Paris could never have had complete autonomy over her appearance, since social and cultural cues would have influenced her. See Solomon-Godeau, "The Legs of the Countess," for a paradigmatic analysis of the ways in which female subjectivity is defined vis-à-vis cultural markers.

42. This concept of woman being able to seduce men only from a critical distance is not new to the nineteenth century. A contemporary use of this idea is Jacques Derrida's critical reading of Nietzsche's claim, in *Beyond Good and Evil,* that woman must be seen from a distance, from behind a veil, in order to be desirable. For Nietzsche, when a woman is seen from up close, her flaws are immediately evident, and she is thus unable to be viewed as pleasurable. See Derrida, *Spurs,* 49.

43. Baudelaire, "Woman," in *The Painter of Modern Life and Other Essays,* 30.

44. Within this context, Manet's representations of Berthe Morisot (see chapter 3), especially the later paintings, are particularly overdetermined. By building up her face, by encasing her in veils, fabrics, and furs, he is, in a sense, borrowing a language of unrespectability and forcing a comparison between Morisot and the improper woman.

45. "Roses et épines," *L'express des modes* 17 (August 7, 1866): 4. "L'apparance des femmes est aussi trompeuse que le reflet des objets sur la surface de l'eau."

46. For an analysis of women's desire vis-à-vis nineteenth-century fashion plates through the lens of queer theory, see Marcus, "Reflections on Victorian Fashion Plates."

47. Warwick and Cavallaro, *Fashioning the Frame,* 50.

48. *Le miroir parisien, journal des dames et des demoiselles* (July 1861): 134. "Autour de ce chapeau se pose une demi-voilette en dentelle noire, qui, formant une ombre légère sur les yeux, leur donne une douceur indescriptible et un charme de plus."

49. Uzanne, *L'art et les artifices de la beauté,* 181.

50. As Peter Brooks points out in "Storied Bodies, or Nana at Last Unveil'd," in *Body Work,* 160: "[T]here appears to be a recognition that hidden within absence is that which really makes the difference. That which is hidden is the source of narratives." Since the veil's presence renders something hidden and visually absent, it essentially catalyzes the construction of a narrative of mystery.

51. See also Georg Simmel, who acknowledges this dialectic when he writes that the veiled woman awakens "delight and desire by means of a unique antithesis and synthesis; through the alternation or simultaneity of accommodation and denial, by a symbolic allusive assent and dissent . . . through placing having and

not having in a state of polar tension even as she seems to make them felt concurrently. . . . The man feels the proximity and interpenetration of the ability and inability to acquire something." Simmel, *Georg Simmel,* 134.

52. Flaubert, *La première éducation sentimentale,* 18. "Il allait au bois de Boulogne, il regardait les jolis chevaux et les beaux messieurs, les carrosses vernis et les chausseurs panaches, et les grandes dames à figure pale, dont le voile remué par le vent et s'échappant de la portière lui passait sous le nez, avec le bruit des gourmettes d'argent."

53. See Baudrillard, *Seduction,* 34.

54. Baudrillard, *The Ecstasy of Communication,* 73–74.

55. Barthes, *The Pleasure of the Text,* 9–10.

56. Barthes, *The Fashion System,* 137.

57. Bouchot, *Les élégances du Second Empire,* 161–62. "Après l'exposition de 1855 une femme de qualité est . . . la plus mystérieuse et la plus indéchiffrable personne qui se puisse; tout au plus un bout de frimousse s'aperçoit-il dans l'amas des falbalas, parmi les ruches, les rubans ou les voilettes."

58. *Le moniteur de la mode* 373 (September 1853): 182. "Rien n'est plus joli qu'un capuchon en dentelle qui vient gracieusement encadrer le visage et le préserver en même temps du froid."

59. Zola, *The Ladies' Paradise,* 74–75.

60. See Lacan, *The Four Fundamental Concepts of Psychoanalysis,* 103 and 111–12. Lacan recounts the story of Parrhasios, who paints a veil on a wall, thus encouraging his friend Zeuxis, who is fooled by the "veil so lifelike," to ask what was behind the veil.

61. Doane, *Femmes Fatales,* 46.

3. Unmasking Manet's Morisot, or Veiling Subjectivity

1. The prints were multiply reproduced, so many more than eleven extant images of Morisot by Manet are in circulation.

2. Higonnet, *Berthe Morisot,* 56.

3. Meurent's name also appears in the 1862 studio register of Manet's teacher, Thomas Couture. See Goedorp, "*L'Olympia* n'etait pas une Montmartoise."

4. The Manet literature has concentrated almost exclusively on the pictures of Meurent, while little, and certainly less controversial, analysis has been produced about his paintings of Morisot. I would contend that the pictures of Meurent have inspired and sustained critical inquiry more than the Morisot paintings because of the clarity of Meurent's position as a paid model and the interpretive carte blanche that role has given critics. In other words, Meurent's virtue was already called into question by her job and by the guises she assumed in Manet's paintings, whereas Morisot's standing was less likely to be attacked or even attended

to, since her social status was far less obviously intriguing. Of course, the public consumption intended for all but perhaps one of the Meurent paintings in contrast with the selection of Morisot pictures displayed at the Salon may also have something to do with the vast body of critical writing about the representations of Meurent.

5. Lipton, *Alias Olympia,* 57. See also Farwell, *Manet and the Nude,* 158–63, who argues that Meurent posed for semipornographic photographs in the 1850s.

6. Male family members, however, modeled for both Berthe Morisot and Mary Cassatt. For example, Morisot's husband frequently sat for her, often with their daughter, Julie. And Cassatt's nephews and brother occasionally posed for her.

7. Morisot, *Berthe Morisot,* 131.

8. The information on the source of *The Balcony* can be found in the Registre Leenhoff, Bibliothèque nationale, Cabinet des estampes Y64549/8, 10. Like Manet's dialogue with Titian's *Venus of Urbino* in *Olympia,* his engagement with Goya's *Majas on a Balcony* in *The Balcony* is a result of both an attraction and a resistance to certain art historical traditions. Equally, Manet's fascination with things Spanish, his incorporation and manipulation of the visual language of another culture, gives him some freedoms at the same time that it limits him.

9. Léon Leenhoff was probably referring to the study for *The Balcony* when he wrote, "Esquisse du *Balcon.* Première idée du tableaux = C'est Mlle Claus a qui est au première plan. Mlle Berthe Morizot [*sic*] est au second plan tenant une ombrelle—projet arrête." Registre Leenhoff, Bibliothèque nationale, Cabinet des estampes Yb34549/8, 73.

10. Jules Castagnary, quoted in the exhibition catalog *Manet: 1832–1883,* 307.

11. The mystery of Léon's paternity remains. Art historians have speculated about the various possibilities—that he was Manet's son or that he was the son of Auguste Manet, Edouard's father, but raised by Edouard as his own, to keep up appearances. Most recently, Nancy Locke has suggested the latter on the basis of both circumstantial information and legal evidence. See Locke, "Manet père et fils," in *Manet and the Family Romance,* 114–46.

12. See, for example, Morisot's *Young Woman at a Window,* of 1869, in which her sister, Edma, wears a similar white dressing gown.

13. Morisot, *Berthe Morisot,* 36.

14. *Uncanny* comes from the German *Unheimlich,* which roughly translates into English as "unhomely." For Freud, since the idea of the uncanny contains some sense of the home, this misrecognition through recognition, or this detour in signification, becomes a crisis and a perversion of the sense of self. See Freud, "The Uncanny."

15. One could also interpret Manet's inclusion of veils, fans, ribbons, and furs as the mobilization of fetish objects. Freud associated all of these items of clothing with fetishism when he theorized the concept in 1921 in "Fetishism." According

to Freud, certain objects and body parts are invested with fetish value in order to cover over the threat of castration. He wrote: ". . . it is as though the last impression before the uncanny and traumatic one is retained as a fetish. Thus the foot or shoe owes its preference as a fetish . . . to the circumstances that the inquisitive boy peered at the woman's genitals from below, from her legs up. . . . fur and velvet . . . pieces of underclothing, which are so often chosen as a fetish, crystallize the moment of undressing, the last moment in which the woman could still be regarded as phallic" (155). For Freud, the employment of a fetish protects the male subject from perceiving his own lack, for the fetish object becomes a surrogate for the absence of the phallus. Simply put, fetishism displaces the threat of castration by substitution, making less fearful the object of desire. While my reading of Manet's portraits of Morisot is certainly indebted to Freud's understanding of the fetish, the concept does not work unqualifiedly in relation to these images, for Manet's use of certain objects does not fit neatly into Freud's paradigm. While they do obscure and call attention to something, these veils, fans, and furs never replace Morisot, or her threat to Manet, fully.

16. See, for example, Hamilton's *Manet and His Critics,* where Hamilton recapitulates critics' reactions to many of Manet's most scandalous works. Among the varied responses Hamilton cites in relation to *Olympia,* for example, is Félix Jahyer's: "Such indecency! . . . I cannot take this painter's intentions seriously. Up to now he has made himself the apostle of the ugly and repulsive" (71). And Ernest Fillonneau, writing in *Le moniteur des arts,* remarked: "An epidemic of crazy laughter prevails . . . in front of the canvases by Manet. . . . [It is] a subject of general surprise that the jury selected these works" (71). Ernest Chesneau offers yet another perspective on the derisiveness of contemporary Manet criticism: "I must say that the grotesque aspect of his contributions has two causes: first, an almost childish ignorance of the fundamentals of drawing, and then, a prejudice in favor of inconceivable vulgarity" (72).

17. Morisot, *Berthe Morisot,* 40.

18. Ibid., 40.

19. Ibid., 46.

20. Ibid., 48.

21. See Mathews, ed., *Cassatt and Her Circle,* 53, where Mathews reproduces a letter written by Eliza Haldeman, a close friend and colleague of Mary Cassatt's. The letter, dated May 8, 1868, recounts Haldeman's disappointment at the unfortunate location of her painting at the Salon. She attributes this to the retouching of her painting by her teacher, Paul Soyer.

22. Morisot, *Berthe Morisot,* 49.

23. Armstrong, in "Facturing Femininity," discusses formal similarities and borrowings between Morisot's and Manet's toilette pictures of the 1880s.

24. Manet's representations of Morisot posing idly contradict the obvious

respect he had for her as an artist and for her opinion regarding his painting. Indicating that there was, indeed, a close professional dialogue between the two, Manet wrote to Morisot: "Mademoiselle Berthe, I shall ask you to postpone until a later time the visit you promised to make to the studio on Thursday. I have not made enough progress to risk your keen judgment. I am determined not to expose myself to you except to my advantage." Quoted in Brombert, *Edouard Manet,* 320.

25. In each of Manet's two depictions of Gonzalès, she either sits or stands in front of her easel and is at work on a painting. For an insightful reading of *Portrait of Mlle E. G.* and the ways in which Manet inscribes his presence through certain objects, see Garb, "Framing Femininity in Manet's Mlle E. G."

26. Quoted in the exhibition catalog *Manet: 1832–1883,* 315.

27. When Théodore Duret sold the painting at auction in 1894, Morisot herself bought it. *Exposition Edouard Manet,* 110.

28. Quoted in *Manet: 1832–1883,* 334–35.

29. Manet chose to defy both pictorial and bourgeois conventions here, in this more easily distributable form of visual representation. Since prints could circulate more easily than paintings, Manet was, in effect, making more public his complicated feelings toward Morisot.

30. Quoted in Mondor, *La vie de Mallarmé,* 393. "Berthe Morisot . . . le peintre et le poète aiment beaucoup l'intelligence impérieuse, [une] certaine sauvagerie distinguée, le désordre nerveux de sa chevelure brune."

31. Scarry, "Imagining Flowers," 93.

32. Morisot, *Berthe Morisot,* 43.

33. Ibid., 44.

34. Ibid., 45.

35. Speaking for a culture's understanding of the position of the veil in Spain, Manet's contemporary Charles Blanc wrote: "For a Spaniard, all the intrigues of love, all the *manoeuvres* of flirtation, are hidden in the fold of her fan." See Blanc, *Art in Ornament and Dress,* 195.

36. Ibid., 194–95.

37. Manet may also have known that in seventeenth-century England, a closed fan signified that a woman was not available for sex.

38. This painting should be compared with *Berthe Morisot with a Pink Shoe,* which has been dated to 1868 but which is probably contemporaneous with *Berthe Morisot with a Fan,* of 1872. In each, Morisot wears what seems to be the same dress and shoes. Both pictures reference Spanish painting, particularly that of Goya. For a discussion of the influence of Goya on *Berthe Morisot with a Pink Shoe,* see the exhibition catalog *Exposition Edouard Manet,* 100.

39. By choosing to marry Eugène Manet, Morisot enabled herself to maintain a close association with Edouard. As in-laws, they could preserve their easy professional and personal exchange. See Brombert, *Edouard Manet,* 265. Edouard may

have actually set up the romance between Berthe and his brother Eugène so that the two painters could remain close (320).

40. See the exhibition catalog *Berthe Morisot: Impressionist,* 16, on the possibility that a number of the destroyed paintings may have been self-portraits.

41. Morisot, *Berthe Morisot,* 33.

42. Ibid., 75.

43. For an insightful analysis of contemporary critics' responses to Morisot's technique, which they saw as "unfinished," see Garb's "Berthe Morisot and the Feminizing of Impressionism," 57–66.

44. Paul de Man writes in relation to the autobiographical project, which could be considered a kind of textual self-portrait: "The interest of autobiography, then, is not that it reveals reliable self-knowledge—it does not—but that it demonstrates in a striking way the impossibility of closure and of totalization (that is the impossibility of coming into being) of all textual systems made up of tropological substitutions." One could say that this impossibility that de Man identifies as being inherent to the construction of an autobiography may be expressed in visual terms by the inclusion of blank canvas. In other words, the blank spaces become the tropological substitutions standing for the impossibility of closure and of totalization. de Man, "Autobiography as Defacement," 71.

45. Anne Higonnet has pointed out that Morisot is wearing the same clothing and hairstyle here as in *Self-Portrait with Julie.* She is right to argue that "[t]his could be the archetypal artist's self-portrait, were it not so closely paired to Morisot's maternal self-image." Higonnet, *Berthe Morisot's Images of Women,* 206. One could likewise read *Self-Portrait with Julie* in the more professional terms of *Self-Portrait with Palette,* given their similarities.

46. Even though Morisot's self-portraits, unlike some of Manet's paintings of her, were private images and not necessarily meant for public consumption, her possible intent for them does not undermine my point that her images were in some ways a response, however personal, to Manet's depictions of her.

4. The Other Side of the Veil

1. In this chapter I use a language of oppositions, because the colony was constructed binarily in relation to France in the nineteenth century. My main goal here is to articulate the contemporary French representation of the colony, though I have deliberately chosen to report critically on those representations. For excellent treatments of cross-cultural exchange in some Orientalist visual culture, see Beaulieu and Roberts, eds., *Orientalism's Interlocutors.* The essays in this anthology assert Orientalism not as a monolithic but rather as a heterogeneous and reciprocal construct.

2. Jourdain, "Les tisseuses kabyles," 134. "Rien ne peut donner une impression

plus saisissante de moeurs arabes que cet intérieur kabyle, reproduit par notre gravure."

3. The compositional similarities between this drawing and Albrecht Dürer's famous *Draughtsman Drawing a Nude,* of 1538, are perhaps not entirely coincidental, since both assert, in their own ways, cultural and temporal difference. In each, a grid separates two distinct parts of the picture, setting up multiple oppositions. In Dürer's woodcut, a gridded glass pane allows an artist to render the female nude on the other side in what Svetlana Alpers has called "the Italian manner," or using Alberti's theories of perspective. The illustration for the Algerian display does not contest the Western tradition, in which the left side of the picture tends to be associated with the passive and the right side with the active. For a discussion of the ways in which art history has been not only gender biased but geographically biased as well, see Alpers, "Art History and Its Exclusions."

4. This restriction of levels of vision could be related to the ways in which the Muslim veil, which typically covers the body but leaves the eyes bare, limits how much of the colonial woman's body is visible to the outside.

5. Alloula, in *The Colonial Harem,* 17, reproduces a number of late nineteenth- and early twentieth-century postcards of paid models, mainly women of non-European origin, seen from behind or in front of bars. Alloula writes, articulating the idea that the bars help to position the women as "authentic," unobtainable, and desirable members of the harem: "[T]he model will manage, thanks to the art of illusion that is photography, to impersonate, to the point of believability, the unapproachable referent: the *other* Algerian woman. . . . The perfection and the credibility of the illusion are ensured by the fact that the absent other is, by definition, unavailable and cannot issue a challenge."

6. In *Women of Algiers in Their Apartment,* Assia Djebar, though writing at the end of the twentieth century, speaks to issues of relevance to the late nineteenth century as well. She claims that the potential ramification for a woman rejecting the veil is permanent banishment to the barred harem space. She writes: "I have known young women who, when they reached adolescence, refused the principle of having to be veiled when circulating [in public]. The result was that they had to remain cloistered behind windows and bars, and so see the exterior world from afar" (154).

7. Jourdain, "Les tisseuses kabyles," 134. "[D]es femmes accroupies sur les talons travaillent à tisser de la toile sur un métier primitif. Ces fellahs exécutent leur besogne avec régularité et sans lever les yeux sur les visages curieux de la foule qui les entoure."

8. In most analyses of the discourse of Orientalism, the Orient (and I am here including Algeria in this category) has been positioned as feminine in relation to a masculine Europe.

9. On the ways in which the department store liberated female viewing practices, see for example, Bowlby, *Just Looking;* Friedberg, *Window Shopping;* Leach,

Land of Desire; Tiersten, *Marianne in the Market;* and, most recently, Wolff, "Gender and the Haunting of Cities," where she compellingly argues that the masculine was not as central to the notion of an emerging modernity as most studies of the *flâneur* have purported and that it is through this redefinition that we may begin to see how women figured into life in the urban environment.

10. There is no one term to describe the variety of head and body coverings found in Islamic regions and countries, many of which practice related though unique forms of Islam. The general word *hijab,* often misused in the American popular press today, translates from Arabic as "modest dress," which is what all of these garments are. Some cover only the head, while others obscure the head, face, and body. For example, the *chador* in Iran is not the same as the burka worn in various Bedouin cultures. Since the word *veil* was used by late nineteenth-century French people to denote the many variations they saw of the Muslim veil, mainly in paintings and photographs, I too will use the term *veil* as an umbrella concept in this chapter.

11. Michael A. Osborne points out in his study of the intersections between medical, technological, and scientific advancements and colonialism that public enthusiasm for imperialistic practices tended to be somewhat diffuse in France by the second half of the nineteenth century. Osborne, *Nature, the Exotic, and the Science of French Colonialism,* xii.

12. As quoted in Walther, *Women in Islam,* 69.

13. Men too had recourse to the *hijab.* The most powerful man in a Muslim community, for example, could wear the veil to protect himself from the gaze of his followers.

14. Mernissi, *Women and Islam,* 93.

15. Timothy Mitchell, in *Colonising Egypt,* discusses some of the means by which Europe learned about the Orient. He includes in his list the universal exhibitions, museums, Oriental congresses, theater, the zoo, schools, department stores, and street architecture. He writes: "Everything seemed to be set up before the observer as a picture or exhibition of something, representing some reality beyond" (xiv). While I would include those institutions that Mitchell regards as having been important to the formation of knowledge of the East, I would also add novels, periodicals, travel writing, photography, and other popular imagery, not to mention Orientalist painting and everyday French fashion, to his litany.

16. Derek Gregory describes the French occupation of Egypt from 1798 to 1801 as "a decisive moment in the formation of a distinctly modern Orientalism." Gregory, "Emperors of the Gaze." Other significant early examples of French interest in the East include the 1704 translation of *A Thousand and One Nights* and its subsequent popularity in France during the nineteenth century and the publication of Lady Mary Wortley Montagu's letters in 1717. Ali Behdad claims that the first descriptions of the harem came to France through travelogues such as Tavernier's

La nouvelle relation de l'intérieur du serail du Grand Seigneur (1675) and Chardin's *Voyage en Perse* (1686). See also Behdad, "The Eroticized Orient," 110–11.

17. The French government commissioned du Camp to publish *Égypte, Nubie, Palestine et Syrie* in 1852, a collection of calotypes taken during his travels. According to Louis Vaczek and Gail Buckland, this was the first travel book illustrated with photographs. Vaczek and Buckland, *Travelers in Ancient Lands,* 35. For a detailed description of du Camp's photographs of Egypt and his working process, see Gregory, "Emperors of the Gaze," 200–204.

18. Lane quoted in Kabbani, *Europe's Myths of Orient,* 67.

19. Lane, *An Account of the Manners and Customs of the Modern Egyptians,* 54–55.

20. For example, while in the East, Lady Mary Wortley Montagu and Isabel Burton kept diaries and wrote letters that were subsequently published. For analyses of the writing of some women travelers to the East, see Mehlman, *Women's Orients;* and Micklewright, *A Victorian Traveler in the Middle East.*

21. Vallory, *À l'aventure en Algérie,* 28. "Elle ne sort pas seule, sans doute; elle n'a pas la permission de lever son voile dans les rues, de montrer son visage à un étranger."

22. I am, of course, making the argument that the popularity of the veil in France is integrally related to its importance in Muslim cultures. Thus, the fascination with writing about the veil in French colonies is a symptom of that importance, but it is also the embrace of an object in another culture that is similar to, and therefore familiar as, an object in one's own culture.

23. Charles-Lucien Huard, in *Livre d'or de l'exposition: 1889,* called the exhibition of 1889 "une encyclopédie vivant, illustrée par les objets même" (1). And, Ernest Dréolle wrote that "les galeries du Maroc, de la Tunisie, et de l'Égypte nous les montrent très-fidelement dans leurs costumes essentiellement orginaux." Dréolle, "Costumes orientaux," 215. Regarding la rue du Caire, one writer even went so far as to say, "On ne peut visiter la section égyptienne sans se croire transporté dans quelque coin perdue de l'Orient, loin de notre civilisation industrielle, et s'est un bien étrange contraste que cette restitution du vieux Caire à l'ombre de la Tour Eiffel." "Une rue au Caire," *L'Exposition de Paris de 1889* 10 (May 4, 1889): 74. Sylviane Leprun, in her excellent investigation of colonial displays at the universal exhibitions, notes the ways in which the pavilions gave the effect of a scientific or ethnographic view of the colonies by appealing to the viewers' senses. Leprun, *Le théâtre des colonies,* 14.

24. Dréolle, "Costumes orientaux," 214–15. "[L]'Orient pour nous—ce n'est pas l'Orient des astronomes ou des géographes—c'est le pays où l'on dort, où l'on rêve. . . . c'est l'Eden où les femmes, blondes aux yeux noirs ou bruns aux yeux bleus, aux chairs blanches et roses, aux sourires criblés de perles, vivent sans vivre, plongeés dans des nuages de parfums, enveloppées de tissus transparents. . . . les

galeries du Maroc, de la Tunisie et de l'Égypte nous les montrent très-fidèlement dans leurs costumes essentiellement originaux. . . . Une femme passe en long manteau brun, le visage entièrement couvert; c'est la petite bourgeoise de l'Orient; ses vêtements sont plus que modestes, et il faut beaucoup deviner pour découvrir à travers ses grands plis droits un corps souple, une taille élégante."

25. Feydeau, *Alger,* 65. "[L]a peau fine de son visage, cette peau que le soleil n'a jamais mordue de ses rayons, se rose aux pommettes de ses joues, et tire un éclat merveilleux d'une mouche posée à la tempe ou au menton. Enfin, elle a les lèvres rouges, les dents très-blanches, les yeux noirs ombragés de lourdes paupières, les sourcils peints; quelque chose de craintif et de résigné dans toute la physionomie qui ressemble à l'expression d'une bête fauve prise au piège. Mais cette expression s'atténue quand elle marche dans sa chambre."

26. Ibid., 111–13. "[E]lle le complète de façon à déguiser toute sa personne sous des voiles flottants. Un mouchoir de batiste brodée, plié en double est appliqué sur son visage, juste au-dessous de ses yeux, et les deux bouts en sont attachés au sommet de sa tête . . . ses grands yeux, semblables à des diamants noirs et brillants qui palpitent doucement dans leur enveloppe de cils. . . . Rentrée chez elle, elle se débarasse immédiatement de ses habits de rue, enlève son masque, essuie son visage covert de sueur, sa rajuste."

27. For the purposes of this study, I am here focusing exclusively on *cartes-de-visite,* studio cards, and studio photographs that depict veiled women from Algeria and Turkey. This subject matter represents a large percentage of the "Orientalized" photographic output of the time, though there were other popular themes, such as street scenes, men, architecture, and so forth.

28. See also Çelik's *Displaying the Orient,* in which she systematically analyzes not only the architecture used to represent the East at the European universal exhibitions but also the Muslim visitors and the people displayed at the fairs.

29. Edward Said, who was one of the first to formulate an explanation for Orientalism in relation to the Islamic Middle East, in his book *Orientalism,* has more recently been critiqued for not privileging gender as one of the main components in the structure of Orientalism.

30. Çelik and Kinney, "Ethnography and Exhibitionism at the *Expositions Universelles,*" 41.

31. Contemporary writers provide countless and detailed descriptions of the *danse du ventre.* Théophile Gautier, for example, commented on it as a source of extreme fascination for the French traveler in Algeria. He wrote, paying special attention to the movement of the dancer's body: "La danse moresque consiste en ondulations perpétuelles du corps, en torsions des reins, en balancements des hanches, en mouvements de bras agitant des mouchoirs . . . pendant ce temps, la physionomie pâmée, les yeux noyés ou flamboyants, la narine frémissante, la bouche entrouverte, le sein oppressé, le col ployé comme une gorge de colombe étouffée

d'amour, représentent à s'y tromper le mystérieux drame de volupté dont toute danse est le symbole." Gautier, *Voyage en Algérie,* 70. Of course, not all viewers of the dance were equally enthralled. Frantz Jourdain, for example, noted the difference between the belly dance and French ballet and even called the belly dance "un peu banale." Jourdain, "L'Exposition algérienne à l'Esplanade des Invalides," 147. And G. Lenôtre called the belly dance bizarre and disagreeable and doubted whether it was good for the "fonctions et aux devoirs de la maternité." Lenôtre, "La danse des almées," 282.

32. Even though the universal exhibitions themselves occurred only about every ten years in Paris (1855, 1867, 1878, 1889), they could take up to three years of planning and preparation. In addition, widely distributed illustrated and unillustrated journals documented the planning stages and the actual events, further prejudicing public knowledge regarding the exhibitions.

33. Battle scenes in which warriors are depicted in violent combat, in fact, constitute a substantial category of French Orientalist painting.

34. The appearance and subsequent popularity of the *capeline arabe* in 1868, following the Universal Exhibition of 1867, is indicative of how French fashion was influenced by colonial costumes exhibited at the exhibitions. *La mode illustrée, journal de la famille* 1 (January 5, 1868).

35. *Le petit courrier de la mode* (January 7, 1860), 3. "[L]a mode aime l'Orient; c'est là qu'elle puise ses heureuses inspirations. Ses doigts roses et déliés répandent à plaisir les perles et l'or sur toutes nos parures."

36. Zola, *The Ladies' Paradise,* 78–79.

37. Ibid., 352–53.

38. Puisieux, "Mode," 3. "Ces voiles de gaze prêtent une douceur orientale à des créations toutes parisiennes."

39. Cortambert, "Promenade d'un fantaisiste," 30. "L'Orient a façonné les plus grands littérateurs et les peintres les plus éminents de notre siècle."

40. For a fascinating discussion of the significance of the picture's female patronage by Murat, see Ockman, "A Woman's Pleasure: The *Grande Odalisque,*" in her book *Ingres's Eroticized Bodies,* 33–66. Regarding Ingres's use of Lady Mary Wortley Montagu's letters, see Yeazell, "Private Baths and Public Harems," in which Yeazell questions Ingres's use of these letters in his *Turkish Bath.* Ingres's layering of information about the Orient may be understood within the framework of what Ali Behdad has termed the "orientalist intertext." This concept sees any Orientalist representation as "always a re-representation of the Orient." That is to say, any Orientalist work has been inflected by and filtered through long-standing traditions of representations of the Other. Behdad, "Orientalist Desire, Desire of the Orient,"43.

41. Nochlin, "The Imaginary Orient," in *The Politics of Vision,* 37–38.

42. Nochlin sets up an opposition between Gérôme's standard of academic

Orientalism and Delacroix's more impassioned, many would say Romantic, version, which was, to use her words, "greeted with outrage." She continues, "Gérôme's fantasia on the theme of sexual politics has been more successfully ideologized than Delacroix's, and this ideologizing is achieved precisely through the work's formal structure. Gérôme's version was more acceptable because he substituted a chilly and remote pseudoscientific naturalism—small, self-effacing brushstrokes, and 'rational' and convincing spatial effects . . . for Delacroix's tempestuous self-involvement, his impassioned brushwork, subjectively outpouring perspective, and inventive, sensually self-revelatory dancelike poses." Ibid., 44. So, "naturalistic" and seemingly scientific images were more successful and convincing to the public than erratic and impassioned ones, which were considered to be more subjective.

43. Ibid., 35.

44. The way in which clothing could indicate a woman's status and national affiliation is articulated by Théophile Gautier in his comments on the difference between the corseted and thoroughly clothed French woman's body in relation to the uncorseted and only lightly draped body of the Algerian woman: "Les yeux européens, accoutumés aux mensonges de la crinoline, aux exagérations des sous-jupes et autres artifices qui métamorphosent en Vénus Callipyges des beautés fort peu hottentotes, sont surpris de voir ces tailles sans corset et ces corps qu'enveloppe une simple chemise de gaze." Gautier, *Voyage en Algérie,* 40–41.

45. Bhabha, "Signs Taken for Wonders."

46. Whether he knew Manet's painting or not, René Magritte would later pick up on this connection between the face and the body in his painting *The Rape,* of 1934, in which he superimposes a female body across a woman's face (or a woman's face across a female body).

47. Martel Caristie provides just one of many examples of the positive attention that Gérôme received when he exhibited: "Les tableaux de M. Gérôme ont le privilège de passioner presque toujours en leur faveur l'attention de la foule." Caristie, "Salon de 1864: Orientalistes," 493.

48. Hanson, in *Manet and the Modern Tradition,* 88, establishes *Odalisque* as Manet's only other known work with an Orientalized theme. The most obvious examples of reclining odalisques are Ingres's and Delacroix's.

49. Anne Hanson cites Beatrice Farwell's assertion that one woman may have modeled for both images. Hanson, *Manet and the Modern Tradition,* 88 fn. 157.

50. The model for *Young Woman Reclining in Spanish Costume* may well be Nadar's mistress. Manet, in fact, wrote in the bottom right corner of the picture, just above his own signature, "à mon ami Nadar."

51. *Lola de Valence, Young Woman Reclining in Spanish Costume, Mll . . . V in the Costume of an Espada,* and *The Spanish Ballet,* all of 1862, and *Émilie Ambre in the Role of Carmen,* of 1879–80, are all examples of Manet's interest in these dark-haired types. Denis Rouart and Daniel Wildenstein's catalogue raisonné of

Manet's oeuvre includes several images of Spanish dancers painted on tambourines and small wooden panels. One could also add to this list of Manet's depictions of Spanish themes some of his portraits of Berthe Morisot, since several of them, mainly *Berthe Morisot with a Fan, The Balcony,* and *Berthe Morisot with a Veil,* clearly refer to Spanish painting and custom.

52. In his account of his trip to the East, Gérard de Nerval invokes these kinds of stereotypes in describing his experience of seeing dancing *almahs* in a café. He wrote that he was "struck by the brilliant colours of the skull-caps which topped their glossy tresses. Small bells rang and rings jangled as their heels beat the floor, while their raised arms whirled in time with the boisterous rhythm and their hips quivered voluptuously. Under the transparent muslin their waists were naked between their short blouses and their ornate, hanging girdles, but so rapidly did they turn and spin that I could scarcely make out the features of these seductive dancers. Two of them, however, were intoxicating beauties. . . . their Arabic eyes glittered with kohl, their plump but delicate cheeks were lightly painted." No sooner does de Nerval cite all of the stereotypes that nineteenth-century French travelers to the East seem to have associated with the *almah* than he realizes that these intoxicating beauties are, in fact, men. This points out that the objects that were worn by the "*almahs,*" perhaps more than the body beneath, added up to the preconceived notion of an ideal and desirable Eastern woman. de Nerval, *Journey to the Orient,* 26.

EPILOGUE

1. Barthes, *The Pleasure of the Text,* 64.
2. Moffett in the exhibition catalog *Manet: 1832–1883,* 441.
3. Ibid., 442.

Bibliography

Ackerman, Gerald M. *The Life and Work of Jean-Leon Gérôme.* New York: Sotheby's Publications, Harper and Row, 1986.

Adler, Kathleen. *Manet.* Oxford: Phaidon Press, 1986.

Adler, Kathleen, and Tamar Garb. *Berthe Morisot.* Ithaca, NY: Cornell University Press, 1987.

Adriani, Götz. *Renoir.* Exhibition catalog. New Haven, CT: Yale University Press, 1996.

Agrest, Diana, Patricia Conway, and Leslie Kanes Weisman, eds. *The Sex of Architecture.* New York: Harry N. Abrams, 1996.

Agulhon, Maurice, ed. *Histoire de la France urbaine: La ville de l'âge industriel, le cycle haussmannien.* Vol. 4. Paris: Seuil, 1983.

Ahmad, Aijaz. *In Theory: Classes, Nations, Literatures.* London: Verso, 1992.

Ahmed, Leila. *Women and Gender in Islam.* New Haven, CT: Yale University Press, 1992.

Aisenberg, Andrew R. *Disease, Government, and the "Social Question" in Nineteenth-Century France.* Stanford, CA: Stanford University Press, 1999.

Allem, Maurice. *La vie quotidienne sous le Second Empire.* Paris: Librairie Hachette, 1949.

Alloula, Malek. *The Colonial Harem.* Trans. Myrna Godzich and Wlad Godzich. Minneapolis: University of Minnesota Press, 1986.

Alpers, Svetlana. "Art History and Its Exclusions: The Example of Dutch Art." In

Feminism and Art History: Questioning the Litany, ed. Norma Broude and Mary D. Garrard, 183–200. New York: Harper and Row, 1982.

Amato, Joseph A. *Dust: A History of the Small and the Invisible.* Berkeley: University of California Press, 2000.

Amblard, Dr. A. *Hygiène élémentaire publique et privée.* Paris: A. Maloine, 1891.

Angeloglou, Maggie. *A History of Makeup.* London: Studio Vista, 1970.

Ankum, Katharina von. *Women in the Metropolis: Gender and Modernity in Weimar Culture.* Berkeley: University of California Press, 1997.

Apter, Emily. "Female Trouble in the Colonial Harem." *differences* 4 (Spring 1992): 205–24.

———. *Feminizing the Fetish: Psychoanalysis and Narrative Obsession in Turn-of-the-Century France.* Ithaca, NY: Cornell University Press, 1991.

———. "*Figura Serpentinata:* Visual Seduction and the Colonial Gaze." In *Spectacles of Realism: Gender, Body, Genre,* ed. Margaret Cohen and Christopher Prendergast, 163–78. Minneapolis: University of Minnesota Press, 1995.

Arène, Paul. *Vingt jours en Tunisie.* Paris: Alphonse Lemerre, 1884.

Armstrong, Carol. "Counter, Mirror, Maid. Some Infra thin Notes on *A Bar at the Folies-Bergère.*" In *12 Views of Manet's Bar,* ed. Bradford R. Collins, 25–46. Princeton, NJ: Princeton University Press, 1996.

———. "Edgar Degas and the Representation of the Female Body." In *The Female Body in Western Culture: Contemporary Perspectives,* ed. Susan Rubin Suleiman, 223–42. Cambridge, MA: Harvard University Press, 1986.

———. "Facturing Femininity: Manet's *Before the Mirror.*" *October* 74 (Fall 1995): 75–104.

———. *Manet/Manette.* New Haven, CT: Yale University Press, 2002.

———. *Odd Man Out: Readings of the Work and Reputation of Edgar Degas.* Chicago: University of Chicago Press, 1991.

Arnold, Dana. *Re-presenting the Metropolis: Architecture, Urban Experience, and Social Life in London, 1800–1840.* Burlington, VT: Ashgate, 2000.

Ash, Juliette, and Elizabeth Wilson, eds. *Chic Thrills: A Fashion Reader.* Berkeley: University of California Press, 1992.

Atil, Esin, Charles Newton, and Sarah Searight. *Voyages and Visions: Nineteenth-Century European Images of the Middle East from the Victoria and Albert Museum.* Washington, D.C.: Smithsonian Institution Traveling Exhibition Service in association with University of Washington Press, Seattle, 1995.

Bailey, David A., and Gilane Tawadros, eds. *Veil: Veiling, Representation and Contemporary Art.* Cambridge, MA: MIT Press, 2003.

Bal, Mieke. *The Mottled Screen: Reading Proust Visually.* Stanford, CA: Stanford University Press, 1997.

Baldus, Édouard. *Les monuments principaux de la France: Produit en héliogravure.* Paris: Ve. A. Morel et Cie, Libraires-Éditeurs, 1875.

Ballerini, Julia. "The in visibility of Hadji-Ishmael: Maxime du Camp's 1850 Photographs of Egypt." In *The Body Imaged: The Human Form and Visual Culture since the Renaissance,* ed. Kathleen Adler and Marcia Pointon, 147–60. Cambridge: Cambridge University Press, 1993.

———. "'La maison démolie': Photographs of Egypt by Maxime du Camp, 1849–1850." In *Home and Its Dislocations in Nineteenth-Century France,* ed. Suzanne Nash, 103–23. Albany: State University of New York Press, 1993.

Banta, Melissa, and Curtis M. Hinsley. *From Site to Sight: Anthropology, Photography, and the Power of Imagery.* Exhibition catalog. Cambridge, MA: Peabody Museum Press, 1986.

Barnes, David S. *The Making of a Social Disease: Tuberculosis in Nineteenth-Century France.* Berkeley: University of California Press, 1995.

Barnett, Harry V. "Fitness and Fashion." *Magazine of Art* (London, Paris, New York) 5 (1882).

Barrows, Susanna. *Distorting Mirrors: Visions of the Crowd in Late Nineteenth-Century France.* New Haven, CT: Yale University Press, 1981.

Barthes, Roland. "The Face of Garbo." *Mythologies.* Trans. Annette Lavers. New York: Noonday Press, 1957; reprint, Farrar, Strauss and Giroux, 1972.

———. *The Fashion System.* Trans. Matthew Ward and Richard Howard. Berkeley: University of California Press, 1983.

———. *The Pleasure of the Text.* Trans. Richard Miller. New York: Noonday Press, Farrar, Straus and Giroux, 1975.

Bashkirtseff, Marie. *Journals of Marie Bashkirtseff.* Introduced by Rozsika Parker and Griselda Pollock. London: Virago Press, 1985.

Bataille, Georges. *Documents.* Paris: Mercure de France et Éditions Gallimard, 1968.

Baudelaire, Charles. *Baudelaire: Oeuvres complètes.* Paris: Éditions du Seuil, 1968.

———. *The Painter of Modern Life and Other Essays.* Trans. and ed. Jonathan Mayne. New York: Phaidon, 1964.

Baudrillard, Jean. *The Ecstasy of Communication.* Trans. Bernard and Caroline Schutze. New York: Semiotext(e), 1990.

———. "Fetishism and Ideology: The Semiological Reduction." *For a Critique of the Political Economy of the Sign,* 88–101. St. Louis, MO: Telos, 1981.

———. *Seduction.* Trans. Brian Singer. New York: St. Martin's Press, 1990.

———. *Simulations.* Trans. Paul Foss, Paul Patton, and Philip Beitchman. New York: Semiotext(e), 1983.

Beaugrand, Dr. Emile. *L'hygiène ou l'art de conserver la santé.* Paris: Hachette, 1855.

Beaulieu, Jill, and Mary Roberts, eds. *Orientalism's Interlocutors: Painting, Architecture, Photography.* Durham, NC: Duke University Press, 2002.

Beaunier, André. *Visages des femmes.* Paris: Plon-Nourrit, 1913.

Becquerel, A. *Traité élémentaire d'hygiène privée et publique.* Paris: P. Asselin, 1867.

Beebe, Mrs. C. D. *Lace, Ancient and Modern.* New York: Sharps Publishing Company, 1880.

Behdad, Ali. "The Eroticized Orient: Images of the Orient in Montesquieu and His Precursors." *Stanford French Review* 13 (Fall-Winter 1989): 109–26.

———. "Orientalist Desire: Desire of the Orient." *French Forum* 15, no. 1 (January 1990): 37–51.

Bell, Leonard. *Colonial Constructs: European Images of Maori 1840–1914.* Auckland: Auckland University Press, 1992.

Belli, Gabriella. *Boldini, De Nittis, Zandomeneghi: Mondanità e costume nella Parigi fin de siècle.* Exhibition catalog. Milan: Il Museo di Arte Moderna e Contemporanea di Trento e Rovereto, 2001.

Benjamin, Roger. *Orientalist Aesthetics: Art, Colonialism, and French North Africa, 1880–1930.* Berkeley: University of California Press, 2003.

Benjamin, Walter. *The Arcades Project.* Trans. Howard Eiland and Kevin McLaughlin. Cambridge, MA: Belknap Press of Harvard University Press, 1999.

———. *Charles Baudelaire: A Lyric Poet in the Era of High Capitalism.* Trans. Harry Zohn. London: Verso, 1976.

Berchet, Jean-Claude. *Le voyage en Orient: Anthologie des voyageurs français dans le levant au XIX siècle.* N.p.: Robert Laffont, 1985.

Berhaut, Marie. *Gustave Caillebotte: Catalogue raisonné des peintures et pastels.* Paris: Wildenstein Institute, 1994.

Berman, Marshall. *All That Is Solid Melts into Air.* New York: Penguin, 1982.

Bernard, Claude. *An Introduction to the Study of Experimental Medicine.* Translated by Henry Copley Greene. N.p.: Henry Schuman, 1927.

Bernheim, Samuel, and André Roblot. "Tuberculose et blanchisseries." *L'hygiène familiale* (February 1906): 54–57.

Bernheimer, Charles. *Figures of Ill Repute: Representing Prostitution in Nineteenth-Century France.* Cambridge, MA: Harvard University Press, 1989.

Bershad, Deborah. "Looking, Power and Sexuality: Degas' *Woman with a Lorgnette.*" In *Dealing with Degas: Representations of Women and the Politics of Vision,* ed. Richard Kendall and Griselda Pollock, 95–105. New York: Universe, 1991.

Berthe Morisot: Impressionist. Exhibition catalog. Curated by Charles Stuckey and William P. Scott. New York: Hudson Hills Press, 1987.

Bewell, Alan. *Romanticism and Colonial Disease.* Baltimore: Johns Hopkins University Press, 1999.

Bezançon, M. F. *Rapport général sur les travaux du conseil d'hygiène publique et de salubrité du département de la Seine.* Paris: La prefecture de police, 1880–81.

Bhabha, Homi K. *The Location of Culture.* London: Routledge, 1994.

———. "Signs Taken for Wonders: Questions of Ambivalence and Authority under a Tree outside Delhi, May 1817." In *"Race," Writing, and Difference,* ed. Henry Louis Gates, 163–84. Chicago: University of Chicago Press, 1985.

Binder, Polly. *The Truth about Cora Pearl.* London: Weidenfeld and Nicolson, 1986.

Bitard, A., ed. *L'Exposition de Paris* (1878). Paris: M. Dreyfous, 1878.

Blanc, Charles. *Art in Ornament and Dress.* London: Chapman and Hall, 1877.

———. *Voyage de la Haute-Égypte: Observations sur les arts égyptien et arabe.* Paris: Renouard, 1876.

Blanchard, Pascal, and Armelle Chatelier. *Images et colonies: Nature, discours et influence de l'iconographie coloniale liée à la propagande coloniale et à la représentation des Africains et de l'Afrique en France, de 1920 aux indépendances.* Paris: ACHAC, 1993.

Boer, Ingeborg Erica. "Rereading the Harem and the Despot: Changes in French Cultural Representations of the Orient in the Late Eighteenth and Early Nineteenth Centuries." Ph.D. dissertation, University of Rochester, 1992.

———. "This Is Not the Orient: Theory and Postcolonial Practice." In *The Point of Theory: Practices of Cultural Analysis,* ed. Mieke Bal and Inge E. Boer, 211–19. New York: Continuum, 1994.

Bonnier, Gaston. *Science naturelles et hygiène.* Paris: Librairie générale de l'enseignement, n.d.

Bouchardat, M. "Paris au point de vue de l'hygiène." *La revue scientifique* 14 (April 7, 1883): 434–39.

Bouchot, Henri. *Les élégances du Second Empire.* Paris: Librairie Illustrée, 1896.

Bournon-Ginestoux, le Vicomte de. *Les jeunes femmes ou les séductions de la nature et de l'art.* Paris: E. Blanchard, 1856.

Bowie, Karen, ed. *La modernité avant Haussmann: Formes de l'espace urbain à Paris 1801–1853.* Paris: Éditions Rescherches, 2001.

Bowlby, Rachel. *Just Looking: Consumer Culture in Dreiser, Gissing, and Zola.* New York: Methuen, 1985.

Braun, Marta. *Picturing Time: The Work of Etienne-Jules Marey (1830–1904).* Chicago: University of Chicago Press, 1992.

Braunschvig, Marcel. *La femme et la beauté: Le rôle de la beauté dans la nature.* Paris: A. Colin, 1929.

Brennan, Teresa, and Martin Jay. *Vision in Context: Historical and Contemporary Perspectives on Sight.* New York: Routledge, 1996.

Breward, Christopher. *The Culture of Fashion.* Manchester: University of Manchester Press, 1995.

———. *The Hidden Consumer: Masculinities, Fashion and City Life, 1860–1914.* Manchester: University of Manchester Press, 1999.

Breward, Christopher, and Caroline Evans, eds. *Fashion and Modernity.* New York: Berg, 2005.

Brivic, Sheldon. *The Veil of Signs: Joyce, Lacan, and Perception.* Urbana: University of Illinois Press, 1991.

Brombert, Beth Archer. *Edouard Manet: Rebel in a Frock Coat.* Boston: Little, Brown, 1996.

Bronfen, Elisabeth. *Over Her Dead Body: Death, Femininity and the Aesthetic.* New York: Routledge, 1992.

Brooks, Peter. *Body Work: Objects of Desire in Modern Narrative.* Cambridge, MA: Harvard University Press, 1993.

———. "The Text of the City." *Oppositions* 8 (1977): 7–11.

Bruhat, J. *Étude sur la responsabilité du conseil municipal de Paris et de l'administration à propos du laboratoire municipal.* Paris: Veuve Hugonis, 1890.

Buck-Morss, Susan. *The Dialectics of Seeing: Walter Benjamin and the Arcades Project.* Cambridge, MA: MIT Press, 1989.

———. "The Flâneur, the Sandwichman and the Whore." *New German Critique* 39 (Fall 1986): 99–141.

Burbick, Joan. *Healing the Republic: The Language of Health and the Culture of Nationalism in Nineteenth-Century America.* Cambridge: Cambridge University Press, 1994.

Burton, Isabel. *AEI: Arabia, Egypt, India: A Narrative of Travel.* London: William Mullan and Son, 1879.

Butler, Judith. *Bodies That Matter: On the Discursive Limits of "Sex."* New York: Routledge, 1993.

Cadava, Eduardo. *Words of Light: Theses on the Photography of History.* Princeton, NJ: Princeton University Press, 1997.

Calefato, Patrizia. *The Clothed Body.* Trans. Lisa Adams. New York: Berg, 2004.

Callen, Anthea. *The Spectacular Body: Science, Method and Meaning in the Work of Degas.* New Haven, CT: Yale University Press, 1995.

Cardinal, Philippe. *L'Orient d'un photographe.* Paris: Favre, 1987.

Caristie, Martel. "Salon de 1864: Orientalistes." *Revue du monde coloniale* 10 (1864).

Carmona, Michael. *Haussmann: His Life and Times, and the Making of Modern Paris.* Trans. Patrick Camiller. Chicago: Ivan R. Dee, 2002.

Cars, Jean des, and Pierre Pinon. *Paris: Haussmann.* Paris: Pavillon de l'Arsenal, 1991.

Cartwright, Lisa. *Screening the Body: Tracing Medicine's Visual Culture.* Minneapolis: University of Minnesota Press, 1995.

Cartwright, Lisa, and Marita Sturken. *Practices of Looking: An Introduction to Visual Culture.* Oxford: Oxford University Press, 2001.

Casenave, Alphée. *De la decoration humaine: Hygiène de la beauté.* Paris: Paul Daffis, 1867.

Caws, Mary Ann, ed. *City Images: Perspectives from Literature, Philosophy, and Film.* New York: Gordon and Breach, 1991.

Çelik, Zeynep. *Displaying the Orient: Architecture of Islam at Nineteenth-Century World's Fairs.* Berkeley: University of California Press, 1992.

———. "Gendered Spaces in Colonial Algiers." In *Architecture: In Fashion*, ed. Deborah Fausch, Paulette Singley, Rodolphe El-Khoury, and Zvi Efrat, 127–40. Princeton, NJ: Princeton Architectural Press, 1994.

Çelik, Zeynep, and Leila Kinney. "Ethnography and Exhibitionism at the *Expositions universelles*." *Assemblage* (December 1990): 35–59.

Centre Georges Pompidou. *Walter Benjamin: Le passant, la trace*. Exhibition catalog. Paris: Bibliothèque publique d'information au Centre Georges Pompidou, 1994.

Certeau, Michel de. *The Practice of Everyday Life*. Trans. Steven Rendall. Berkeley: University of California Press, 1984.

Challamel, Augustin. *History of Fashion in France: or, The Dress of Women from the Gallo-Roman Period to the Present Time*. Trans. Mrs. Cashel Hoey and Mr. John Lillie. London: Sampson, Low, Marston, Searle, and Rivington, 1882.

Cham [A. de Noé]. *Les tortures de la mode*. Paris: Bureau du *Journal des modes parisienne* et du *Journal amusant*, n.d.

Chambord, Comte de. *Journal de voyage en Orient 1861*. Ed. Arnaud Chaffanjon. Paris: Tallandier, 1984.

Champeux, M. A. de. *Dessins et modèles: Les arts du tissu: Étoffes, tapisseries, broderies, dentelles, reliures*. Paris: J. Rouam and Cie., Éditeurs, 1890.

Chantel, Ch., and G. Viterbo. *Annuaire général de la mode: Couture, mode, corset, lingerie*. Paris, 1901.

Charles Marville: Photographe de Paris de 1851 à 1879. Exhibition catalog. Paris: Bibliothèque historique de la ville de Paris, 1980.

Charles-Roux, J. *Les colonies françaises, l'organisation et le fonctionnement de l'exposition des colonies et pays de protectorat*. Paris, 1902.

Chevalier, Louis, ed. *Le choléra: La première épidémie du XIX siècle*. Paris: Imprimerie Centrale de l'Ouest, 1958.

Cixous, Hélène, and Jacques Derrida. *Veils*. Trans. Geoffrey Bennington. Stanford, CA: Stanford University Press, 2001.

Clark, Linda L. *Schooling the Daughters of Marianne: Textbooks and the Socialization of Girls in Modern French Primary Schools*. Albany: State University of New York Press, 1984.

Clark, T. J. *The Painting of Modern Life: Paris in the Art of Manet and His Followers*. Princeton, NJ: Princeton University Press, 1984.

Clay, Jean. "Ointments, Makeup, and Pollen." Trans. John Shepley. *October* 27 (Winter 1983): 3–44.

Claye, Louis. *Les talismans de la beauté*. Paris: Louis Claye, 1860.

Clayson, Hollis. *Painted Love: Prostitution in French Art of the Impressionist Era*. New Haven, CT: Yale University Press, 1991.

———. *Paris in Despair: Art and Everyday Life under Siege (1870–1871)*. Chicago: University of Chicago Press, 2002.

———. "The Sexual Politics of Impressionist Illegibility." In *Dealing with Degas: Representations of Women and the Politics of Vision,* ed. Richard Kendall and Griselda Pollock, 66–79. New York: Universe, 1991.

Clifford, James. *The Predicament of Culture: Twentieth-Century Ethnography, Literature, and Art.* Cambridge, MA: Harvard University Press, 1988.

Cohen, William A., and Ryan Johnson, eds. *Filth: Dirt, Disgust, and Modern Life.* Minneapolis: University of Minnesota Press, 2005.

Coles, Alex, ed. *The Optic of Walter Benjamin.* London: Black Dog Publishing, 1999.

Connor, Susan P. "Politics, Prostitution and the Pox in Revolutionary Paris 1789–99." *Journal of Social History* 12, no. 1 (1989): 42–51.

"Contre les voilettes." *La fronde,* August 21, 1899.

Coombes, Annie E. *Reinventing Africa: Museums, Material Culture and Popular Imagination in Late Victorian and Edwardian England.* New Haven, CT: Yale University Press, 1994.

Copjec, Joan. "The Sartorial Superego." *October* 50 (Fall 1989): 56–95.

Corbin, Alain. *The Foul and the Fragrant: Odor and the French Social Imagination.* Cambridge, MA: Harvard University Press, 1986.

———. *Women for Hire: Prostitution and Sexuality in France after 1850.* Translated by Alan Sheridan. Cambridge, MA: Harvard University Press, 1990.

Corson, Richard. *Fashions in Makeup: From Ancient to Modern Times.* London: Peter Owen, 1972.

Cortambert, Richard. "Promenade d'un fantaisiste: À l'Exposition des beaux-arts de 1861." *La revue du monde coloniale* 5 (1861).

Courtine, Jean-Jacques, and Claudine Haroche. *Histoire du visage: XVI–XIX siècle.* Paris: Éditions Rivages, 1988.

Crary, Jonathan. *Techniques of the Observer: On Vision and Modernity in the Nineteenth Century.* Cambridge, MA: MIT Press, 1990.

D'Aincourt, Marguerite. *Études sur le costume féminin.* Paris: Éd. Rouveyre et G. Blond, 1884.

Darragon, Eric. *Gustave Caillebotte.* Trans. Marie-Hélène Agüeros. Bergamo, Italy: Bonfini Press, 1994.

Davenport, Milia. *The Book of Costume.* Vol. 1. New York: Crown Publishers, 1976.

Dawkins, Heather. "Frogs, Monkeys and Women: A History of Identification across a Phantastic Body." In *Dealing with Degas: Representations of Women and the Politics of Vision,* ed. Richard Kendall and Griselda Pollock, 202–17. New York: Universe, 1991.

———. "Grief and Fascination." *differences* 4 (Fall 1992): 66–90.

———. "Managing Degas." In *Dealing with Degas: Representations of Women and the Politics of Vision,* ed. Richard Kendall and Griselda Pollock, 133–45. New York: Universe, 1991.

Dayot, Armand. *L'image de la femme.* Paris: Hachette, 1889.

Degas. Exhibition catalog, with essays by Jean Sotherland Boggs, Douglas W. Druick, Henri Loyrette, Michael Pantazzi, and Gary Tinterow. New York: Metropolitan Museum of Art, 1988.

Delaporte, François. *Disease and Civilization: The Cholera in Paris, 1832*. Translated by Arthur Goldhammer. Cambridge, MA: MIT Press, 1986.

Deleuze, Gilles. *Cinema 1: The Movement Image*. Minneapolis: University of Minnesota Press, 1986.

———. *The Fold: Leibniz and the Baroque*. Translated by Tom Conley. Minneapolis: University of Minnesota Press, 1993.

Deleuze, Gilles, and Félix Guattari. *A Thousand Plateaus: Capitalism and Schizophrenia*. Translated by Brian Massumi. Minneapolis: University of Minnesota Press, 1987.

Delord, Taxile. *Physiologie de la Parisienne*. Paris: Aubert, Levigne, n.d.

Del Plato, Joan. *Multiple Wives, Multiple Pleasures: Representing the Harem, 1800–1875*. Madison and Teaneck, NJ: Fairleigh Dickinson University Press, 2002.

de Man, Paul. "Autobiography as Defacement." *The Rhetoric of Romanticism*. New York: Columbia University Press, 1984.

Démy, Adolphe. *Essai historique sur les expositions universelles de Paris*. Paris: Alphonse Picard et Fils, 1907.

de Nerval, Gérard. *Journey to the Orient*. Selected and translated by Norman Glass. New York: New York University Press, 1972.

Denes, Agnes. *Book of Dust: The Beginning and the End of Time and Thereafter*. Rochester, NY: Visual Studies Workshop Press, 1989.

Dennis, Kelly. "Ethno-pornography: Veiling the Dark Continent." *History of Photography* 18, no. 1 (Spring 1994): 22–28.

Derrida, Jacques. *Spurs: Nietzsche's Styles*. Translated by Barbara Harlow. Chicago: University of Chicago Press, 1978.

Descamps, Hubert. *L'Europe découvre l'Afrique occidentale*. Paris: Berger Levrault, 1967.

des Cars, Jean, and Pierre Pinon. *Paris: Haussmann*. Paris: Picard Éditeur, 1991.

Didi-Huberman, Georges. *L'invention de l'hystérie: Charcot et l'iconographie photographique de la Salpêtrière*. Paris: Macula, 1982.

Djebar, Assia. *Women of Algiers in Their Apartment*. Translated by Marjolijn de Jager. Charlottesville: University Press of Virginia, 1992.

Doane, Mary Ann. "The Close-Up: Scale and Detail in the Cinema." *differences* 14, no. 3 (Fall 2003): 89–111.

———. *Femmes Fatales: Feminism, Film Theory, Psychoanalysis*. New York: Routledge, 1991.

Donald, James. *Imagining the Modern City*. London: Athlone Press, 1999.

Douglas, Mary. *Purity and Danger: An Analysis of Concepts of Pollution and Taboo*. New York: Frederick A. Praeger, 1966.

Doy, Gen. *Drapery: Classicism and Barbarism in Visual Culture.* London: I. B. Tauris, 2002.

Dréolle, Ernest. "Costumes orientaux." *L'Exposition universelle de 1867 illustrée* 14 (1867).

Drouineau, Gustave. *L'hygiène et la mode.* Paris: La Rochelle, 1886.

D'Souza, Aruna, and Tom McDonough, eds. *The Invisible Flâneuse? Gender, Public Space, and Visual Culture in Nineteenth-Century Paris.* Manchester: Manchester University Press, 2006.

du Camp, Maxime. *Voyage en Orient (1849–1851) Notes.* Messina, Italy: Peloritana, 1972.

Duval, Jules. *L'Algérie et les colonies française.* Paris: Librairie Guillaumin, 1877.

Duvernois, Clément. *L'Algérie pittoresque.* Paris: J. Rouvier, 1863.

Edelstein, T. J., ed. *Perspectives on Morisot.* New York: Hudson Hills Press, 1990.

Edwards, Elizabeth. *Raw Histories: Photographs, Anthropology and Museums.* Oxford: Berg, 2001.

Ellis, Jack. *The Physician-Legislators of France: Medicine and Politics in the Early Third Republic, 1870–1914.* Cambridge: Cambridge University Press, 1990.

En Égypte au tempts de Flaubert 1839–1860: Les premiers photographes. Exhibition catalog. Curated by Marie-Thérèse and André Jammes. N.p., n.d.

L'exotisme oriental dans les collections de la Bibliothèque Forney. Exhibition catalog. Paris: Bibliothèque Forney, 1983.

Exposition Edouard Manet. Exhibition catalog. Copenhagen: Ordrupgaardsammlungen, 1989.

Fage, Jean, André Fage, and Alain Challande. *Histoire de la photographie française des origines à 1920.* Paris: Creatis, 1980.

Farwell, Beatrice. *Manet and the Nude.* New York: Garland, 1981.

Fauque, Claude. *La dentelle: Une industrie de l'arabesque.* Paris: Syros, 1995.

Fausch, Deborah, Paulette Singley, Rodolphe El-Khoury, and Zvi Efrat, eds. *Architecture: In Fashion.* Princeton, NJ: Princeton Architectural Press, 1994.

Feeney, Maura. *À la Mode: Women's Fashions in French Art, 1850–1900.* Exhibition catalog. Williamstown, MA: Sterling and Francine Clark Art Institute, 1982.

Les femmes d'aujourd'hui, études sur la toilette: Extraits de la vie parisienne. Paris: La Vie Parisienne, 1887.

Fer, Briony. "The Hat, the Hoax, the Body." In *The Body Imaged: The Human Form and Visual Culture since the Renaissance,* ed. Kathleen Adler and Marcia Pointon, 161–74. Cambridge: Cambridge University Press, 1993.

———. "Poussière/peinture: Bataille on Painting." In *Bataille: Writing the Sacred,* ed. Carolyn Bailey Gill, 154–71. London: Routledge, 1995.

Ferguson, Priscilla Parkhurst. "The *Flâneur* on and off the Streets of Paris." In *The Flâneur,* ed. Keith Tester, 22–42. London: Routledge, 1994.

———. *Paris as Revolution: Writing the 19th-Century City.* Berkeley: University of California Press, 1994.

Festa-McCormick, Diana. *Proustian Optics of Clothes: Mirrors, Masks, Mores.* Saratoga, CA: ANMA Ubri, 1984.

Feydeau, Ernest. *Alger.* Paris: Michel-Lévy Frères, 1862.

———. *Du luxe, des femmes, des moeurs, de la littérature et de la vertu.* Paris: Calmann Lévy, 1873.

Flahault, François. *Face à face: Histoire de visages.* Paris: Plon, 1989.

Flaubert, Gustave. *Madame Bovary.* Trans. Paul de Man. New York: W. W. Norton, 1965.

———. *La première éducation sentimentale.* Ed. F. R. Bastide. Paris: Éditions du Seuil, 1963.

Fortassier, Rose. *Les écrivains française et la mode de Balzac à nos jours.* Paris: Presses Universitaires de France, 1988.

Foucault, Michel. *The Birth of the Clinic: An Archaeology of Medical Perception.* Trans. A. M. Sheridan Smith. New York: Vintage Books, 1973.

———. *Discipline and Punish: The Birth of the Prison.* Trans. Alan Sheridan. New York: Vintage Books, 1979.

Fournel, Victor. *Ce qu'on voit dans les rues de Paris.* Paris: Adolphe Delahays, 1858.

Fournier, Édouard. *Paris démoli.* Paris: Librairie de la Société des gens de lettres, 1883.

Fowle, Frances. *Soil and Stone: Impressionism, Urbanism, Environment.* Burlington, VT: Ashgate, 2003.

Freud, Sigmund. "Fetishism." *The Standard Edition of the Complete Psychological Works of Sigmund Freud.* Vol. 21, 149–57. Trans. James Strachey. London: Hogarth Press, 1953.

———. "The Uncanny." *The Standard Edition of the Complete Psychological Works of Sigmund Freud.* Vol. 17, 219–52. Trans. James Strachey. London: Hogarth Press, 1953.

Friedberg, Anne. *Window Shopping: Cinema and the Postmodern.* Berkeley: University of California Press, 1993.

Frisby, David. *Cityscapes of Modernity: Critical Explorations.* Cambridge: Polity Press, 2001.

Frizot, Michel. *Nouvelle histoire de la photographie.* Paris: Bordas, 1994.

Gaillard, Marc. *Paris sous le Second Empire: Au temps de Charles Baudelaire.* Etrepilly: Presses du Village, 2004.

Galignani's New Paris Guide for 1867. Paris: A. et W. Galignani et Co., 1867.

Galtier-Boissière, Dr. *Notions élémentaire d'hygiène pratique suivres d'un appendice.* Paris: A. Colin, 1896.

Garb, Tamar. "Berthe Morisot and the Feminizing of Impressionism." In *Perspectives on Morisot,* ed. T. J. Edelstein, 57–66. New York: Hudson Hills Press, 1990.

———. *Bodies of Modernity: Figure and Flesh in Fin-de-Siècle France.* New York: Thames and Hudson, 1998.

———. "The Forbidden Gaze: Women Artists and the Male Nude in Late Nineteenth-Century France." In *The Body Imaged: The Human Form and Visual Culture since the Renaissance,* ed. Kathleen Adler and Marcia Pointon, 33–42. Cambridge: Cambridge University Press, 1993.

———. "Framing Femininity in Manet's Mlle E. G." In *Self and History: A Tribute to Linda Nochlin,* ed. Aruna D'Souza, 76–89. London: Thames and Hudson, 2001.

———. *Sisters of the Brush: Women's Artistic Culture in Late Nineteenth-Century Paris.* London: Yale University Press, 1994.

Garelick, Rhonda. "Bayadères, Stéréorama, and Vahat-Loukoum: Technological Realism in the Age of Empire." In *Spectacles of Realism: Gender, Body, Genre,* ed. Margaret Cohen and Christopher Prendergast, 294–319. Minneapolis: University of Minnesota Press, 1995.

———. "Electric Salomé: Loie Fuller at the Exposition Universelle of 1900." In *Imperialism and Theatre: Essays on World Theatre, Drama and Performance,* ed. J. Ellen Gainor, 85–103. New York: Routledge, 1995.

Garnier, Charles. *L'habitation humaine.* Paris: Hachette, 1892.

Gastineau, Benjamin. *Les femmes et les moeurs de l'Algérie.* Paris: Librairie de Michel Lévy, 1861.

Gastou, Paul. *Hygiène du visage: Cosmétique, esthétique et massage.* Paris: J.-B. Baillière et Fils, 1910.

Gautier, Émile. "Les 'Balyayeuses.'" *Journal* (April 1, 1901).

Gautier, Hippolyte. *Les curiosités de l'Exposition universelle de 1867.* Paris: Ch. Delagrave et Companie, 1867.

Gautier, Théophile. *L'Orient.* Paris: G. Charpentier, 1877.

———. *Voyage en Algérie.* Ed. Denise Brahimi. Paris: La Boîte à Documents, 1989.

Geist, Johann Friedrich. *Arcades: The History of the Building Type.* Cambridge, MA: MIT Press, 1983.

Gilloch, Graeme. *Myth and Metropolis: Walter Benjamin and the City.* Cambridge, MA: Blackwell Publishers, 1996.

Gilman, Sander. "Black Bodies, White Bodies: Toward an Iconography of Female Sexuality in Late Nineteenth-Century Art, Medicine, and Literature." *Critical Inquiry* 12 (Autumn 1985): 204–42.

———. *Difference and Pathology: Stereotypes of Sexuality, Race, and Madness.* Ithaca, NY: Cornell University Press, 1985.

———. *Disease and Representation: Images of Illness from Madness to AIDS.* Ithaca, NY: Cornell University Press, 1988.

Gléon, Delort de. *La rue du Caire à l'Exposition universelle de 1889.* Paris: E. Plon, Nourrit et Cie, Éditeurs, 1889.

Glucq. *Trois visites à l'Exposition universelle 1889.* Paris, 1889.

Godfrey, Sima. "Baudelaire, Gautier, and *une toilette savamment composé.*" In *Modernity and Revolution in Late Nineteenth-Century France,* ed. Barbara T. Cooper and Mary Donaldson-Evans, 74–87. Newark: University of Delaware Press, 1992.

———. "The Fabrication of *Salammbô:* The Surface of the Veil." *MLN* 95, no. 4 (May 1980): 1005–16.

———. "Lamartine and My Shoes: French Fashion, 'la terreur et la sympathie.'" *Nineteenth-Century French Studies* 24, nos. 1–2 (Fall–Winter 1995–96): 58–73.

Goedorp, Jacques. "*L'Olympia* n'etait pas une Montmartoise." *Journal de l'amateur de l'art* (February 23, 1967): 7.

Golan, Romy. *Modernity and Nostalgia: Art and Politics in France between the Wars.* London: Yale University Press, 1995.

Goldstein, Jan. *Console and Classify: The French Psychiatric Profession in the Nineteenth Century.* Cambridge: Cambridge University Press, 1987.

Gordon, Rae Beth. *Ornament, Fantasy, and Desire in Nineteenth-Century French Literature.* Princeton, NJ: Princeton University Press, 1992.

Grace, Daphne. *The Woman in the Muslin Mask: Veiling and Identity in Postcolonial Literature.* London: Pluto Press, 2004.

Graham-Brown, Sarah. *Images of Women: The Portrayal of Women in Photography of the Middle East, 1860–1950.* New York: Columbia University Press, 1988.

Grain de beauté: Un siècle de beauté par la publicité. Exhibition catalog. Paris: Bibliothèque Forney, 1993.

Grandière, Dr. A. Benoist de la. *Notions d'hygiène a l'usage des instituteurs et des élèves des écoles normales primaires.* Paris: V. Adrien Delahaye, 1877.

Granveau, A. *L'ouvrier devant la société.* Paris: Libr. Marrinon, 1868.

Gravures des modes du XIX siècle, extrait de périodique. N.p., n.d.

Green, Nancy, L. "Art and Industry: The Language of Modernization in the Production of Fashion." *French Historical Studies* 18, no. 3 (Spring 1994): 722–48.

Green, Nicolas. *The Spectacle of Nature: Landscape and Bourgeois Culture in Nineteenth-Century France.* Manchester: University of Manchester Press, 1990.

Greenhalgh, Paul. *Ephemeral Vistas: The Expositions Universelles, Great Exhibitions and World's Fairs, 1851–1939.* New York: St. Martin's Press, 1988.

Gregory, Derek. "Emperors of the Gaze: Photographic Practices and Productions of Space in Egypt, 1839–1914." In *Picturing Place: Photography and the Geographical Imagination,* ed. Joan M. Schwartz and James R. Ryan, 195–225. London: I. B. Tauris, 2003.

Grigsby, Darcy Grimaldo. *Extremities: Painting Empire in Post-revolutionary France.* New Haven, CT: Yale University Press, 2002.

Gronberg, Tag A. *Manet: A Retrospective.* New York: Park Lane, 1988.

———. "Dumbshows: A Carefully Staged Indifference." In *12 Views of Manet's Bar,* ed. Bradford R. Collins, 189–213. Princeton, NJ: Princeton University Press, 1996.

Gustave Caillebotte: Urban Impressionist. Exhibition catalog. New York: Abbeville Press, 1994.

Hamilton, George Heard. *Manet and His Critcs.* New Haven, CT: Yale University Press, 1954.

Hamilton, Peter. "Policing the Face." In *The Beautiful and the Damned: The Creation of Identity in Nineteenth-Century Photography,* Peter Hamilton and Roger Hargreaves, 57–107. Exhibition catalog. London: Lund Humphries, 2001.

Hamon, Philippe. *Expositions: Literature and Architecture in Nineteenth-Century France.* Trans. Katia Sainson-Frank and Lisa Maguire. Berkeley: University of California Press, 1992.

Hanson, Anne Coffin. *Manet and the Modern Tradition.* New Haven, CT: Yale University Press, 1977.

Harris, Jean C. *Edouard Manet: Graphic Works: A Definitive Catalogue Raisonné.* New York: Collectors Editions, 1970.

Harris, Michael. *The History of the Hat.* London: Herbert Jenkins Ltd., 1960.

Hartman, Elwood. *Three Nineteenth-Century French Writer/Artists and the Mahgreb: The Literary and Artistic Depictions of North Africa by Théophile Gautier, Eugène Fromentin, and Pierre Loti.* Tübingen, Germany: Gunter Narr Verlag, 1994.

Harvey, David. *Consciousness and the Urban Experience: Studies in the History and Theory of Capitalist Urbanization.* Baltimore: Johns Hopkins University Press, 1985.

———. *Paris, Capital of Modernity.* New York: Routledge, 2003.

Helfand, William H., ed. *The Picture of Health: Images of Medicine and Pharmacy from the William H. Helfand Collection.* Philadelphia: University of Pennsylvania Press, 1991.

Herbert, James D. "Privilege and the Illusion of the Real." In *12 Views of Manet's Bar,* ed. Bradford R. Collins, 214–32. Princeton, NJ: Princeton University Press, 1996.

Herbert, Robert L. *Impressionism: Art, Leisure, and Parisian Society.* New Haven, CT: Yale University Press, 1988.

Herelle, F. d'. *Études sur le choléra.* Alexandria, Egypt, 1929.

Heynan, Hilde. *Architecture and Modernity: A Critique.* Cambridge, MA: MIT Press, 1999.

Higonnet, Anne. *Berthe Morisot.* New York: Harper and Row, 1990.

———. *Berthe Morisot's Images of Women.* Cambridge, MA: Harvard University Press, 1992.

———. "The Other Side of the Mirror." In *Perspectives on Morisot,* ed. T. J. Edelstein, 67–78. New York: Hudson Hills Press, 1990.

———. "Real Fashion: Clothes Unmake the Working Woman." In *Spectacles of Realism: Gender, Body, Genre,* ed. Margaret Cohen and Christopher Prendergast, 137–62. Minneapolis: University of Minnesota Press, 1995.

Hiner, Susan. "Lust for *Luxe:* 'Cashmere Fever' in Nineteenth-Century France." *Journal for Early Modern Cultural Studies* 5, no. 1 (Spring-Summer 2005): 76–98.

Holden, W. H. *The Pearl from Plymouth: Eliza Emma Crouch Alias Cora Pearl; with Notes on Some of Her Celebrated Contemporaries.* London: British Technical and General Press, 1950.

Homer. *The Odyssey.* Trans. Richmond Lattimore. New York: HarperCollins, 1991.

Hoodfar, Homa. "The Veil in Their Minds and on Our Heads: Veiling Practices and Muslim Women." In *The Politics of Culture in the Shadow of Capital,* ed. Lisa Lowe and David Lloyd, 248–79. Durham, NC: Duke University Press, 1997.

Huard, Charles-Lucien. *Livre d'or de l'exposition: 1889: Journal hebdomadaire illustré.* Vols. 1–14. Paris: L. Boulanger, 1889.

Huyssen, Andreas. *After the Great Divide: Modernism, Mass Culture, Postmodernism.* Bloomington: Indiana University Press, 1986.

Hyde, Melissa, "The 'Make-up' of the Marquise: Boucher's Portrait of Pompadour at Her Toilette." *Art Bulletin* 82, no. 3 (September 2000): 453–75.

Irigaray, Luce. "Veiled Lips." *Mississippi Review* 33 (Winter-Spring 1983): 98–131.

Jacobs, Michael. *The Painted Voyage: Art, Travel, and Exploration, 1564–1875.* London: British Museum Press, 1995.

J. H. "L'hygiène et la mortalité à Paris." *La revue scientifique* 20, no. 16 (November 1889).

Johnson, Barbara. "My Monster, My Self." *A World of Difference.* Baltimore: Johns Hopkins University Press, 1987.

Johnson, Sharon P. *Boundaries of Acceptability: Flaubert, Maupassant, Cézanne, and Cassatt.* New York: Peter Lang Publishing, 2000.

Jordanova, Ludmilla. *Defining Features: Scientific and Medical Portraits, 1660–2000.* London: Reaktion, 2000.

———. *Sexual Visions: Images of Gender in Science and Medicine between the Eighteenth and Twentieth Centuries.* Madison: University of Wisconsin Press, 1989.

Jourdain, Frantz. "L'Exposition algérienne à l'esplanade des Invalides." *L'Exposition de Paris de 1889* 19 (July 6, 1889).

———. *Pour servir à l'histoire de l'habitation humaine.* Paris: Librairie Central des Beaux-Arts, 1889.

———. "Les tisseuses kabyles." *L'Exposition de Paris de 1889* 17 (June 22, 1889).

Juin, Hubert. *La parisienne: Les élégantes, les célébrités et les petites femmes, 1880–1914.* Paris: Tresors de la Photographie, 1978.

Jullian, Philippe. *The Orientalists: European Painters of Eastern Scenes.* Oxford: Phaidon, 1977.

Kabbani, Rana. *Europe's Myths of Orient.* Bloomington: Indiana University Press, 1986.

Kalff, Elsbeth, "La sensibilisation à l'hygiène à Paris 1850–1880: La loi sur les logements insalubrités." *Les annales de la recherche urbaine* 33 (March–April 1987): 97–104.

Keddie, Nikki R., and Beth Baron, eds. *Women in Middle Eastern History: Shifting Boundaries in Sex and Gender.* New Haven, CT: Yale University Press, 1991.

Kendall, Richard. *Degas: Beyond Impressionism.* Exhibition catalog. New Haven, CT: Yale University Press, 1996.

Kessler, Marni. "Dusting the Surface: The Veil, the *Bourgeoise*, and the City Grid." In *The Invisible Flâneuse? Gender, Public Space, and Visual Culture in Nineteenth-Century Paris,* ed. Aruna D'Souza and Tom McDonough, 49–64. Manchester: Manchester University Press, 2006.

———. "Filters and Pathologies: Caillebotte and Manet in Haussmann's Paris." *Nineteenth-Century Contexts* 27, no. 3 (September 2005): 245–68.

———. "Restructuring Relationships: Berthe Morisot's Edma Series." *Woman's Art Journal* 12, no. 1 (Spring-Summer 1991): 24–28.

———. "Unmasking Manet's Morisot." *Art Bulletin* 81, no. 3 (September 1999): 473–89.

Khanna, Ranjana. *Dark Continents: Psychoanalysis and Colonialism.* Durham, NC: Duke University Press, 2003.

Kinney, Leila. "Fashion and Figuration in Modern Life Painting." In *Architecture: In Fashion,* ed. Deborah Fausch, Paulette Singley, Rodolphe El-Khoury, and Zvi Efrat, 270–313. Princeton, NJ: Princeton Architectural Press, 1994.

Knibiehler, Yvonne, and Régine Goutalier. *La femme au temps des colonies.* Paris: Éditions Stock, 1985.

Kostof, Spiro. "His Majesty the Pick: The Aesthetics of Demolition." In *Streets: Critical Perspectives on Public Space,* ed. Zeynep Çelik, Diane Favro, and Richard Ingersoll, 9–22. Berkeley: University of California Press, 1994.

Krauss, Rosalind. "Grids, You Say." In *Grids: Format and Image in 20th-Century Art.* Exhibition catalog. New York: Pace Gallery, 1978.

Krell, Alan. "Dirt and Desire: Troubled Waters in Realist Practice." In *Impressions of French Modernity: Art and Literature in France 1850–1900,* ed. Richard Hobbs, 135–52. Manchester: University of Manchester Press, 1998.

Kuryluk, Ewa. *Veronica and Her Cloth: History, Symbolism, and Structure of a "True" Image.* Cambridge, MA: Basil Blackwell, 1991.

Kybalova, Ludmila, Olga Herbenova, and Milena Lamarova. *The Pictorial Encyclopedia of Fashion.* Trans. Claudia Rosoux. London: Paul Hamlyn, 1968.

Labédollière, Émile de. *Le nouveau Paris: Histoire de ses 20 arrondissements.* Paris: Gustave Barba, n.d.

La Berge, Ann F. *Mission and Method: The Early Nineteenth-Century French Public Health Movement.* Cambridge: Cambridge University Press, 1992.

Lacan, Ernest. *Esquisses photographiques à propos de l'Exposition universelle et de la guerre d'Orient.* Paris: A. Gaudin et Frère, 1856.

Lacan, Jacques. *The Four Fundamental Concepts of Psychoanalysis.* Ed. Jacques-Alain Miller, translated by Alan Sheridan. New York: Norton, 1973.

Lajer-Burcharth, Ewa. "Fragonard in Detail." *differences* 14, no. 3 (Fall 2003): 34–56.

Lane, Edward William. *An Account of the Manners and Customs of the Modern Egyptians: Written in Egypt during the Years 1833–1838.* The Hague and London: East-West Publications, Livres de France, 1978.

Laporte, Laurent. *L'Égypte à la voile.* Paris: Hachette, 1870.

La Selve, Edgar, ed. *La revue exotique des pays étrangers et des colonies européennes.* Paris: La Librairie E. Dente, n.d.

Lassablière, P. *Annuaire et guide pratique d'hygiène par un comité d'hygiènistes.* Paris: Jouve et Companie, 1911.

Latour, Marie L. *L'Orient en question 1825–1875: De Missolonghi à Suez ou l'orientalisme de Delacroix à Flaubert.* Marseille: Musée Cantini, 1975.

Leach, William. *Land of Desire: Merchants, Power, and the Rise of a New American Culture.* New York: Pantheon Books, 1993.

Leatherbarrow, David, and Mohsen Mostafavi. *Surface Architecture.* Cambridge, MA: MIT Press, 2002.

Lefébure, Ernest. *Broderies et dentelles.* Paris: Ernest Gründ, 1888.

Lehmann, Ulrich. *Tigersprung: Fashion in Modernity.* Cambridge, MA: MIT Press, 2000.

Leichner. *L'art du maquillage et ses auxiliaires indispensibles: Guide pour artistes au théâtre.* Paris: L'Édition Publicitaire, n.d.

Lemoine, Bertrand. *La France du XIXe siècle.* Paris: Éditions de la Martinière, 1993.

Lenôtre, G. "La danse des almées." *L'Exposition de Paris de 1889* 36 (September 18, 1889).

Leprun, Sylviane. *Le théâtre des colonies: Scénographie, acteurs et discours de l'imaginaire dans les expositions 1855–1937.* Paris: Éditions l'Harmattan, 1986.

Lester, Katherine Morris, and Bess Viola Oerke. *An Illustrated History of Those Frills and Furbelows of Fashion Which Have Come to Be Known as: Accessories of Dress.* Peoria, IL: Chas. A. Bennett Co., 1954.

Levey, Santina M. *Lace: A History.* London: W. S. Maney and Son, 1983.

Lévy, Michel. *Traité d'hygiène publique et privée.* Paris: Librairie J.-B. Baillière, 1879.

Lewis, Reina. *Gendering Orientalism: Race, Femininity, and Representation.* London: Routledge, 1996.

Lipton, Eunice. *Alias Olympia: A Woman's Search for Manet's Notorious Model and Her Own Desire.* New York: Charles Scribner's, 1992.

———. *Looking into Degas: Uneasy Images of Women and Modern Life.* Berkeley: University of California Press, 1986.

Le livre des expositions universelles, 1851–1889. Paris: Union central des arts décoratifs, 1983.

Livre d'or de l'exposition: 1889. Paris, 1889.

Locke, Nancy. *Manet and the Family Romance.* Princeton, NJ: Princeton University Press, 2001.

Lowe, Lisa. *Critical Terrains: French and British Orientalisms.* Ithaca, NY: Cornell University Press, 1991.

MacKenzie, John M. *Orientalism: History, Theory, and the Arts.* Manchester: University of Manchester Press, 1995.

Madanipour, Ali. *Public and Private Spaces of the City.* London: Routledge, 2003.

Magli, Patrizia. "The Face and the Soul." In *Fragments for a History of the Human Body,* ed. Michel Feher, vol. 2, 86–127. New York: Zone, 1989.

Mainardi, Patricia. *Art and Politics of the Second Empire: The Universal Expositions of 1855 and 1867.* New Haven, CT: Yale University Press, 1987.

Malet, Henri. *Le Baron Haussmann et la renovation de Paris.* Paris: Les Éditions Municipales, 1973.

Malgras, G. J. *Les peintres de l'Afrique noire.* Paris: ABC, 1982.

Manegeglier, Hervé. *Paris impérial: La vie quotidienne sous le Second Empire.* Paris: Armand Colin, 1990.

Manet, Julie. *Growing Up with the Impressionists: The Diary of Julie Manet.* Translated and edited by Rosalind de Boland Roberts and Jane Roberts. New York: Harper and Row, 1987.

Manet: 1832–1883. Exhibition catalog. Curated by Françoise Cachin and Charles S. Moffett. New York: Harry N. Abrams, 1983.

Marcus, Sharon. *Apartment Stories: City and Home in Nineteenth-Century Paris and London.* Berkeley: University of California Press, 1999.

———. "Reflections on Victorian Fashion Plates." *differences* 14, no. 3 (Fall 2003): 4–33.

Masson, F. "J. L. Gérôme, peintre de l'Orient." *Figaro illustrée* (July 1901).

Mathews, Nancy Mowll, ed. *Cassatt and Her Circle: Selected Letters.* New York: Abbeville, 1984.

———. *Mary Cassatt: A Life.* New York: Villard Books, 1994.

Matlock, Jann. *Scenes of Seduction: Prostitution, Hysteria, and Reading Difference in Nineteenth-Century France.* New York: Columbia University Press, 1994.

Maxwell, Anne. *Colonial Photography and Exhibitions: Representations of the "Native" and the Making of European Identities.* London: Leicester University Press, 2000.

McCabe, James D., Jr. *Paris by Sunlight and Gaslight: A Work Descriptive of the Mysteries and Miseries, the Virtues, the Vices, the Splendors, and the Crimes of the City of Paris.* Philadelphia: National Publishing Co., 1869.

McClintock, Anne. *Imperial Leather: Race, Gender and Sexuality in the Colonial Contest.* New York: Routledge, 1995.

McGrath, Roberta. *Seeing Her Sex: Medical Archives and the Female Body.* New York: Palgrave, 2002.

Mehlman, Billie. *Women's Fictions: English Women and the Middle East, 1718–1918.* London: Macmillan, 1992.

Meissirel-Duguay, Élisabeth. *Élégantes: Modes d'avant-hier 1850–1866 à travers la photographie et la gravure.* Paris: Gaston Lachurié, 1887.

Mernissi, Fatima. *Beyond the Veil: Male-Female Dynamics in a Modern Muslim Society.* Cambridge: Schenkman, 1975.

———. *Women and Islam: An Historical and Theological Enquiry.* Trans. Mary Jo Lakeland. Oxford: Basil Blackwell, 1991.

Mesnil, O. du. *Nettoiement de la voie publique: Enlèvement et utilisation des ordures ménagères.* Paris: J.-B. Baillière et Fils, 1884.

Micale, Mark S., ed. *The Mind of Modernism: Medicine, Psychology, and the Cultural Arts in Europe and America, 1880–1940.* Stanford, CA: Stanford University Press, 2004.

Michelet, Jules. *Oeuvres complètes de Michelet.* Vol. 18. Paris: Flammarion, 1985; originally published 1858–60.

Mickel, Emanuel J., Jr. "Orientalist Painters and Writers at the Crossroads of Realism." *Nineteenth-Century French Studies* 23, nos. 1–2 (Fall–Winter 1994–95): 1–34.

Micklewright, Nancy. *A Victorian Traveler in the Middle East: The Photography and Travel Writing of Annie Lady Brassey.* London: Ashgate, 2003.

Midgley, Claire, ed. *Gender and Imperialism.* Manchester: University of Manchester Press, 1998.

Missac, Pierre. *Walter Benjamin's Passages.* Trans. Shierry Weber Nicholsen. Cambridge, MA: MIT Press, 1995.

Mitchell, Timothy. *Colonising Egypt.* Berkeley: University of California Press, 1991.

Mondor, M. *La vie de Mallarmé.* Vol. 2. Paris: Gallimard, 1941.

Monin, E. *La propreté de l'individu et de la maison.* Paris: Charles Senlaeber, 1886.

Monti, Nicolas. *Africa Then: Photographs 1840–1918.* London: Thames and Hudson, 1987.

Morisot, Berthe. *Berthe Morisot: The Correspondence with Her Family and Her Friends Manet, Puvis de Chavannes, Degas, Monet, Renoir, and Mallarmé.* Ed. Denis Rouart, trans. Betty W. Hubbard. Newly introduced and edited by Kathleen Adler and Tamar Garb. London: Camden Press, 1986.

Mulvey, Laura. *Fetishism and Curiosity.* Bloomington: Indiana University Press, 1996.

Myers, J. Arthur. "The Development of Knowledge of Unity of Tuberculosis and the Portals of Entry of Tubercle Bacilli." *Journal of the History of Medicine and Allied Sciences* 29 (April 1, 1974): 213–28.

Napias, H., and A.-J. Martin. *L'étude et les progrès de l'hygiène en France de 1878 à 1882.* Paris: G. Masson, 1883.

Nead, Lynda. *The Female Nude: Art, Obscenity and Sexuality.* London: Routledge, 1992.

———. *Victorian Babylon: People, Streets, and Images in 19th-Century London.* New Haven, CT: Yale University Press, 2000.

Nesbit, Molly. "'In the Absence of the *Parisienne.*'" In *Sexuality and Space,* ed. Beatriz Colomina, 307–26. Princeton, NJ: Princeton Architectural Press, 1992.

The New Oxford Annotated Bible: New Revised Standard Version with Apocrypha. Ed. Michael D. Coogan et al. Oxford: Oxford University Press, 2001.

Nochlin, Linda. *Bathtime: Renoir, Cézanne, Daumier and the Practices of Bathing in Nineteenth-Century France.* Gröningen, The Netherlands: Gerson Lectures Foundation, 1991.

———. "A House Is Not a Home: Degas and the Subversion of the Family." In *Dealing with Degas: Representations of Women and the Politics of Vision,* ed. Richard Kendall and Griselda Pollock, 43–65. New York: Universe, 1991.

———. *The Politics of Vision: Essays on Nineteenth-Century Art and Society.* New York: Harper and Row, 1989.

———. *Representing Women.* London: Thames and Hudson, 1999.

———. *Women, Art, and Power and Other Essays.* New York: Harper and Row, 1988.

Norinsr, Panivong. "Representing Indochina: The French Colonial Fantasmatic and the Exposition Coloniale de Paris." *French Cultural Studies* 6, no. 16 (February, 1995): 35–60.

Nye, Robert. *Crime, Madness, and Politics in Modern France: The Medical Concept of National Decline.* Princeton, NJ: Princeton University Press, 1984.

Ockman, Carol. *Ingres's Eroticized Bodies: Retracing the Serpentine Line.* New Haven, CT: Yale University Press, 1995.

Ory, Pascale. *Les expositions universelles de Paris.* Paris: Ramsay, 1982.

Osborne, Michael A. *Nature, the Exotic, and the Science of French Colonialism.* Bloomington: Indiana University Press, 1994.

Palmer, Alexandra. *Couture and Commerce: The Transatlantic Fashion Trade in the 1950s.* Ontario: Royal Ontario Museum, 2001.

Parent-Duchâtelet, Alexandre. *De la prostitution dans la ville de Paris.* Brussels: Dumont, 1837.

Paris à l'Exposition 1855. Paris: Librairie d'Alphonse Taride, 1855.

Parsons, Deborah L. *Streetwalking the Metropolis: Women, the City, Modernity.* Oxford: Oxford University Press, 2000.

Patin, Ch. *Rapport général sur les travaux du conseil d'hygiène publique et de salubrité du département de la Seine depuis 1878 jusqu'a 1880 inclusivement.* Paris: Chaix, 1884.

Peiss, Kathy. *Hope in a Jar: The Making of America's Beauty Culture.* New York: Metropolitan Books, 1998.

———. "Making Faces: The Cosmetics Industry and the Cultural Construction of Gender, 1890–1930." *Genders* 7 (Spring 1990): 143–69.

Perez, Nissan N. *Focus East: Early Photography in the Near East (1839–1885).* New York: Harry N. Abrams, 1988.

Perrot, Philippe. *Fashioning the Bourgeoisie: A History of Clothing in the Nineteenth Century.* Trans. Richard Bienvenu. Princeton, NJ: Princeton University Press, 1994.

Peyenson, Lewis. *Civilizing Mission: Exact Sciences and French Overseas Expansion, 1830–1940.* Baltimore: Johns Hopkins University Press, 1993.

Piesse, S. *Des odeurs, des parfums, et des cosmetiques.* Paris: J.-B. Baillière et Fils, 1865.

Pinkney, David. *Napoleon III and the Rebuilding of Paris.* Princeton, NJ: Princeton University Press, 1958.

Pinon, Pierre. *Atlas du Paris haussmannien: La ville en heritage du Second Empire à nos jours.* Paris: Éditions Parigramme, 2002.

Plum, Werner. *Les expositions universelles au 19e siècle, spectacles du changement socio-culturel.* Bonn: Hildesheimer Druck-und-Verlags-Gmbh, 1977.

Plumandon, J. R. *Les poussières atmosphériques: Leur circulation dans l'atmosphère et leur influence sur la santé.* Paris: Société d'Éditions Scientifiques, 1897.

Pointon, Marcia. *Naked Authority: The Body in Western Painting 1830–1908.* Cambridge: Cambridge University Press, 1990.

Pollock, Griselda. "Feminism/Foucault Surveillance/Sexuality." In *Visual Culture: Images and Interpretations,* ed. Norman Bryson, Keith Moxey, and Michael Ann Holly, 1–41. Middletown, CT: Wesleyan University Press, 1994.

———. "The Gaze and the Look: *Woman with Binoculars*—a Question of Difference." In *Dealing with Degas: Representations of Women and the Politics of Vision,* ed. Richard Kendall and Griselda Pollock, 106–32. New York: Universe, 1991.

———. "The 'View from Elsewhere': Extracts from a Semi-public Correspondence about the Visibility of Desire." In *12 Views of Manet's Bar,* ed. Bradford R. Collins, 278–314. Princeton, NJ: Princeton University Press, 1996.

———. *Vision and Difference: Femininity, Feminism and the Histories of Art.* London: Routledge, 1988.

Porter, Dennis. *Haunted Journeys: Desire and Transgression in European Travel Writing.* Princeton, NJ: Princeton University Press, 1991.

Pouchet, F. A. *Hétérogénie ou traité de la génération spontanée.* Paris: J.-B. Baillière et Fils, 1859.

Prendergast, Christopher. *Paris and the Nineteenth Century.* Oxford: Basil Blackwell, 1992.

Prochaska, David. *Making Algeria French: Colonialism in Bône 1870–1920.* Cambridge, MA: Harvard University Press, 1990.

Puisieux, Julie de. "Mode." *La mode actuelle: Journal professionel des couturières et des modistes* (November 15, 1869).

Purdy, Daniel Leonhard, ed. *The Rise of Fashion: A Reader.* Minneapolis: University of Minnesota Press, 2004.

Rabinow, Paul. *French Modern: Norms and Forms of the Social Environment.* Cambridge, MA: MIT Press, 1989.

Ramsey, Matthew. *Professional and Popular Medicine in France, 1770–1830.* Cambridge: Cambridge University Press, 1988.

Raymond, Emmeline. "Hygiène du visage." *La mode illustrée, journal de la famille* 14 (April 1, 1860).

Rendell, Jane. *The Pursuit of Pleasure: Gender, Space and Architecture in Regency London.* London: Athlone Press, 2002.

Richter, Gerhard, ed. *Benjamin's Ghosts: Interventions in Contemporary Literary and Cultural Theory.* Stanford, CA: Stanford University Press, 2002.

Rifkin, Adrian. *Street Noises: Parisian Pleasure, 1900–1940.* Manchester: Manchester University Press, 1993.

Rochard, Dr. Jules. *Encyclopédie d'hygiène et de médecine publique.* Paris: Bataille et Companie, 1895.

Roth, Michael S., with Claire Lyons and Charles Merewether. *Irresistible Decay: Ruins Reclaimed.* Los Angeles: Getty Research Institute, 1997.

Rounding, Virginia. *Grandes Horizontales: The Lives and Legends of Marie Duplessis, Cora Pearl, La Païva and La Présidente.* New York: Bloomsbury Press, 2003.

Rowe, Dorothy. *Representing Berlin: Sexuality and the City in Imperial Weimar Germany.* Burlington, VT: Ashgate, 2003.

Sagne, Jean. *L'atelier du photographie 1840–1940.* Paris: Presse de la Renaissance, 1984.

Said, Edward. *Orientalism.* New York: Vintage Books, 1978.

———. "Representing the Colonized: Anthropology's Interlocutors." *Critical Inquiry* 15 (Winter 1989): 205–25.

Sartory, A., and Marc Langlais. *Poussière et microbes de l'air.* Paris: A. Poinat, 1912.

Scarry, Elaine. "Imagining Flowers: Perceptual Mimesis (Particularly Delphinium)." *Representations* 57 (Winter 1997): 90–115.

Schneider, William H. *An Empire for the Masses: The French Popular Image of Africa, 1870–1900.* Westport, CT: Greenwood Press, 1982.

Schueller, Malini Jonar. "Harems, Orientalist Subversions, and the Crisis of Nationalism: The Case of Edgar Allen Poe." *Criticism* 37, no. 4 (Fall 1995): 601–24.

Schwartz, Joan M., and James R. Ryan, eds. *Picturing Place: Photography and the Geographic Imagination.* London: I. B. Tauris, 2003.

Scott, Joan Wallach. *Gender and the Politics of History.* New York: Columbia University Press, 1988.

La sculpture ethnographique de la Vénus Hottentote à la Tehura de Gauguin. Paris: Réunion des musées nationaux, 1994.

Sedgwick, Eve Kosofsky. *The Coherence of Gothic Conventions.* New York: Arno Press, 1980.

Seguin, Joseph. *La dentelle: Histoire, description, fabrication, bibliographie.* Paris: J. Rothschild, Éditeur, 1875.

Sennett, Richard. *The Fall of Public Man.* London: Faber and Faber, 1974 and 1976.

Shapiro, Ann-Louise. "Paris." In *Housing the Workers, 1850–1914: A Comparative Perspective,* ed. M. J. Daunton, 33–66. London: Leicester University Press, 1990.

Sharpe, Jenny. *Allegories of Empire: The Figure of Woman in the Colonial Text.* Minneapolis: University of Minnesota Press, 1993.

Sheets-Pyenson, Susan. *Cathedrals of Science: The Development of Colonial Natural History Museums during the Late Nineteenth Century.* Kingston, Ont.: McGill-Queen's University Press, 1988.

Sheringham, Michael, ed. *Parisian Fields.* London: Reaktion, 1996.

Shirazi, Faegheh. *The Veil Unveiled: The Hijab in Modern Culture.* Gainesville: University Press of Florida, 2001.

Shirrmeister, Anne. "La dernière mode: Berthe Morisot and Costume." In *Perspectives on Morisot,* ed. T. J. Edelstein, 103–15. New York: Hudson Hills Press, 1990.

Shonfield, Katherine. *Walls Have Feelings: Architecture, Film and the City.* New York: Routledge, 2000.

Sidlauskas, Susan. *Body, Place, and Self in Nineteenth-Century Painting.* Cambridge: Cambridge University Press, 2000.

———. "Painting Skin: John Singer Sargent's *Madame X.*" *American Art* (Fall 2001): 9–33.

Silverman, Debora L. *Art Nouveau in Fin-de-Siècle France: Politics, Psychology, and Style.* Berkeley: University of California Press, 1992.

Silverman, Kaja. "Fragments for a Fashionable Discourse." In *Studies in Entertainment: Critical Approaches to Mass Culture,* ed. Tania Modleski, 139–52. Bloomington: Indiana University Press, 1986.

Simmel, Georg. *Georg Simmel: On Women, Sexuality, and Love.* Translated by Guy Oakes. New Haven, CT: Yale University Press, 1984.

Simon, Jules. *La femme du XIXe siècle.* Paris: Calmann Lévy, 1892.

Smith, Bonnie G. *Ladies of the Leisure Class: The Bourgeoises of Northern France in the Nineteenth Century.* Princeton, NJ: Princeton University Press, 1981.

Société de médecine publique et d'hygiène professionelle de Paris 1877–1887. Paris: G. Rougier, 1887.

Société française de photographie numéro speciale: Expositions universelles. Paris, 1983.

Solomon-Godeau, Abigail. "The Legs of the Countess." *October* 39 (Winter 1986): 65–108.

———. *Photography at the Dock: Essays on Photographic History, Institutions and Practices.* Minneapolis: University of Minnesota Press, 1991.

Spivak, Gayatri Chakravorty. *The Post-colonial Critic: Interviews, Strategies, Dialogues.* Ed. Sarah Harasym. New York: Routledge, 1990.

Staffe, Baronne. *Le cabinet de toilette.* Paris: Victor-Havard, 1893.

Stallybrass, Peter, and Allon White. *The Politics and Poetics of Transgression.* Ithaca, NY: Cornell University Press, 1986.

Stansell, Christine. *City of Women: Sex and Class in New York 1789–1860.* New York: Alfred A. Knopf, 1986.

Staum, Martin S. *Labeling People: French Scholars on Society, Race, and Empire 1815–1849.* Montreal: McGill-Queen's University Press, 2003.

Steedman, Carolyn. *Dust: The Archive and Cultural History.* New Brunswick, NJ: Rutgers University Press, 2001.

Steele, Valerie. *Paris Fashion: A Cultural History.* New York: Berg, 1998.

Stern, Radu. *Against Fashion: Clothing as Art, 1850–1930.* Cambridge, MA: MIT Press, 2004.

Stevens, Mary Anne, ed. *The Orientalists: Delacroix to Matisse: European Painters in North Africa and the Near East.* London: Weidenfeld and Nicolson, 1984.

Stewart, Susan. *On Longing: Narratives of the Miniature, the Gigantic, the Souvenir, the Collection.* Durham, NC: Duke University Press, 1993.

Suleri, Sara. *The Rhetoric of English India.* Chicago: University of Chicago Press, 1992.

Tagg, John. *Grounds of Dispute: Art History, Cultural Politics and the Discursive Field.* Minneapolis: University of Minnesota Press, 1992.

Taithe, Bertrand. *Defeated Flesh: Medicine, Welfare, and Warfare in the Making of Modern France.* Lanham, Md.: Rowman and Littlefield, 1999.

Ten Years of Imperialism in France: Impressions of a Flâneur. Edinburgh: William Blackwood and Sons, 1862.

Terdiman, Richard. *Discourse/Counter-discourse: The Theory and Practice of Symbolic Resistance in Nineteenth-Century France.* Ithaca, NY: Cornell University Press, 1985.

Tester, Keith, ed. *The Flâneur.* London: Routledge, 1994.

Thézy, Marie de. *Charles Marville: Paris disparu.* Paris: Paris-Musées, 1994.

Thornton, Lynne. *Les africanistes peintres voyageurs 1860–1960.* Paris: ACR Édition, 1990.

———. *La femme dans la peinture orientaliste.* Tours: Mame Imprimeurs, 1993.

Tiersten, Lisa. *Marianne in the Market: Envisioning Consumer Society in Fin-de-Siècle France.* Berkeley: University of California Press, 2001.

Tissandier, Gaston. *Les poussières de l'air.* Paris: Gauthier-Villars, Imprimeur-Librairie, 1877.

Troy, Nancy J. *Couture Culture: A Study in Modern Art and Fashion.* Cambridge, MA: MIT Press, 2003.

Tyndall, M. J. "Poussières et maladies." *Revue des cours scientifique de la France et de l'étranger* 15 (March 12, 1870): 235–40.

"Une rue au Caire." *L'Exposition de Paris de 1889* 10 (May 4, 1889).

Uzanne, Octave. *L'art et les artifices de la beauté.* Paris: Juven, 1902.

———. *La femme et la mode: Métamorphoses de la parisienne de 1792 à 1892.* Paris: Ancienne Maison Quantin, 1893.

———. *Les ornements de la femme: L'éventail, l'ombrelle, le gant, le manchon.* Paris: Librairies-Imprimeries Réunies, 1892.

———. *Son altesse la femme.* Paris: A. Quantin, 1885.

Vaczek, Louis, and Gail Buckland. *Travelers in Ancient Lands: A Portrait of the Middle East, 1839–1919.* New York: New York Graphic Society, 1981.

Valéry, Paul. *Degas, Manet, Morisot.* Trans. David Paul. Princeton, NJ: Princeton University Press, 1989.

Vallory, Louise. *A l'aventure en Algérie.* Paris: J. Hetzel, 1863.

Van Zanten, David. *Building Paris: Architectural Institutions and the Transformation of the French Capital, 1830–1870.* Cambridge: Cambridge University Press, 1994.

Varnedoe, Kirk. "Caillebotte's *Pont de l'Europe:* A New Slant." In *Gustave Caillebotte and the Fashioning of Identity in Impressionist Paris,* ed. Norma Broude. New Brunswick, NJ: Rutgers University Press, 2002.

———. *Gustave Caillebotte.* New Haven, CT: Yale University Press, 1987.

Vaucaire, Dr. *La femme: Sa beauté, sa santé, son hygiène.* Paris: J. Rueff, 1900.

Veblen, Thorsten. *The Theory of the Leisure Class.* London: Allen and Unwin, 1957.

Veillon, Dominique. *Fashion under the Occupation.* Oxford: Berg, 2002.

Vidler, Anthony. *Warped Space: Art, Architecture, and Anxiety in Modern Culture.* Cambridge, MA: MIT Press, 2001.

Vigarello, Georges. *Histoire de la beauté: Le corps et l'art d'embellir de la renaissance à nos jours.* Paris: Éditions du Seuil, 2004.

Vigne, Georges. *Ingres.* Paris: Citadelles and Mazenod, 1995.

Vinken, Barbara. "Temples of Delight: Consuming Consumption in Emile Zola's

Au Bonheur des dames." In *Spectacles of Realism: Gender, Body, Genre*, ed. Margaret Cohen and Christopher Prendergast, 247–67. Minneapolis: University of Minnesota Press, 1995.

Visions of the Ottoman Empire. Exhibition catalog. Edinburgh: Scottish National Portrait Gallery, 1994.

Vogelsang-Eastwood, G. M. *For Modesty's Sake?* Tilburg, The Netherlands: Syntax Publishers, 1996.

Walker, Lynne, "Home and Away: The Feminist Remapping of Public and Private Space in Victorian London." In *The Unknown City: Contesting Architecture and Social Space*, ed. Iain Borden, Joe Kerr, and Jane Rendell, 297–310. Cambridge, MA: MIT Press, 2001.

Walther, Wiebke. *Women in Islam*. Princeton, NJ: Princeton University Press, 1993.

Ward, Janet. *Weimar Surfaces: Urban Visual Culture in 1920s Germany*. Berkeley: University of California Press, 2001.

Warwick, Alexandra, and Dani Cavallaro. *Fashioning the Frame: Boundaries, Dress and the Body*. Oxford: Berg, 1998.

Wigley, Mark. *White Walls, and Designer Dresses*. Princeton, NJ: Princeton University Press, 1994.

Wilcox, R. Turner. *The Mode in Hats and Headress*. New York: Charles Scribner's Sons, 1945.

Willsdon, Clare A. P., "'Promenades et plantations': Impressionism, Conservation and Haussmann's Reinvention of Paris." In *Soil and Stone: Impressionism, Urbanism, Environment*, ed. Frances Fowle and Richard Thomson, 107–24. Burlington, VT: Ashgate Publishing Limited, 2003.

Wilson, Elizabeth. *The Contradictions of Culture: Cities, Culture, Women*. London: Sage Publications, 2001.

———. *The Sphinx in the City: Urban Life, the Control of Disorder, and Women*. Berkeley: University of California Press, 1991.

Winkel, Marieke de. "Fashion or Fancy? Some Interpretations of the Dress of Rembrandt's Women Re-evaluated." In *Rembrandt's Women*, exhibition catalog, ed. Julia Lloyd Williams, 55–63. Munich: Prestel, 2001.

Wolff, Janet. "Gender and the Haunting of Cities: Or, the Retirement of the Flâneur." *AngloModern: Painting and Modernity in Britain and the United States*, 65–85. Ithaca, NY: Cornell University Press, 2003.

———. "The Invisible Flâneuse: Women and the Literature of Modernity." *Theory, Culture, and Society* 2, no. 3 (1985): 37–46.

Woodhull, Winifred. "Unveiling Algeria." *Genders* 10 (Spring 1991): 112–31.

Worboys, Michael. *Spreading Germs: Disease Theories and Medical Practice in Britain, 1865–1900*. Cambridge: Cambridge University Press, 2000.

Wrigley, Richard. *The Politics of Appearance: Representations of Dress in Revolutionary France*. Oxford: Berg, 2002.

Yanni, Carla. *Nature's Museums: Victorian Science and the Architecture of Display.* Baltimore: Johns Hopkins University Press, 1999.

Yeazell, Ruth Bernard. *Harems of the Mind: Passages of Western Art and Literature.* New Haven, CT: Yale University Press, 2000.

———. "Public Baths and Private Harems: Lady Mary Wortley Montagu and the Origins of Ingres's *Bain Turc.*" *Yale Journal of Critcisim* 7, no. 1 (Spring 1994): 111–38.

Yegenoglu, Meyda. "Supplementing the Orientalist Lack: European Ladies in the Harem." In *Orientalism and Cultural Differences,* ed. Mahmut Mutman and Meyda Yegenoglu, 43–80. Santa Cruz: Center for Cultural Studies, University of California, Santa Cruz, 1992.

Zéghidour, Slimane. *Le voile de la bannière.* Paris: Hachette, 1990.

Zola, Émile. *L'assommoir.* Trans. Leonard Tancock. New York: Penguin Books, 1970.

———. *La bête humaine.* Paris: Pocket, 1991.

———. *The Ladies' Paradise.* Trans. Henry Vizetelly. Introduction by Kristin Ross. Berkeley: University of California Press, 1992.

———. *Nana.* Trans. George Holden. New York: Penguin, 1972.

Periodicals

Actes de la Société d'ethnographie

Annale de médecine publique

Bulletin de l'Académie de médecine

Bulletin et memoire de la Société de médecine de Paris

Exposition de Paris de 1855, L'

Exposition de Paris de 1867 illustrée, L'

Exposition de Paris de 1878, L'

Exposition de Paris de 1889, L'

Exposition universelle de 1889, L'

Express des modes, L'

Gazette de France, La

Hygiène: Journal des familles, L'

Illustration, L'

Journal des dames et des modes

Journal des demoiselles, Le

Magasin des demoiselles, Le

Miroir parisien, journal des dames et des demoiselles, Le

Mode: Revue française illustrée, La

Mode actuelle: Journal professionel des couturières et des modistes, La

Mode de la style

Mode de Paris

Mode et beauté
Mode illustrée, journal de la famille, La
Modes parisiennes, Les
Modes parisiennes illustrées, Les
Monde illustré, Le
Moniteur de la mode, Le
Moniteur des arts, Le
Moniteur des dames et des demoiselles, Le
Paris élégant
Paris-exposition
Paris-moderne
Petit courrier de la mode, Le
Petit moniteur de la santé, Le
Revue de la mode
Revue d'hygiène et de police sanitaire de médecine
Revue du monde coloniale, La
Santé publique, La
Siècle medical, Le
Vie parisienne, La

Index

MARNI REVA KESSLER is assistant professor in the Kress Foundation Department of Art History at the University of Kansas.